Early Praise for *Technical Blogging, Second Edition*

I'm in absolute awe at this amazing book, which has the best advice I've ever heard on the subject, with helpful "Do this" suggestions. I wish I'd read this years ago, because I had to learn the hard way. This book inspired me to write and publish more.

➤ **Derek Sivers**
Founder, CD Baby

New consultants often ask me how to market themselves. I recommend blogging. Then, I recommend *Technical Blogging* as the one book they should read and use as a guide. Even after blogging for 16+ years, I found gems that I put on my list to address.

➤ **Johanna Rothman**
Author, *Create Your Successful Agile Project*

Antonio covers everything from the philosophy of what makes good blog content to the nitty-gritty of what software plugins to use and the best time of day to publish articles. Every few pages, I added another item to my to-do list to improve my blog.

➤ **Andy Lester**
Author, *Land the Tech Job You Love*

A lot of us drag our heels on blogging because we have so many decisions to make before we even get started: the name, the audience, the platform, the style, and so on. Antonio will deftly steer you through these crucial early stages while your enthusiasm is still fresh, and he'll be your steady guide as you start writing and building momentum. You'll say to yourself, "I have no excuses any more. Let's do this!"

➤ **Erin Dees**
Principal Software Engineer, Stitch Fix

Technical Blogging, Second Edition

Amplify Your Influence

Antonio Cangiano

The Pragmatic Bookshelf

Raleigh, North Carolina

Many of the designations used by manufacturers and sellers to distinguish their products are claimed as trademarks. Where those designations appear in this book, and The Pragmatic Programmers, LLC was aware of a trademark claim, the designations have been printed in initial capital letters or in all capitals. The Pragmatic Starter Kit, The Pragmatic Programmer, Pragmatic Programming, Pragmatic Bookshelf, PragProg and the linking *g* device are trademarks of The Pragmatic Programmers, LLC.

Every precaution was taken in the preparation of this book. However, the publisher assumes no responsibility for errors or omissions, or for damages that may result from the use of information (including program listings) contained herein.

Our Pragmatic books, screencasts, and audio books can help you and your team create better software and have more fun. Visit us at *https://pragprog.com*.

The team that produced this book includes:

Publisher: Andy Hunt
VP of Operations: Janet Furlow
Managing Editor: Susan Conant
Development Editor: Michael Swaine
Copy Editor: Molly McBeath
Indexing: Potomac Indexing, LLC
Layout: Gilson Graphics

For sales, volume licensing, and support, please contact *support@pragprog.com*.

For international rights, please contact *rights@pragprog.com*.

ISBN-13: 978-1-68050-647-1
Book version: P1.0—June 2019

To my incredible wife, Jessica. And to all the kind souls who helped us in the aftermath of losing our home in an arson fire.

Contents

Acknowledgments

It's customary for authors to thank everyone who has even remotely touched their book and offer platitudes about the invaluable contributions these people have made.

In the case of this book, there is no false modesty. I genuinely have to thank a great many folk who have helped make it possible. The volume of feedback I received shaped the book and made it far more useful than it would have been otherwise.

I want to start by thanking my unofficial editor, my beautiful wife, Jessica. She put in countless hours helping me refine my message and providing me with endless support and patience as I worked on each chapter. Without her, this book would be a lot less clear.

I must thank the whole team at the Pragmatic Bookshelf, in particular my editor, Mike Swaine, for his insightful suggestions and for demanding nothing but the utmost quality from me throughout the writing of this book, both in its original incarnation and in this revised second edition; my publisher, Andy Hunt, for believing in this project from the very beginning; my managing editor, Susan Conant, for providing important advice on the development of the book from its earliest stages onward; my production manager, Janet Furlow, for ensuring the book would end up in your hands as a polished product; and last but not least, Gilson Graphics, for withstanding my incessant search for the perfect cover.

Between the first and second edition, I was privileged to have a team of world-class technical reviewers who cannot be thanked enough for their contributions. The impressive list includes Andy Lester, Brian Hogan, Dan Wohlbruck, Derek Sivers, Giles Bowkett, Gregg Pollack, Ian Dees, Ilya Grigorik, Jeff Langr, Johanna Rothman, John C. Dvorak, Kent Beck, Lukas Mathis, Patrick McKenzie, Peter Cooper, Satish Talim, Scott Mace, Sebastian Marshall, Steve Yegge, Susan Visser, and Thom Hogan.

My list of informal reviewers—a small group of family, friends, and colleagues who read early drafts—must also be thanked for their feedback and support. In particular, I wish to thank Lynn Schill, Bradley Steinfeld, Davide Varvello, Henrique Zambon, Kalid Azad, Laurent Sansonetti, Leon Katsnelson, Ludovico Magnocavallo, Marco Beri, Marius Butuc, Ninh Bui, Piergiuliano Bossi, and Rav Ahuja.

Finally, I'd like to thank the customers who purchased the first edition and beta versions of this book. Their detailed feedback, suggestions, encouragement, and early success (having put the advice in this book into practice) motivated me to keep going. In particular, I'd like to acknowledge Paul Cochrane for his suggestions during the beta of this second edition.

For allowing me to create a relentlessly useful book I'm proud to put my name on, all these people have my sincere respect and gratitude.

The reports of my death are greatly exaggerated.

    Mark Twain

Introduction

You may not know it yet, but blogging has the potential to change your life.

I didn't know it either when I first began writing online, well over a decade ago. I thought blogging would be a way to perform a brain dump from time to time. Maybe something would come out of it, but I wasn't holding my breath.

Boy, was I wrong.

Every day we face many decisions. Most of them turn out to be inconsequential, but occasionally a choice ends up shaping our future. Starting to blog did just that for me.

In fact, I count blogging as one of three decisions that drastically affected my career and personal life: the other two being leaving Italy—my home country—in 2003 and getting into the Ruby programming language before Rails was released to the world.

You might think I'm overstating the impact blogging has had on me. Allow me to briefly recap some highlights that might convince you otherwise.

- My manager found me through a post on my programming blog. I moved to Canada, my wife's native country, as a result and I've been employed by IBM for over twelve years now.

- Blogging has afforded me extra income, every single month, for more than a decade.

- I've received dozens of technical books and other freebies over the years.

- When we lost our home and virtually everything we owned to an arson fire in October 2016, a crowdfunding campaign was set up on our behalf. Simply posting it on my blog (and also on my wife's blog) led to a staggering 297 donations.[1] Family, close friends, and colleagues all generously helped and we were very appreciative. What surprised us was that the majority

---

1.   programmingzen.com/programming-zen-will-be-on-a-hiatus-due-to-tragic-circumstances/

of donors were blog readers and friends we'd made through blogging. My wife received numerous care packages as well. What a great help to receive such an outpouring of support during a time of complete loss.

- Last year I sold one of my blogs about mathematics to a British company and used the profits for the down payment on a new house.

The positive impact that blogging has had on my career, income, and life in general is what persuaded me to write this book. I'm certain that by the end of it, you'll have the skills required to benefit from sharing your knowledge online.

This book teaches you the art and science of technical blogging and shows you how to be a successful blogger. Whenever possible, I've tried to back up my assertions with direct experiences and statistics.

Nevertheless, this is an opinionated book. It's the distilled form of what I've learned from trial and error over the course of the past fourteen years through several blogs that I started, either in English or Italian. As you read it, you may disagree with me, much like the readers of my blogs sometimes contest a point I've made in one of my posts.

That's OK.

My goal is to provide you with a roadmap to achieve success with your own blog. I'll supply you with step-by-step instructions, starting with the planning phase and going all the way to creating, promoting, benefiting from, and maintaining your blog. I won't shy away from expressing my opinion about what you should do and what is best avoided.

But you're not me, and this is a team effort. So I also want to get you thinking in new ways, experimenting, and ultimately reaching your own conclusions about what does and doesn't work for your technical blog. I'll be your mentor, gently guiding you in the right direction while still allowing you to find your own way.

What Is Technical Blogging?

The most generic definition of *blog* (an amalgamation of the words *web* and *log*) is a site that contains a series of posts organized in reverse chronological order. This sterile definition doesn't quite convey what people really think when they hear the word *blog*, though.

In the collective mind, the word *blog* sometimes calls forth a picture of a writer in pajamas, talking about his or her daily life. Many of the concepts we'll cover in this book will be beneficial to those who want to start such a personal blog; however, our focus is specifically centered around technical blogging.

A technical blog is a nonfiction blog, the main subject matter of which is technical—rather than personal—in nature. Generally, you won't delve into what you had for lunch or include pictures of your newborn nephew. Instead, you'll use your blog as a way to share your expertise with others in your field.

Examples of some popular technical blogs that you might already be familiar with include *TechCrunch* (tech news), *Engadget* (gadget news), *Joel on Software* (programming), *Signal v. Noise* (entrepreneurship), *Coding Horror* (programming), *Troy Hunt* (tech security), and *Seth's Blog* (marketing),[2] to name a few.

Figure 1—A sample of a popular blog

As a developer and web entrepreneur, I imagine my ideal readers to be developers and technically minded entrepreneurs who are blogging about software development and business-related subjects, respectively.

Fitting into one camp or the other isn't a requirement, though. You may be launching a blog about biotechnology, dentistry, or photography, and the content of this book would still apply to you. In fact, you could be using the information from within this book to promote a mom-and-pop type of shop, and you'd still be able to derive useful guidance to succeed in your content marketing efforts.

---

2. techcrunch.com, engadget.com, joelonsoftware.com, m.signalvnoise.com, blog.codinghorror.com, troyhunt.com, and seths.blog, respectively.

Blogging Isn't Dead

You may have heard that blogging is dead and thus are wary of investing your time and effort in an activity that's obsolete. Don't be! To adapt a famous quote by Mark Twain, rumors of blogging's death have been greatly exaggerated. The blogging ecosystem is now extremely mature and well established. Individuals and companies continue to reap incredible benefits from blogging, and if anything they have fewer competitors willing to invest the time and energy required to produce longer content. So they're more likely to stand out.

Among many reasons why publishing quick content on social media (say, on Twitter) is so popular is the fact that it takes minimal effort to do so. You can share a link or a short thought with your followers in a matter of seconds. Conversely, a well-written article for a traditional blog could take a couple of hours to craft. Some see platforms like Twitter as an evolutionary branch of blogging, targeted toward an Internet audience that's stereotypically perceived as having a short attention span.

As a technical blogger, you have nothing to fear from these microblogging platforms. They don't compete with your blog. They are a complementary tool to reach your audience. A maximum of 280 characters is sufficient to enable you to share what you're watching on TV, crack a joke, link to an article, or share a quick thought, but it is ill-suited for essays or HOWTOs on technology (long Twitter threads notwithstanding). Instead, think of social media as a complementary way of blogging and broadcasting your message. Later in the book, we'll outline a complete strategy to take advantage of such platforms in that capacity.

By the way, exact blogging statistics are hard to come by; but using available numbers from some of the larger players like Tumblr and WordPress, it's quite likely that there are well over 500 million blogs in the world. This number has roughly tripled since the first edition of this book, published five years prior to this second edition. Blogging is indeed alive and well.

Blogging as a Megaphone

An established blog is like a megaphone: it amplifies your voice, allowing you to reach a wider audience. Creating such a following takes time and hard work, but the payoff is that the audience you've built up is going to be there for you when you need it (as I've literally experienced firsthand).

This megaphone also has the wonderful advantage of coming with a built-in echo generator, since your audience may rebroadcast your message through social networks or their own blogs, helping you reach an even larger pool of interested readers.

It's up to you to decide how to use this type of megaphone, but you'll be surprised by just how handy it is to have the same circulation as a local newspaper. Announcing a new project or product? Looking for a new hire? Having an issue with a company that's ignoring your valid complaint? Fear not; your audience can help.

Here's a case in point: I once had a problem with a computer store chain that wouldn't repair a brand-new but defective laptop I had just purchased for my wife's birthday. I wrote about the situation on my technical blog; and after a few days, the story had been read by over a hundred thousand people. Among those readers were members of the traditional media, some of whom became interested in my story and wanted to interview me. After the whirlwind of attention that my story generated, the company agreed to do the right thing and reluctantly repaired the laptop under warranty.

As with all situations in life, with great power comes great responsibility. Don't abuse your position of influence, but know that thousands of regular readers will be there for you when you need them. At times, it may feel as though you have an unfair advantage in this respect, and that's because you do.

Blogging as a Conversation

Blogging is not just about broadcasting a message to thousands of readers; it's also an ongoing conversation with a portion of them.

Most blogs have comment sections for this specific purpose, and they're definitely good for relationship building and engagement. Some readers may even contact you directly by email or quote you on their own blog. Other discussions about your content may pop up on sites or communities such as Twitter, Facebook, Instagram, LinkedIn, Reddit, or Hacker News.[3]

Thinking of blogging as a conversation can also be freeing because you don't need to have all the answers before approaching a subject you intend to write about. You are not expected to.

A blog post is a conversation starter that can lead to lengthy discussions that have the potential to spread far and wide across the Internet. It's important that you treat blogging as a conversation that will help you grow and learn, and not just as a megaphone.

---

3. news.ycombinator.com

As a blogger, you are part of the blogosphere, a world with its own expectations, most of which are based around the idea of a community of bloggers and commenters interacting with one another.

Be part of this conversation by replying to comments whenever they're posted on your site and by linking to other blogs that are relevant to your articles. In doing so, your blog stands a good chance of growing and quickly attracting a community of like-minded individuals. To boot, you may establish professional relationships and make new friends in the process.

Bloggers with Benefits

As an author, I'm aware that different readers will have different goals and, consequently, different expectations of this book.

Some readers may be solely interested in sharing their knowledge with the world. Writing and expressing thoughts for these kinds of readers is enough reward and motivation to blog on a regular basis. It's their way of giving back by sharing a part of themselves for the benefit of others.

At the other end of the spectrum are readers who are mostly interested in learning how to make a second income for themselves or how to better market their company's products via blogging.

This book is meant to be useful regardless of where you land on this spectrum. The only common assumption I make is that you have the honest intent to share your expertise with an audience and aren't afraid of working toward that goal.

Throughout the book you'll find a fair bit of information about how to build a large audience and, in the process, benefit to the fullest (including economically) from the success of your blog. I don't think anyone reading this book will object to attracting a large following, but a minority might not be interested in the monetary benefits of blogging. That's OK. Bear with me or feel free to skip those parts. Just understand that I've covered such topics in detail to satisfy those readers who may have goals that differ from your own.

And consider this: any time you spend blogging is time you're not spending on paying pursuits or, more importantly, with your family/loved ones. A time may come when this weighs on you. You're likely to blog more consistently and longer if your blogging pays for itself in some form or another (even if the reward isn't directly monetary).

With that clarification out of the way, let's briefly list what some practical and tangible benefits of blogging are. Most benefits, you'll notice, derive directly from your blog being the effective megaphone and conversation tool we discussed earlier.

- Blogging can advance your career. You could land a dream job, improve your standing and visibility within your current company, or book more consultancy gigs if you're a freelancer. If the latter applies to you, then blogging could also help you be more in demand and therefore enable you to command a higher rate.

- Blogging can help you become well known in your field. You might receive invitations to speak at conferences, receive an offer to write a book on the subject you blog about, or have the awesome benefit of being able to quickly bring attention to your latest projects with a single post. And, if you're into technical books, make some room on your shelves for the free review copies you'll likely be offered by publishers.

- Blogging can help you earn extra income. This can range from pizza money all the way to thousands of dollars a month. Blogging is by no means a get-rich-quick scheme, but it has the potential to handsomely provide you with economic rewards, both directly and indirectly.

In addition to these benefits, if you are blogging to promote a business, you can also expect to achieve the following:

- Finding new customers—blogging is an extremely cost-effective marketing tool (often referred to as inbound marketing); it can definitely help you attract a large number of new customers for your products.

- Building loyalty—customers who regularly interact with companies tend to develop greater loyalty to those companies, their brands, and their products. A blog that allows for comments and has an approachable social media presence is the ideal means by which to keep that communication channel open.

- Finding new employees, partners, and investors—when you put your business out there through a blog, you have the chance to meet an array of people online, including prospective hires. With a bit of luck, you may even catch the interest of potential business partners and investors. Blogging can enable you to network with the right type of people to help bolster the growth of your business.

Chapter 11, Advancing Your Career with Blogging, on page 199, and Chapter 12, Promoting Your Own Business, on page 229, will show you how to obtain all of these benefits.

How to Get the Most Out of This Book

Before proceeding with this journey, I feel it's important to highlight how this book is intended to be read.

If you don't have a blog yet, it's worth reading this book from cover to cover, as you'll be provided with a complete set of steps that you can take to become a successful blogger. After reading each chapter, write down the steps you plan to undertake for your site. To take full advantage of the book, you must actively put at least some of the advice housed within it into action.

If you already have a blog, you'll still benefit from reading the book in its entirety, but doing so is not quite as mandatory. You can focus on the chapters that interest you right now and come back to others whenever you need assistance with a specific topic.

Regardless of whether you're a new blogger or not, think of blogging as an experiment. You'll try suggestions from this book, and many of them will work for your blog (though a few might not). By using traffic statistics and user feedback, you'll be able to validate what works for you and what doesn't. Then iterate, constantly improving your blog with small enhancements. As you gain more experience, you'll be able to test your own theories to discover what helps your blog grow.

Remember that everything we do as bloggers is intended to showcase our content. Yet this book contains many chapters that focus on other aspects of blogging. These other chapters are necessary because they'll help you maximize your ability to promote and benefit from your content. As you approach each chapter, however, you should remember the mantra "Content first." The underlying assumption throughout this book is that you're reading these pages with the intent of producing the best content you can.

If you've already read the first edition of this book, welcome back. The world has changed in the past five years, and so have some of my blogging recommendations. I'm confident that you'll find the updates throughout the book, and the additional content, well worth reading this second edition for.

This book is written in the belief that each of us has something worth sharing. Each of us has a blogger within. I'm here to help you let your blogger out.

Part I

Plan It

The Internet is really about highly specialized information, highly specialized targeting.

> *Eric Schmidt*

CHAPTER 1

What Kind of Blog Are You Going to Run?

The first step when planning your blog is to determine the type of blog you're going to run. We've already established that it's likely not going to be about your personal life, but you still have some choices to make.

The decisions you make now will affect many aspects of how you develop your blog down the road, so you should try to answer these important questions before proceeding with the next chapters of this book.

Solo vs. Collective

I would expect the majority of readers to be interested in creating (or resuming) a single-author blog. This is the most common type of blog and it makes for a sensible default. There is a chance, though, that a collective blog might be a better option for you. To help you figure out which of the two is best suited to your circumstances and goals, let's briefly consider the advantages and disadvantages of solo and collective blogs.

Solo blogs are relatively easy to start. They allow you to be the boss, and you don't need to collaborate with other people. Being the only author for your blog also lowers the expectations in terms of how much content you produce. With a solo blog, you're just a person expressing his or her thoughts on the web.

The Joys and Perils of Collective Blogs

Collective blogs are a team effort. Not only do you have to worry about getting this whole blogging thing going, but you have to factor in the overhead and typical issues that arise when trying to collaborate with multiple people on the same project.

You'll have to figure out who's going to cover what topics—and on what days—as well as the time commitment each blogger is willing to put in, the acceptable styles and conventions, and who's going to handle the editing, comment moderation, and article promotion. Furthermore, if the authors are not blogging on behalf of a company, the issue of fairly splitting the financial rewards will have to be sorted out.

But the biggest challenge, in my experience, is to keep everyone motivated enough to continue writing and meeting the agreed-upon deadlines. Sound familiar? Right, it's not that different from coordinating a team of developers working on a software project.

Just as with a software team, you'll probably want to have someone in charge (i.e., an editor-in-chief) who can oversee the project management and coordination as well as ensure that the writing meets the standards you set for your group blog (or online magazine).

> Tip 1   Collective blogs can benefit greatly from an editor-in-chief.

That's the hard part. On the plus side, you can crank out content very quickly thanks to the sheer number of authors, rapidly accelerating the blog's growth. You'll also offer a greater variety of topics and viewpoints. At the very end of that spectrum are blogs with multiple paid authors that post as much as news sites. Such sites can hardly be seen as blogs anymore. They are full-blown online tech news outlets. Among this group, you'll find well-known sites such as *TechCrunch, Ars Technica,*[1] and *InfoQ.*[2]

Several years ago I started a collective Italian blog called *Stacktrace* with more than a dozen unpaid authors.[3] We were able to quickly publish more than a hundred articles and grow our list of feed subscribers to well over ten thousand members.

Our articles were rather technical (e.g., Linux kernel hacking, JavaScript closures) and written in Italian, so these figures are far more respectable than they may seem at first glance. In fact, in a matter of months, this collective blog became, arguably, one of the most respected aperiodic technical publications in Italy.

It would've been impossible for me to achieve the same results if I'd launched *Stacktrace* on my own. Unfortunately, as my interest in publishing in Italian waned, so did the interest of the group of volunteers who had been contributing to it.

---

1.   arstechnica.com
2.   infoq.com
3.   stacktrace.it

Due to the challenges associated with running a collective blog, I would discourage you from attempting this type of site if you're a novice blogger. This is particularly true when the group of bloggers you are trying to coordinate with is larger than two or three friends.

The Team Blog

The one notable exception to this recommendation is this: if you have a group of colleagues all working for the same company, it may make sense to set up a team blog. In fact, if you aren't a seasoned blogger, this is the only type of collective blog I'd ever consider recommending. When writing for such a team blog is part of your work duties and you're held accountable to some extent for its success, you're far less likely to abandon the site (and so are your colleagues).

The perfect example of a collective blog that's run by a team from the same company is the previously mentioned *Signal v. Noise* by Basecamp as shown in as shown in Figure 2, One of the most successful team blogs in the world, on page 6. This is a company that literally owes its fame and fortune to the constant blogging activities of a handful of founders and employees (along with its remarkable product, open source contributions, and recent best-selling books).

If you end up being the editor-in-chief for your team blog, expect to nag people to deliver articles. Professionals are busy and might not give any priority to the marketing efforts you're championing. You might also want to be prescriptive and assign specific articles around their expertise, as opposed to hoping that your colleagues will come up with their own.

In my experience, asking that your colleagues commit to one article every couple of months leads to a manageable workload for them. Depending on the number of participants and how much editing you'll do, it may not be so for you. Take all these factors into consideration before setting deadlines for your team blog.

Abandoned Blogs

Sadly, the most common type of blog is the abandoned one. It's not unusual for new bloggers to start a blog and post for a while, only to discover that they don't have the time or patience required to keep it alive. The incentives to continue blogging will also be relatively few at first. The average blog fails to attract a wide readership and consequently, the rewards can also be scarce.

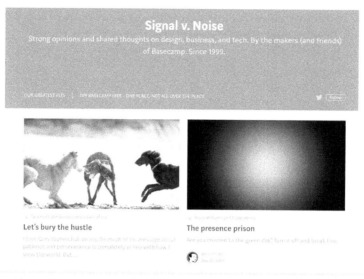

Figure 2—One of the most successful team blogs in the world

If you follow the blueprint outlined in this book, you should have no problem avoiding most pitfalls and the common fate of abandoning your blog. If you already have an abandoned blog, this is the perfect opportunity to reboot it.

General vs. Niche

Now that you have thought about and hopefully decided to run a blog by yourself or with the help of a few people, it's time to consider another important question: is your blog going to be general or will it cover a specific topic?

It's the old conundrum of choosing between being a generalist or a specialist, something that many developers have to deal with at some point in their careers, only this time it's applied to blogging.

This is an important question because your choice truly defines the type of content you'll typically include, as well as affecting other vital aspects of running a blog, such as promotion and monetization.

The choice you make has a lot to do with your personality and interests. If programming in Python is your pride and joy, you may opt for a *niche* (i.e., a topic that is somewhat narrow in scope) blog on that subject. If you have a thousand interests within the grand scope of programming, as I do, you may find a general blog gives you more room to express your thoughts.

Remember that the distinction between general and niche blogs has to do with the expectations your readers have. People who subscribe to your Python blog expect you to speak about Python-related subjects. That's their main interest and the reason why they subscribed in the first place. You risk disappointing your readers if you start publishing rants about Apple and HOWTOs on developing apps for Android in Kotlin. The occasional off-topic article might be okay, but don't make it a habit if your blog is a niche one.

> Tip 2   Don't betray your readers' expectations.

If you feel that you're the kind of person who needs to express your thoughts on a multitude of subjects, then publishing a general blog is the safer choice. You can still post mostly about Python on *John's thoughts on programming*, for example, but then you're not restricted to that niche.

I experienced the restriction of a niche blog myself when I started my current programming blog. It was originally called *Zen and the Art of Ruby Programming*. Despite its success as a Ruby blog, I simply couldn't stand not talking about other programming languages, frameworks, and even more generic tech topics. As a result, I renamed it *Programming Zen* and I now cover programming and technology within a broader scope.[4]

It may be tempting to assume that a larger scope of subjects necessarily correlates to, or even implies, a larger readership that's easier to attract. After all, if you're posting about Ruby, Python, C#, Apple, and Arduino, you'll definitely attract the attention of multiple communities, right? Wrong. The truth is that it's much harder to succeed with a general blog than it is with a niche one. Let's see why this counterintuitive notion applies.

Imagine that Alice, a passionate Rust programmer, discovers a link to an interesting article on a blog called *Rusty Adventures*. It may be very tempting for her to subscribe to that blog if she likes what she reads.

Now imagine the same article on *John's thoughts on programming*. Alice doesn't know John, nor does she have any reason to trust him as an authority on the subject of Rust. Why would she subscribe to John's personal blog? Sure, the article was good, but John also seems to talk about Python and Swift, which Alice is not interested in. In the end, Alice is far more likely to subscribe to and continue following the niche blog.

> Tip 3   Do one thing, but do it well.

---

4.   programmingzen.com

Niche blogs tend to make why a visitor should subscribe more obvious, but there are other reasons why it's easier to succeed with a niche blog. For one, there's less competition. Performing SEO (search engine optimization) is easier when your blog's name, domain name, and most of its content already contain popular keywords you're targeting (we'll talk more about SEO throughout the book). Blog aggregators and other bloggers are more prone to link to you if you cover their specific niche (and establishing relationships with them is also more likely).

Niche blogging makes you part of a community, and if you play your cards right, it can make you rather famous within such a community. It's not just easier to promote your blog and actually succeed when you opt to go this route; a niche blog can also simplify the process of reaping the benefits of your blogging efforts.

I can think of very few ways to better establish yourself as an expert on a given topic than by running an excellent, informative niche blog on that subject. It doesn't hurt either that such a targeted audience is gold if you decide to directly monetize your blog.

For all these reasons, I recommend you start a niche blog rather than a general one that spans a whole industry—unless you really feel compelled to write about a large variety of topics that can't be contained in a well-defined niche. For an example of an excellent (fairly large) niche blog, check out *Real Python*.[5]

> **Tip 4** Niche blogs are more likely to become successful.

If you see yourself as a polymath, opting for a general blog may still be a worthwhile trade-off if that will make you feel less constrained, more satisfied with your writing, and less likely to abandon your blog.

Pundit vs. Instructional

Look at many of the technical blogs out there, and you'll quickly feel daunted by what looks like a bewildering range of approaches. But they really boil down to providing commentary, giving actual technical instructions, or a mix of both.

A pundit blog showcases an author's insights into an industry or a particular niche. It's typically filled with essays on relevant topics or quotes from other

---

5.   realpython.com

interesting blogs and news stories to which an opinion is added. The perfect example of a pundit who mostly blogs about Apple is John Gruber and his popular blog, *Daring Fireball.*[6]

An instructional blog focuses on HOWTOs. The aim of this type of blog is to provide tutorials or reference material for readers. There may be an opinion here and there, but these are mostly a collection of factual posts. For an example, check out the excellent *John D. Cook's Blog.*[7]

Which should you choose—pundit or instructional? In my experience, this is a false dichotomy and you should opt for both styles—at least in the beginning. Offer variety to your readers by including a mix of pundit-style commentary and tutorials.

Depending on how your readership responds to either type of post, you'll be able to focus more on one or the other. Consider your readers' feedback before cornering yourself into a specific blogging style. You'll also quickly discover which of the two you enjoy writing the most, and that's just as important. You can always evolve and change your blog style at a later stage.

Business Blogs

Note: If you don't own, operate, or promote a company, you can safely skip this section.

It's extremely common for companies to have an official blog. If you're trying to connect with existing customers, reach new ones, and sell more of your products or services, it definitely makes sense to have such a site in place.

The real issue is figuring what sort of style you intend to give to your company blog. During this initial planning phase, you may wonder if the writing should be technical or business-oriented. Should the blog include product updates and announcements?

Although we'll cover the promotion of your own products and company in detail, particularly starting with Chapter 12, Promoting Your Own Business, on page 229, it's worth having a few preliminary thoughts on the matter in mind beforehand.

---

6.   daringfireball.net
7.   johndcook.com/blog/

Who Is Your Audience?

Before you write a single word, it's important to decide who the audience of your company blog is.

Make your blog ultra-technical, with scores of behind-the-scene details regarding how you develop the software that you sell, and you'll attract the attention of fellow developers. If your ideal customer base is developers or if you're trying to hire some new talent, this could be a solid strategy. If that's not the case, however, the explanation of your fancy continuous integration setup or dockerized architecture for your SaaS (software as a service) won't mean a thing to your customers and might even alienate them.

Likewise, taking an all-business approach in which you either share the details of how you run your startup or go into business topics at great length will tend to attract fellow entrepreneurs. Again, if they're your potential customers (e.g., your product is B2B), this approach can pay off.

The aforementioned Basecamp (formerly 37signals) produces SaaS aimed at helping companies better handle communication and collaboration. Its unique and opinionated take on the way a business should be run, broadcast through its blog and books, has attracted many of its customers. Its approach worked because their content attracts entrepreneurs who in turn are primary candidates for its software.

In most other cases, you'll find that your customers won't be particularly interested in learning how your Facebook ad campaign generated a 300 percent ROI (return on investment).

More commonly and realistically, you'll find that your end users are interested in learning about offers and discounts, product updates and announcements, server issues that might affect them, and ways to use your products that will help them be more productive or solve certain problems. The last two on the list will help the most in attracting new customers.

You'll also want to throw testimonials and success stories into the mix, showcasing how other clients are using your products in unique or interesting ways, as well as including general topics of interest that are relevant to the industry your company operates in. The occasional behind-the-scenes post, either technical or business-oriented, is definitely OK too, but it shouldn't be the main point of your blog unless people interested in such posts coincide with your product audience.

If you have the staff to maintain them, you might even opt to have two blogs for your company. Your *product blog* could be dedicated to announcements, status updates, and product news. The other could be broader in scope and mostly aimed at prospective customers and peers. (Though this is quite ambitious and I wouldn't recommend starting off with this approach.)

The secret is to understand who your ideal customers are and then write the sort of content they want, search for, understand, and relate to.

Take Action

Before moving on, take a minute to honestly answer each of the following questions for your blog. Consider writing down your answers, rather than just thinking about them.

1. Is it going to be your blog or a team effort?
2. Is it going to be a niche or a general blog?
3. Do you plan to focus on industry commentary or tutorials?
4. Who is your ideal audience?

What's Next

With a clearer idea of the type of blog you plan to run, we can proceed to the next chapter, where we'll define the main topic of your site and a series of related choices. The next chapter also completes our plan before moving onto chapters that are dedicated to setting up your blog.

Plans are worthless, but planning is everything.

> *Dwight D. Eisenhower*

CHAPTER 2

Rock-Solid Planning for Your Blog

In the previous chapter, we made some broad, preliminary decisions that impact the direction of your blog. In this chapter, we're going to finalize our plan by fleshing out further details.

In particular, we'll define goals for your blog, clarify its raison d'être and topic, and demystify audience expectations. We'll also discuss finding a good domain name that works well both from human and search-engine-optimization perspectives.

Define Your Blog's Main Topic

Whether you opted for a niche blog or a more general one, your site is going to have a main theme. In the case of a niche, the scope will be well defined and easy to identify. For general blogs, it can be much looser and less defined. Nevertheless, you need to have a clear, if preliminary, idea of what your blog will be about.

Identify Your Niche

You should identify the main topic for your niche based on your interests and motivations. For example, an iPhone freelancer may want to start a blog about Swift and iOS development. That's a relatively large niche, but it provides the blog with a well-defined scope. You'll know immediately what the boundaries for the blog are, as well as what does and doesn't belong on your site.

After picking the main topic, jot down a list of ten articles you could write for your blog. You don't need to write the actual articles yet, just the titles. When you're done with this task, ask yourself whether doing this exercise left you excited or frustrated. Was it hard to come up with ten titles, or could you have kept going for ages? The main point of this exercise is to understand if you do in fact have enough to say about the topic at hand.

In most cases, you won't have to worry about this, but if you pick a tiny niche that's highly specific, you may quickly run out of ideas for articles and face other obvious problems, such as only being able to attract a small audience. We'll discuss how to estimate the size of a niche in Analyze the Size of Your Niche, on page 15.

Define the Main Theme for Your General Blog

If you intend to publish a blog on programming in general, web development, or a similarly broad topic in another industry, you don't have to worry about the possibility of running out of ideas or having too small of an audience to capture.

Your pre-setup exercise will be a bit different from the niche one. Start by coming up with a main theme for your blog (e.g., web development). Follow that by listing several relevant topics that you're passionate and knowledgeable about.

For example:

- Python
- Django
- JavaScript
- Deployment and scaling
- Relational and NoSQL databases
- Technical reviews

As you can see, these are very broad topics, each of which would roughly correspond to a different category within your blog. The argument could be made that a general blog is just a niche blog with a much larger niche. I can live with this interpretation, but the much wider latitude will definitely affect your blog in ways that warrant the niche/general distinction.

This task is not just meant to help you figure out what kind of topics you'll be covering in your blog. The real point of this exercise is to determine if you're willing to cover enough variety of topics to warrant creating a general blog on your main subject.

How did you feel as you jotted them down? Were you excited about the prospect of writing articles for them? Was coming up with this list easy or did you struggle to write more than two or three topics? If you find that your passion and expertise really lies with only one or two categories, you may be better off picking one and running a laser-focused niche blog that's dedicated solely to that subject instead.

Analyze the Size of Your Niche

Before committing to your blog, you may want to assess the size of your potential audience. For most niches, this is more of a curiosity than a requirement, but if you're trying to establish yourself in a very small niche and are uncertain about its size, this step can help you determine if it's worth pursuing or not.

We're after an estimate rather than exact numbers. More importantly, the process you'll go through in order to estimate the size of your niche will also turn out to be useful when researching keywords and topics for your articles later on.

Determine the Search Volume for Your Niche

As you probably know, Google makes the bulk of its profits from selling ads. And ads are annoying, right? Well, in this case it actually works in our favor. Google has released a series of tools for advertisers that are meant to help its Ads (formerly AdWords) users find new keywords to advertise with, as well as helping them estimate search volumes for those keywords.

We have no intention of buying ads from Google through its Ads program now, but we can still use the information Google makes available to do some research into the size of our niche.

In the first edition of this book, I advocated using the Google Keyword Tool, which has since been rebranded to the Keyword Planner tool.[1] It's still a viable option, but these days I find it to be more focused toward (and therefore more useful to) actual advertisers rather than bloggers. Nevertheless, at this stage, we're not doing advanced SEO research. We're looking for broad ranges, and the Keyword Planner does provide us with those.

For example, let's say that your blog niche is TypeScript. The Keyword Planner currently suggests a U.S. monthly volume of searches for that exact keyword to be in the 10K–100K range, as shown in Figure 3, Google Keyword Planner, on page 17. This gives us an idea of the size of the audience, and it's good enough for now.

Alternatively, you could use one of the many free keyword tools available by searching for "free keyword tool" in...well, likely Google. Some of these services don't require registration and provide specific numbers instead of broad ranges like Google does. The catch is that the estimates will be different, depending on the site you use, but the general order of magnitude should be consistent across the board.

---

1. ads.google.com/home/tools/keyword-planner

Whichever tool you decide to use, plug in some keywords related to your specific blog topic and see what kind of search volume shows up. Use generic keywords with one or two words at most, and not something specific like "python programming for data science." Instead, search for "python," "data science," and perhaps "numpy" to better gauge the interest level in the topic.

One of the tools I use shows a volume of 42,000 U.S. monthly searches for "TypeScript," and much more globally (200K+). That's certainly a sizable-enough audience to build a blog around.

Although worldwide data is provided by the Keyword Planner, if you're primarily targeting countries like China, Russia, or South Korea, you might be better off using the keyword research tools offered by the most popular search engines in those respective countries—namely Baidu, Yandex, and Naver. The same is true for any market where Google isn't the de facto search engine.

Going Pro with Premium SEO Tools

SEO experts tend to use premium tools that offer amazing features and insight. It's a crowded market, but the three tools that stand out are Ahrefs,[2] SEM-Rush,[3] and Moz.[4] Personally, I'm partial to Ahrefs, but they're all roughly equivalent and invaluable to bloggers who are serious about ranking in Google.

There are two downsides:

1. They are as complex as they are powerful, so there's a bit of a learning curve.
2. Their price tends to be rather premium.

Pricing can vary over time, but think "$100/month and up" kind of premium. The good news is that they are total overkill for someone who's just starting out. I included them because in a few months or years from now, you might decide to take your SEO efforts to the next level. If you do, one of the three tools shown in Figure 3, Google Keyword Planner, on page 17 will serve you well.

Use Google Trends

Just as important as the current search volume is the search trend. Is your keyword becoming increasingly popular over time, or are you setting yourself up to create a blog about a technology whose adoption is regressing?

---

2. ahrefs.com
3. semrush.com
4. moz.com

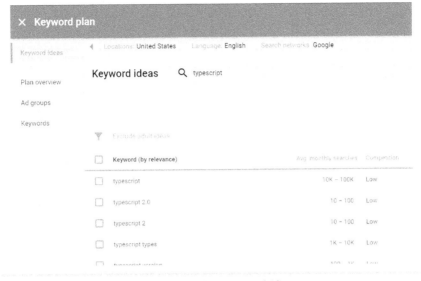

Figure 3—Google Keyword Planner

Thankfully we don't have to rely on intuition. We can verify our gut feeling about the trend of a given technology by using another Google tool called Google Trends.[5] By searching in Google Trends for our language, technology, or main keyword, we can easily assess its search volume over time. The specific example of TypeScript (Figure 4, Google Trends, on page 18) shows decent growth over the past few years. Past performance is never a guarantee of future results, but a chart like this can be somewhat reassuring.

Google Trends offers details about the regions and cities in which a given keyword is popular. TypeScript seems to be searched for primarily in Redmond/Seattle (its birthplace), San Francisco, Minsk, Bengaluru, and other hotbeds of startup activity.

This kind of information is particularly useful to you if you live in one of the cities in which your niche is going strong. Along with starting a blog on the subject, you could decide to become active in your local tech community (and perhaps even launch a relevant Meetup group). A local environment favorable to your technology of choice would also be beneficial if you're looking for a job, intending to offer your freelance services to local companies, or hiring talent for your own business.

---

5. google.com/trends

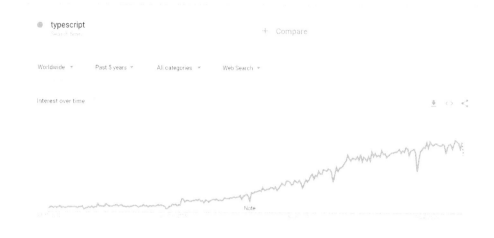

Figure 4—Google Trends

Make an Executive Decision

Perform similar searches for your own niche. It's hard to recommend a minimum threshold because it depends on many factors, including the type of niche, your reasons for blogging, and how specific you were while picking a keyword to search for. "It depends" answers are truthful but deeply unsatisfying. So if I truly had to provide you with a number, I would suggest opting for niches whose main keyword has at least 10,000 monthly searches. If you are creating a more generic blog, you don't have to worry about this.

If only 1,000 people search for your main keyword in a given month, your topic might be too niche to attract a sizable audience. It's up to you to decide whether it's still worth pursuing, but you can probably broaden the scope of your blog, at least slightly, to attract more people.

The exception to this is a brand-new technology that has just been announced (particularly by a well-established company like Apple or Microsoft). While such technologies may show zero search results initially, they're virtually guaranteed to become popular—at least to a certain extent—in the future. Also, keep in mind that, as a rule of thumb, the larger the niche, the bigger the competition.

Some Internet marketers make a very comfortable living through a series of microniche blogs (usually affiliate sites) that have a much smaller target audience than that. However, their business model and approach to blogging are quite different from the ones recommended in this book. Here we favor quality over quantity.

Give Readers a Compelling Reason to Stick Around

At this point, you should have determined the style and topic of your blog, as well as validated the existence of a sizable potential audience. Now you can start thinking about how to answer a question that many of your visitors will ask themselves: *Why should I subscribe to this blog?*

I phrased that question to intentionally imply a subscription to your upcoming posts via email or feed, the latter being less common these days but still used to a degree among a technical readership. Another way of phrasing the question would be to inquire why people should come back to your blog.

Whatever the exact question you ask, you need a convincing answer. What's the reason why your blog exists? Why did you start it in the first place? What's your compelling story? Answer these questions and you'll have a much clearer picture of what your blog is really about and why visitors will want to return.

The Elevator Pitch

The business world has a concept called the *elevator pitch*. Its name derives from the hypothetical scenario of finding yourself in an elevator with a potential investor. In such a context, you only get between thirty and ninety seconds to summarize what your product or company is all about before the doors of the fictional elevator spring open. While you don't need to raise money for your blog, considering your pitch is still a worthwhile exercise.

> Tip 5 Focus your elevator pitch on the why, not the how.

Your elevator pitch should quickly summarize the essence of your product or company. Why does it exist? What problem does it solve? What is its value proposition?

We are dealing with a blog here, but the same principle applies. Characterize your blog in one or two sentences at most and give people a reason why they should come back and visit again.

Case Study: Popular Tech Blogs

To help you with this task, let's look briefly at a few blogs (listed by URL) and analyze the compelling reasons for their existence.

- daringfireball.net: News and opinions about Apple by an unrepentant advocate of Apple products. Reason to read it: It provides fresh insight, interesting controversy, and news about Apple and its competitors delivered by an established community pundit.

- thedailywtf.com: Daily examples of bad programming. Reason to read it: To learn more about antipatterns in programming and for amusement.

- troyhunt.com: The personal blog of security expert Troy Hunt. Reason to read it: To learn more about security and the latest threats.

- seths.blog: The personal blog of marketing expert Seth Godin. Reason to read it: To improve your marketing skills with the aid of a leader in the marketing world via thought-provoking ideas and bite-sized insight.

- techcrunch.com: News about startups and technology. Reason to read it: To stay up-to-date with the world of technology and startups.

- engadget.com: News about gadgets. Reason to read it: To stay abreast of the latest gadgets.

- flowingdata.com: A visualization and statistics blog. Reason to read it: To learn, in the blog's words, "how designers, programmers, and statisticians are putting data to good use." It's a must for those interested in data visualization and statistics.

In each example above, the reason why you should follow these blogs is pretty obvious and can be stated in a single sentence.

Come Up with Your Blog's Reason for Being

Your goal is to make it just as obvious, to yourself first and then to your readers, why your blog is worth following. Remember the elevator pitch we discussed earlier. You only have from a few seconds (most commonly) to a few minutes (rarely and at the very most) to effectively win your readers over. You want to state your blog's intent through your title, tagline/motto, "about" blurb in the sidebar, and on the About page. Be as direct as possible: don't be subtle about stating what your blog is about and who it's for.

In the example of the TypeScript niche, we could set our sights on becoming a one-stop resource for folks who are interested in TypeScript news. Alternatively, we could make the blog about tutorials on how to accomplish various tasks or, again, create a blog that's dedicated solely to converting from JavaScript to TypeScript programming. What about one that is devoted to documenting your journey as you try to become proficient in TypeScript and related frameworks (e.g., Angular)?

Pick the idea that suits you best for your own subject; pretty much any will do as long as you give it an angle and clearly communicate the point of your blog to your visitors.

Over time you'll find that many other elements corroborate with your effort to make your blog compelling for your readers. These include the quality and usefulness of your articles, the type of visitors and comments that your blog attracts, the design of your site, and even how catchy your headlines are. We'll examine each of these points in further detail in the coming chapters.

Set Goals for Your Blog

With this clearer picture of your blog's topic and the reason for its existence, it's time to start thinking big and coming up with some goals for the months ahead. Don't worry if this looks like more planning than you bargained for. This is a practical book, and we'll take off in the next chapter. But as with many situations in life, it's important to develop a plan first.

Write down your goals. What do you want to get out of the blog you're starting? What do you expect from it in a month, three months, a year, three years?

Clarify your initial expectations now so that you can revisit and compare them to the results you actually achieve from your blog later on. If you're on track, well done. If not, you'll be able to make adjustments to your blogging efforts or even readjust your goals if your initial ones have proven to be unrealistic.

Don't write down vague goals. Try to be as specific as you can. One of your first-year goals shouldn't be phrased as, "Make some extra money from my blog." It should be more along the lines of, "Earn an extra $500 USD per month from my blog." Or if you're a startup blogger, you could have a goal such as "Use the blog to increase sales by 30 percent over the next twelve months."

> **Tip 6**   Always set verifiable goals.

If you're not presently interested in supplementing your income or increasing your product sales via blogging, then focus on different points while still aiming for goals that are verifiable.

As you set your short-term goals, please understand that most of the benefits you'll get from blogging are likely to kick in after a few months to a year. So don't jot down goals that are too ambitious for your one-month milestone.

Good first-month goals can include ensuring you've determined your blogging strategy with the help of this book. You may also want to throw in a goal about respecting the schedule you set throughout the month (more on this in Chapter 6, Producing Content Regularly, on page 111). Longer-term goals (say, one year) can be more focused on the desired positive impact on your career, project, or company, for example.

Readership Expectations

As you work on this goal-setting exercise, you may be tempted to define a specific numerical readership goal. I wouldn't focus on this. It's seriously hard to predict the readership of your own blog before you launch, because so many variables can affect the outcome.

For this reason, I wouldn't explicitly define an arbitrary number of readers by a certain date as a goal. Nevertheless, you may wonder what realistic traffic expectations should be for your first year of blogging.

Readership can be evaluated by using a number of key metrics, like subscribers, visitors, or page views. I like to focus on subscribers, since they're visitors who put some skin in the game.

The following numbers refer to total subscribers—via feed (increasingly rarer) or email—that you can expect to attract in your first year of blogging. These are your regular readers, so this figure tends to be a less transient metric of the popularity of your blog (and less of a vanity metric as well).

- *0–100 subscribers*: Your blog is still struggling to attract an audience. Unless you're in a very tiny niche, you may need to improve your strategy, content quality and quantity, promotion, and so forth to help bolster your readership.

- *100–500 subscribers:* Not a bad number for a technical blog. You're off to a decent start.

- *500–1,000 subscribers:* Above-average readership. I expect many of my readers will able to pull these kinds of numbers off.

- *1,000–5,000 subscribers:* Very successful blog. Few bloggers can boast such figures in their first year.

- *5,000–10,000 subscribers:* An extremely successful site that has quickly established itself as an authority blog in its field.

- *Over 10,000 subscribers:* Statistical outlier. Huge potential for the blog to become one of the most popular sites in its field, as well as a major source of income.

If you want a realistic single number to shoot for as your traffic milestone, try to reach the 1,000-subscriber mark as quickly as you can. In my experience, the magic of blogging and its many benefits start to manifest themselves visibly after you reach the general ballpark of a thousand subscribers.

With such a large fan base, your other metrics will no doubt be equally impressive. It's not uncommon to get an order of magnitude more monthly visitors than email and feed subscribers combined. We'll discuss the subject of subscribers (i.e., email, feed, and social) repeatedly in the book, and we'll also cover how to count them. For email subscribers, this is straightforward, but for feed subscribers, we'll need to get creative.

Choose and Register a Domain Name

The last step of this initial planning process is to choose a name and register a domain name for your new blog. If you already have a blog, it might still be worth reading this section. You could decide to start afresh with a new name and domain name, redirecting the existing one, particularly if your existing blog is new or unpopular at the moment.

Keep Your Blog on the Same Domain as Your Company

If the blog you are creating is for your company, the domain name choice is very straightforward. Assuming you already have a site for your company, you don't need to register a new domain name for your blog; simply define a subfolder, such as yourcompany.com/blog.

The reason for going this route isn't limited to URL consistency and the need to make a connection between your blog and company obvious to your customers. When you use the same domain for your main site as well as your blog, any SEO efforts you make on either side will end up benefiting (to a lesser extent) the other as well. This is because they both reside on the same domain. Your blog will also have better positioning from day one, thanks to the existing authority—in the eyes of search engines—of the main domain name.

Many companies will opt for a subdomain instead of a subfolder (e.g., blog.yourcompany.com). I don't recommend that you do. Although it arguably looks better, it's not as effective from an SEO standpoint. The existing authority of your domain name will not benefit your articles as much, and popular blog posts won't end up benefiting your main site's rankings in Google to the same degree, either.[6]

---

6. www.mattcutts.com/blog/subdomains-and-subdirectories

For company blogs, prefer a subfolder over a subdomain.

Blog Name or Domain Name?

Before delving into the topic of picking a good name for your blog, let me state one important distinction that's often overlooked. The name of your blog and your domain name are two different entities. You may opt for a domain name that's different from your blog name for brevity reasons (nobody likes overly long domain names) or because the exact domain name is not available.

That said, having a domain name that matches your blog name is definitely recommended. It helps cut down on confusion and ensures that visitors remember your domain name more easily. So I strongly suggest you strive to find a domain name that matches your desired blog name. However, if a perfect match isn't possible, do not turn your back on a short, easy-to-remember domain name.

Naming the Baby

Bestowing names on things looks easy from the outside, but the process can quickly become a time-consuming endeavor. You might think that it would take only a few minutes to find the perfect name, but once you start searching for a name, your brainstorming sessions can sometimes end up lasting for hours or even span the course of several days.

To help you decide on a good domain name for your blog (and its own corresponding name) much more quickly, I've listed a series of guidelines below that I tend to use when I find myself in this situation. Most of them should be common sense, but there might be a few novel ideas that will make the process of coming up with a good name easier and quicker for you.

Which TLDs?

As soon as you start searching for a domain name, you'll realize that a ton of .com domain names have already been taken at this point in time. Often, this extends to the .net and .org TLDs (top-level domains) as well. So it can be tempting to simply opt for one of the many new TLD domains made available by the ICANN (Internet Corporation for Assigned Names and Numbers). These are increasingly more common and accepted, but I would still recommend that you try as hard as you can to acquire a .com domain. At the end of the day, it's still the king of TLDs.

Failing that, you should consider a .net or .org domain name. But you'll need to accept that registering a .net or .org domain name when the .com version is held by a *domainer* (a domain name speculator who mainly buys domain names with the intent of reselling them for a large profit margin) implies that you'll inevitably end up sending some of your traffic to the .com version of your site, as users may assume that your site is located on the .com address.

Conversely, if the .com is actually being used by someone with a real site, it's common courtesy not to register the exact (or very similar) .net or .org version of the domain name, even if available. I'm pointing this out because you'll inevitably create confusion for readers of both sites if you decide to go down this path.

A litigious individual or business may also decide to pursue legal action, which is annoying to deal with, whether the case is legitimate or not (this is even worse in the case of registered trademarks, where the owner is often required by law to protect it by going after violators).

.com, .net, and .org are the most SEO-friendly options and what most people expect to type in. SEO isn't an exact science (by design) so there's a debate on whether alternative TLDs will rank as well as .com, .net, and .org. In my opinion, you can rank any domain, but Google still has a bias toward the big three. If you must consider other options, I suggest staying away from confusing TLDs like ".co." People will inevitably type ".com" instead.

In fact, SEO debates aside, the key problem is people's perception of your domain name and their ability to remember it. Case in point, avoid .info because it was historically very cheap to acquire and therefore used and abused by spammers and scammers. Its reputation is somewhat tarnished.

In recent years, the TLD .io has become particularly popular among startups and programmers. If your blog is mostly aimed at programmers and you really cannot find any suitable .com domain name, .io might be an acceptable, if suboptimal, option. The same can be said for the increasingly popular .blog or even .codes. They aren't my first choice, but they can work, and the latter lends itself to some neat-sounding domain names (e.g., yourname.codes).

If you're trying to break into a local market with your blog, it may make sense to register a country-specific domain name. For example, a Canadian freelancer who's interested in promoting her web design services locally may opt for a ccTLD (country code top-level domain) .ca domain name. Doing so also makes sense from an SEO standpoint, as search engines like Google absolutely love country-specific domain names when showing local search results.

> **Tip 8** If your target audience is local to a specific country, favor ccTLDs.

In the example of the Canadian site, all things being equal, the .ca will edge out the .com's SERP (search engine results page) positioning on Google.ca. Hosting your blog through a Canadian host would also help the cause, eh?

Keyword- or Brand-Based?

Search engines love keyword-based domain names and generally give them an unfair advantage in the result pages. Having the one or two main keywords you are targeting placed within your domain name will boost your blog ranks on Google and Bing (as well as on other search engines that, quite frankly, very few people in the Western world use).

The reason for this is that search engines take the keywords within your domain name as an indication of your site's relevance to a given user's query. If I'm looking for "old-fashioned programmer keyboards," all things being equal, Google will assume that oldfashionedprogrammerkeyboards.com is more relevant than undermyfingertips.com (note that these are entirely fictional names, even if these sites do exist).

An SEO-friendly domain name is not the only aspect to consider, though. The human perception of your domain name is incredibly important in the case of a reputable technical blog. Most programmers I know would probably guess that oldfashionedprogrammerkeyboards.com is a commercial or spammy site of some sort. undermyfingertips.com on the other hand, would be seen as a clever name that could easily host a blog that reviews all kinds of keyboards.

In short, humans tend to remember and love good brand names, while search engines favor domain names with keywords. The trouble with brand names is that they take time and effort to establish, even when we're just dealing with blogs and not company names.

My suggestion is to find the right balance. If your keyword-based domain name makes for a decent, catchy brand, definitely go for it. If not, see if mixing it up with other words can help. The textbook example of this is engadget.com, which managed to include the word *gadget* and the pun on *engage* in such a short brand domain name.

As a less clever example, I went with programmingzen.com because it's easy to remember and is fairly "brand-ish" sounding while also containing the keyword *programming.*

A few years ago, it made sense to err on the side of keyword-rich domain names. These days, there's some evidence that Google is giving this particular signal less weight than it did in the past. Ideally, a niche blog about Python should include the word Python in it, if only for no other reason than it immediately showcases what the blog is about to readers. But don't obsess over having an exact match between your topic's main keywords and your domain name.

Other Suggestions for Picking the Right Domain Name

So far we've covered the essentials of picking a domain name, but what about using hyphens in your name, choosing your domain length, and other things like that? Let's briefly look at some other criteria that are important to keep in mind when picking out good domain names.

- Keep your domain name as short as possible. A short domain name is easier to type and is more memorable. (It also fits better on printed materials, such as T-shirts and business cards.) As a general rule of thumb, I try to keep domain names under twenty characters at most (TLD extension excluded) and comprise them of three words at the very most (ideally two).

- Choose a domain name that's easy to pronounce and communicate. Any ambiguity in the way the domain name could be spelled should be eliminated. In light of this, I would also avoid using numbers if at all possible, because of the general ambiguity of spelling them in full vs. typing numerals (e.g., "ten" vs. "10"). Of course, between search engines, social media, bookmarking, and feeds, many of your visitors won't actually type your URL into their browsers.

- Avoid hyphens if possible, and if not, limit them to one at most (like I did when I registered math-blog.com). Multiple hyphens have a tendency to cheapen your brand and make your site look less trustworthy. In fact, many Internet marketers have abused them over the years in an effort to register keyword-rich domain names.

- Use your own name as the domain name (provided that it's not particularly complicated to spell and that you're mostly aiming at promoting yourself through your blog). If such is the case, securing namelastname.com is a good idea. Just keep in mind that blogs of this kind tend to be perceived as more general and personal than your typical niche blog.

- Be careful with unintentional double meanings. The classic example of this faux pas is expertsexchange.com, which was intended to represent "Experts Exchange" but could all too easily be read as "Expert Sex Change." That URL was abandoned in favor of experts-exchange.com, a hyphenated version with a much less ambiguous pronunciation.

- Use tools to quickly check results for your name ideas. As you try to come up with your unique domain name, you'll struggle to find available names. Guaranteed. Tools like instantdomainsearch.com and domainsbot.com can help. I also recommend bustaname.com to generate and check many domain name variations from a few seed keywords.

Aftermarket Domains

Aftermarket domains are domains that have been registered and are available for sale by their owners, or that have expired and will soon become available for sale after a grace and redemption period.

It is possible to purchase a domain from a domainer either directly or via marketplaces like sedo.com or flippa.com. Whether you should take this approach, however, is an entirely different matter. Good domain names tend to be very expensive (e.g., thousands of U.S. dollars), so I wouldn't recommend that you start your blogging career by making such a large investment. (If you find that your absolutely perfect domain name is for sale for a few hundred dollars, by all means, consider purchasing it.)

Expired domain names are also an option. You may be able to get some great names if you wait for the domains to become available. The grace period in effect allows existing owners ample time to change their minds and renew the domain after the expiration date. If they don't do so after the redemption period is over, however, you can register the expired domain just as you would a regular domain name.

In practice, expired domain names are watched carefully by domainers. Valuable ones are hard to snap up, and there's a whole industry around helping you get such domain names (for a hefty but not unreasonable fee, of course).

Register Your Domain

Countless ICANN accredited registrars exist, and the only real distinction between the lot comes down to TLD availability, price, ease of use, and the handling of disputes.

Based on this criteria, for .com domains, I've found namecheap.com and dynadot.com to be reasonable choices. Opt for one of the two, unless you register your domains with someone else already.

Once you've decided on an available name, the next step is to register your domain name (this should cost about $10–$15 USD per year for a .com domain).

Albeit not universally accepted, empirical evidence suggests that search engines prefer—all things being equal—domain names that won't expire soon. The reason for this is that spammers rarely commit to domains for multiple years. Registering the domain for multiple years may offer a slight SEO advantage and, potentially, a cheaper yearly rate (provided you're committed to this endeavor).

When you register a domain name, your own name, mailing address, and other personal information will be made available in a public WHOIS database.[7]

> **Tip 9**   Enable WHOIS privacy when registering your domain name.

If you wish to protect your privacy, many registrars offer WHOIS protection services in which their mailing address and business details are listed on your behalf. Namecheap, at the time of writing, offers this service for free.

If your WHOIS data is publicly available, you can expect to receive junk mail and assorted scams at the indicated mailing address. A common scam is to send you an official-looking form indicating that you might lose your domain name if you don't renew it right away. They prey on the less-technically inclined, of course, but should someone fill out the form, they'd now be using the scammers as their domain registrar at the tune of outrageous yearly fees. In Canada, where I live, they even send it in envelopes that resemble actual, official government communication. Trust me on this, WHOIS privacy is worth enabling with your registrar.

Take Action

If you haven't already, complete the actions suggested within this chapter.

To recap:

1. Define your blog's main topic.

2. If it's a niche blog, brainstorm ten articles for your niche—just the titles.

3. If it's a general blog, list the main categories that compose your blog.

4. Answer this question: what's your reason for starting this blog?

5. Write the "elevator pitch" for your blog.

---

7.   www.internic.net/whois.html

6. Set verifiable goals for both the short term (1–3 months) and the long term (1–3 years).

7. Come up with a compelling name for your blog.

8. Unless it's a company blog, find and register a matching domain name.

What's Next

OK, you've planned it. Now it's time to jump right in and start implementing your blog.

In the next two chapters, you'll learn everything you need to know in order to create the perfect initial setup, whether you opt for the recommended WordPress self-hosted solution or an alternative blogging solution.

Even if you own a blog already, don't skip these two chapters. They'll teach you tips and tricks to help fine-tune your existing setup.

Let's build it!

Part II

Build It

They say Rome wasn't built in a day, but I wasn't on that particular job.

        Brian Clough

CHAPTER 3

Setting Up Your Blog

You've identified your topic and your niche, and you've done a sanity check on these decisions in terms of market and trends. You've set some reasonable goals and expectations for your blogging. You've also, I hope, found a name and registered a domain name already.

Now you're ready to get your hands dirty. In this and the next chapter, you'll install, configure, style, and fine-tune your blog. But first, let's make some crucial decisions about blogging software and hosting.

Choose Your Blogging Software and Hosting

One positive side effect of the maturity and popularity of blogging is the wealth of blogging solutions you can choose from. So many options are available these days that it can be overwhelming for newcomers. I like to say that having too many options is a curse, not a blessing. Fear not, however; I'm here to guide you toward the right choice for you.

Your Three Main Software Options

To keep things manageable, let's reduce the scope to three main categories of blogging software:

- *Self-hosted blogging software*: These are (typically open source) software projects that you install and run on a web server. WordPress is the absolute leader in this space.[1] It powers a sizable portion of all websites worldwide, not just blogs. WordPress and its alternatives are fully fledged CMS (content management systems) that can be easily customized through a system of plugins and themes. The WordPress ecosystem in particular is enormous. Speaking of alternatives, Ghost is a premium hosted blogging

---

1. wordpress.org

service, but it also provides a self-hosted option that has a number of loyal fans.[2]

- *Static site generators*: Increasingly popular among developers, site generators such as Jekyll and Hugo generate your blog from folders of text files that you can edit in a markup language like Markdown.[3] You won't need a database or a complex server setup. The compiled output will be a static site with HTML and CSS files that you can upload to any web server (even Amazon S3 and GitHub Pages).[4] Consequently, you'll also gain in performance and security.

- *Blogging services*: A variety of providers offer the ability to host a blog using their web platform without you needing to install anything. Common services of this nature include WordPress.com (not .org, which is where you download WordPress for self-hosting), Blogger,[5] Medium,[6] and Tumblr (however, blogs hosted on the latter tend to be shorter and considerably more akin to micro/nano-publishing).[7]

It's worth noting that the popular website builder Squarespace can also be used for blogging purposes.[8] It offers a simple and user-friendly blogging platform that will appeal to some. The lack of sophisticated features might be a turn-off for very technical audiences, however.

Let's quickly review the pros and cons of each of these solutions.

Self-Hosted Blogs: The Committed Way

As the most popular blogging software, self-hosted WordPress is able to boast thousands of plugins and themes that let you customize your blog however you like. It has one of the richest online ecosystems, even when compared to software outside the blogging world.

Should you ever need help with WordPress or wish to have custom features created, plenty of developers are familiar with the system and ready to help for a fee. If you're a PHP developer, you can even customize it yourself. Likewise, countless designers have worked with WordPress themes before, so finding help on that front is, thankfully, fairly easy as well.

---

2. ghost.org
3. jekyllrb.com and gohugo.io, respectively.
4. pages.github.com
5. blogger.com
6. medium.com
7. tumblr.com
8. support.squarespace.com/hc/en-us/articles/206543727-Blogging-with-Squarespace

As a self-hosted solution, WordPress has the disadvantage of requiring a server to host it on (unless you opt for the commercial hosted solution provided by WordPress.com). Your server will need a web server such as Nginx and MySQL for storing and retrieving data (plus support for a recent version of PHP).

You'll also need to update WordPress itself, its themes, and its plugins pretty frequently in order to avoid security vulnerabilities that crop up from time to time. WordPress is not the most nimble piece of software (particularly when loaded up with numerous plugins), but there are excellent caching plugins that make it snappy enough.

Self-hosted Wordpress is what many serious bloggers end up using, and I personally believe that it's worth the hassle—or I wouldn't use it for all my blogs. But it does require a certain degree of commitment when compared to the other two main options presented here. I recommend it, but only if you are a developer and are familiar with deploying software on a server. If you don't know what iptables is, for example, I'd skip the self-hosted option or pay for a fully managed hosting plan that takes care of server setup and maintenance for you.

Several commercial services provide managed WordPress hosting. WP Engine is a popular one, but a look at its pricing page at wpengine.com/plans/ is likely to persuade many readers to explore cheaper options described later in this chapter.

What about Ghost? Most of the pros and cons of self-hosted WordPress apply to self-hosted Ghost as well. You can think of it as a simpler version of WordPress. It's much more focused on blogging rather than attempting to be a general CMS platform, and its ecosystem is much smaller. It's a faster, nimbler option, if you will. ghost.org/vs/wordpress offers a good, if inherently biased, comparison of the two.

Static Site Generators: The Hacker Way

Static site generators are still very much a niche, but their increasing popularity with (the good kind of) hackers may be justified. Such generators offer you the ability to directly edit your posts, blog structure, and design by using a text editor such as Vim, Visual Studio Code, or Sublime Text. (An interesting take on this concept is offered by blot.im, a service that publishes posts from files within your Dropbox account.)

Many of these generators are simple, small, and written in popular languages such as Python, Ruby, and Go. If you're familiar with these languages, you'll be able to easily extend the generators to customize their behavior. This process is arguably much simpler than learning how to customize a large and complex system like WordPress.

Other points in favor of Jekyll, Hugo, and similar static site generators are the ability to store your blog under revision control tools like Git, the simplicity of being able to host the generated site pretty much anywhere, the security advantages of not running server-side stacks, and the performance implications. In fact, since your blog ends up being a static HTML site, its performance should be very good—even on cheap hosting plans.

The major disadvantage of static site generators is that you're on your own if you need or want more advanced functionalities. Few premade add-ons will aid you in accomplishing even a fraction of what you can do with software like WordPress. Using a static generator, you'll most likely have to write the code yourself. Depending on the type of blog you envision and your coding abilities, this may or may not be a deal breaker for you. I'll say that they're definitely fine for simpler blogs, even if you don't plan to do any coding yourself.

Blogging Services: The Easy Way

Blogging services have the major advantage of not having to worry about servers and their configuration. The company behind the service is responsible for the blog software and the server upkeep. You can be up and running in minutes.

Even large organizations will routinely use hosted services for their official blogs. This choice allows companies to immediately inject themselves into an existing community, but above all it guarantees a long-form communication channel with their customers should their main site become unavailable. Twitter is quite useful as well in such instances, but the short-form nature of the service limits the type of communication that can happen there.

Status updates become crucial to placating irate customers during outages. So if you're blogging for a company, consider hosting your blog on a different hosting solution from the one you use for your company site.

I'm conflicted when it comes to these blogging services. They're the easiest way to get started and therefore highly recommendable, particularly to beginners. But proprietary platforms come with many caveats. The main problems with blogging services are a relative lack of flexibility and customization, the possibility of being kicked out at the discretion of the service owners, vendor lock-in, and other arbitrary restrictions imposed by the vendor.

While some blogging services are better than others, they all share certain kinds of restrictions when compared to a self-hosted solution. With some platforms, you'll also have to pay a monthly or yearly fee. WordPress.com, the hosted version of the software downloadable from wordpress.org, is free, but it requires that you pay for every small customization, including associating your own domain name to the blog and installing plugins. And I definitely don't recommend that you use one of their subdomains, such as yourusername.wordpress.com for your blog. It doesn't look professional and it can cause a URL-based lock-in should you decide to move your blog later on.[9] Most people don't find WordPress's prices particularly cheap, either.

> **Tip 10**   Do not use a free subdomain for your blog URL.

By the way, you really should serve your blog over HTTPS. It's more secure, your visitors won't see scary warnings in their browsers, and you get some SEO rewards as well. The SEO benefits, by the way, are not a myth. When I switched my blogs to HTTPS all at once, I saw an immediate bump in SERP (search engine result page) performance across all of my sites. There's really no reason not to. If you're using a blogging service, HTTPS is usually a one-click option. If you're self-hosting your blog, look into a free SSL certificate service like Let's Encrypt. Its guides are quite helpful.

It's worth mentioning that third-party services can go under or get acquired and shut down. Before you think I'm being paranoid here, let me bring forth exhibit A. The first edition of this book included Posterous, a popular blogging service, as an option for those looking to quickly set up a blog without having to host anything themselves. It went offline in 2013. Now, Posterous was kind enough (and funded enough) to provide export facilities to other platforms, but that's not something you can bank on with every service.

Should you decide to go this route, you should carefully evaluate features, customization options, policies, and export facilities before committing. This latter point is particularly important. Were the service to shut down, you'd need to be able to move your existing content elsewhere. If you opt for WordPress.com, you can always export the content and import it onto a self-hosted installation of WordPress at a later stage (the same is true of Ghost, which offers both hosted and self-hosted options). Other services might not offer such an easy exit strategy. Aside from WordPress.com, Blogger, Medium, and Typepad are all popular turnkey blogging solutions.

Medium, with its social features and its revenue-sharing program,[10] is a particularly popular option these days, both for solo blogs and for collective blogs ("publications" in Medium's parlance). This site has a massive readership

---

9.   wordpress.com/pricing
10.   medium.com/creators

and there are plenty of famous and influential writers who use it. If you're a developer, you might have come across hackernoon.com, who currently uses it successfully.

Unfortunately, Medium's content discovery system tends to promote a power law distribution that "makes the rich richer," so to speak. If you're already popular there, the site will send plenty of new eyeballs your way. If you're not, it's hard to take advantage of its existing audience.

Aside from being one of the most limited services in terms of customization, with Medium I can't help but feel that you're simply building on top of someone else's land. It can decide at any moment to change the rules or the algorithm, drastically changing who gets to see your content on its platform, for example. Of course, people will still be able to discover you through Google and other channels we'll discuss later on, but the true advantage of Medium could easily disappear for you, even if you're lucky enough to gain traction there in the first place.

Still, that's not my main issue with Medium. A lot of the benefits of blogging come from people discovering you as much as your content. Medium, with its focus on content, and content alone, puts less emphasis on you—the brand—compared with other platforms. Just the fact that every single blog there looks more or less the same affects your ability to stand out and build your personal brand.

Medium recently announced that it won't allow new bloggers to use a custom domain name.[11] Whether it sticks to this decision or not, to me it's further evidence of the point I'm trying to convey here.

So I would recommend using Medium as a way to announce or rebroadcast your content from your main blog if you wish, but not as your main platform. Keep in mind that Google penalizes duplicate content, so care must be taken to specify a canonical URL pointing to your original article. We'll discuss how to do this in the chapter on promotion strategies.

> **Tip 11** Specify a canonical URL when republishing your content.

The same considerations and concerns apply to many of the other numerous services now offering some form of blogging facility, including LinkedIn and Quora. They're good as syndication tools—not as your main blogging platform.

---

11. help.medium.com/hc/en-us/articles/115003053487-Custom-Domains-service-deprecation

Which Blogging Platform Is Right for You?

So which one should you go with? Opt for a self-hosted WordPress installation if you're the kind of person who doesn't mind dealing with a remote Linux box in the Cloud. The chief reason is that you'll be working with what is a de facto standard in blogging that offers you maximum flexibility and independence. If you don't have an IT background or would like to test the waters before committing to something that requires you to rent and manage hosting, then, by all means, go for a hosted blogging solution. Doing so will be a much easier and friendlier choice that will get you up and blogging in very little time.

In such a case, I would recommend WordPress.com, if you're willing to pay its monthly fees, and Blogger (from Google) if you are not. Blogger is entirely free, it allows you to use your own domain name, and it has somewhat lax policies when it comes to ads and affiliate links. Customization is more limited than WordPress, but the ecosystem around it is still pretty big. Google has shut down popular services before, but WordPress offers the option to import Blogger posts. Migrations between different platforms are never perfect, in my experience; but should things go south with Blogger, you wouldn't be entirely out of luck.

Given the technical audience of this book and my recommendation that most committed bloggers opt for a self-hosted WordPress platform, I will provide a lot of guidance for those who have chosen WordPress in both this and the next chapter.

If you go with an alternative solution like Blogger, however, do *not* skip these two chapters. You'll find plenty of useful information about DNS, SEO considerations, sidebar configuration, subscribers, and much more that still fully applies to you!

I've provided hints for Blogger users in these two chapters, but it would've been impractical for me to provide detailed instructions for each major blogging platform that exists. If you didn't opt for WordPress (or Blogger), you may have to figure things out on your own or look online for how—and if—a given feature discussed is available to you. While references to WordPress (and Blogger) may still appear here and there throughout the book, all other chapters will be blog-engine agnostic. (Figure 5, Using a custom domain with Blogger, on page 40).

Select a Hosting Service

Unless you opt for a blogging service like WordPress.com or Blogger, you need a web hosting provider in order to run your blog. Hosting options exist for all

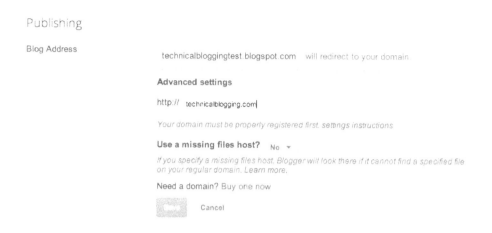

Figure 5—Using a custom domain with Blogger

budgets. Favor the bottom rung of the price range ladder while still aiming for quality providers. In the beginning, spending as little as you can on hosting is the key to keeping your blogging expenses to a minimum before your blog has proven itself as a viable income generator or worthwhile endeavor. Various kinds of hybrid and complex hosting arrangements are available from hosting providers, but the spectrum can be roughly divided into the following four types of hosting plans.

- *Shared hosting*: As many as several hundred sites from many different customers are hosted on the same web server. The hosting provider takes care of managing and maintaining the server, while the customer tends to have limited access to system administration tools and little flexibility in terms of what can be installed on the machine. Often costing you only a few dollars a month, shared web hosting is the most inexpensive option.

- *VPS (virtual private server)*: The resources of a powerful server are divided among a handful of customers through virtualization software. Each customer gets his or her own virtual server running in a virtual machine that uses a proportional share of the physical resources available on the host machine. This option is more expensive than shared hosting, but it also provides you with much better and more predictable performance. It can be provided as an unmanaged service, in which the customer needs to take care of installing and maintaining the server's software, or as a managed service, where the staff handles the system administration for you.

- *Dedicated servers*: A server is entirely dedicated to you. Just like VPS hosting, dedicated servers come in managed and unmanaged forms, depending on the provider. Some people even go so far as to provide their own machines that are hosted in a local data center as part of a so-called *colocation* arrangement.

- *Cloud computing*: Computing resources are provided and billed based on usage. You could rent three instances (think the equivalent resources of three dedicated servers) an hour and switch back to a single instance an hour later when the traffic spike is gone. The value of cloud computing mainly resides in the ability to easily scale your computing needs without requiring a data center investment up front. The cost scales accordingly with the resources you need. The difference between cloud computing and VPS/dedicated servers has become somewhat blurrier over the past few years. In common parlance, the Cloud encompasses pretty much any computing resource that's made available on demand in a data center somewhere (excluding shared hosting).

Unless you already rent web servers and have experience working with them, start with shared hosting. Without a doubt, it's both the most inexpensive and the easiest way to get started with self-hosted blogging. Keep in mind, though, that shared hosting is not as reliable or as fast as the other options, and that you may eventually get kicked out if your blog starts experiencing heavy traffic on a daily basis (this happened to me once several years ago). For the time being, which may be many months, this option should do the trick. To make your life even easier, many hosting providers are now offering WordPress-specific hosting plans that come with WordPress preinstalled and optimized for you. Premium options like WP Engine are of course much better, but you pay for it.

> Tip 12   Opt for WordPress-specific hosting plans.

Do your homework when it comes to these kinds of services, and be aware of the many fake reviews posted by some unscrupulous affiliate marketers, who are after the hefty commissions hosting companies provide for referrals.

If the subject of your blog is truly controversial in nature, you may need to take extra steps to prevent an overzealous registrar or host from kicking you out. Such companies can't take away your right to freedom of speech, but they're usually able to get rid of you as a customer for violating their own terms of service. I wholeheartedly recommend nearlyfreespeech.net as both your registrar and hosting provider if you feel that a regular provider may take issue with your content.

The majority of tech bloggers don't have to worry about all this, of course, but it's something to keep in mind if you were to engage in legal yet highly controversial topics, such as discussions about security exploits, file sharing, and so on.

For everyone else, as far as shared hosting goes, I recommend SiteGround, Namecheap, and DreamHost.[12] They're inexpensive and generally reliable—even though virtually all shared hosting companies tend to oversell and overcrowd their servers. The official list of recommended WordPress shared hosting companies can be found at wordpress.org/hosting.

For unmanaged VPS, it's hard to beat the SSD-based services provided by DigitalOcean. It's what I currently use for my blogs and side projects.[13] Linode is another highly recommended option.[14] For managed VPS, Liquid Web is pretty decent and popular (albeit fairly expensive).[15]

How about dedicated servers? You don't really need to look at these options quite yet; nevertheless, SoftLayer (now merged with IBM Cloud) and ServInt are both excellent choices.[16]

Finally, for Cloud computing solutions in the stricter sense, Amazon AWS, Microsoft Azure, and IBM Cloud are popular advanced options (though I wouldn't say that they're particularly popular options for WordPress itself, since they're best suited for complex web app deployments).[17]

Oh, and don't forget about companies that specialize in WordPress hosting and provide you with WordPress.com-like simplicity, convenience, and performance despite allowing virtually the same degree of flexibility that you'd find with self-hosted WordPress.

Many existing hosting companies have encroached into this space, and new ones dedicated to WordPress hosting are showing up every year. Nevertheless, most will find WP Engine and Flywheel to be sensible choices.[18] They offer a premium service that's priced accordingly, however. I don't have direct experience

---

12. siteground.com, namecheap.com, and dreamhost.com, respectively.
13. digitalocean.com
14. linode.com
15. liquidweb.com
16. softlayer.com and servint.com, respectively.
17. aws.amazon.com, azure.microsoft.com, and ibm.com/cloud, respectively.
18. getflywheel.com

with this service, but for a more affordable option, I've heard good things about PeoplesHost as well.[19]

In the unlikely event that your blog becomes one of the most popular sites on the Internet, you may also consider the incredibly expensive WordPress.com VIP option at vip.wordpress.com. (We are talking about a five-figure budget per month.)

As you can see, you have an almost endless array of options at your disposal. Do a bit of research and see what appeals to you (and your wallet) the most. Just remember not to go crazy in the beginning. Chances are you'll receive limited traffic initially, so you don't need to go all out from day one.

Configure Your Domain Name

Regardless of your blogging platform, you need to ensure that the domain name you registered is properly configured. If you're using a hosted service like WordPress.com, Blogger, or Tumblr, simply follow the instructions provided by your vendor. If you're self-hosting WordPress, Jekyll, or similar software, pay close attention to the following instructions.

For a self-hosted blog to be associated with a domain name, you'll need to take two steps: set the DNS (domain name system) servers for the domain, and then add your domain to the appropriate DNS zone.

The first step usually requires you to use the domain registrar's interface to set the nameservers to those of your hosting company (e.g., "ns1.digitalocean.com," "ns2.digitalocean.com," and "ns3.digitalocean.com").

Next, you'll need to use the interface provided by your hosting company (such as cPanel, Linode DNS Manager, and so on) to add your domain name or subdomain to its DNS zone. If you can't find the option, it's usually located under the Networking menu, but it understandably varies depending on the hosting company. If you declared your domain name during the registration of your hosting account, the association of your domain name with your server IP should've already been taken care of for you.

If you aren't sure how to go about these two tasks, any reputable domain or hosting company will have instructions on how to accomplish them. If you're truly stuck, feel free to contact the company's customer support folks; they should definitely be able to help you out with the process.

If you prefer, you can also use a hosting-agnostic DNS management service such as DNS Made Easy, DNSimple, Amazon Route 53, or a more comprehensive

---

19. www.peopleshost.com/wordpress-hosting/

offering such as Cloudflare.[20] You can set your domain's nameservers to those provided by one of these services and then configure which server IP the domain should be pointed to at any time through the interface. These services can simplify DNS management, speed up switching to a different server, and centralize your DNS organization, particularly if you own multiple sites.

One way to verify if your domain has been properly set up is by running the commands whois yoursitename.com and dig yoursitename.com, which should show you the nameserver and the IP your domain points to, respectively. The nameservers should be the ones that you just set. Dig is usually available by default on *nix systems. Windows users can either install a version that runs on Windows or use a web version of the tool (search for "web-based dig" to find one).

Note that DNS propagation can take several hours, so if you want to work with your domain name right away, you can edit your local hosts file to have the domain name point to the right server IP locally. This change enables you to use your domain name instead of the server IP as you configure your self-hosted blog, even before the DNS records have become visible to the world. On *nix systems this is usually located at /etc/hosts. For Windows, consult the Wikipedia page at en.wikipedia.org/wiki/Hosts_(file).

In your hosts file, you should include a line that looks like this:

```
174.122.8.30 yoursitename.com
```

Replace the fictitious IP and domain name with your real ones. If you don't know the IP of your server, you should check the emails your hosting company sent you when you registered with them, because it's usually located there. Logging in to your hosting account will also typically provide you with this information. If all else fails, just ask your hosting company.

As mentioned earlier, the rest of this chapter shows you how to install and perform a basic configuration of your blog using self-hosted WordPress as the main tool. Tips to guide Blogger users are provided as well. If you opted for Jekyll, Hugo, Ghost, TypePad, Medium, or any other alternative blogging platform, this information will still be useful to you. So consider reading on.

Install WordPress

WordPress can be installed in several ways. I recommend you install it from scratch, which is a quick, straightforward process. Taking this step will allow

---

20. dnsmadeeasy.com, dnsimple.com, aws.amazon.com/route53, and cloudflare.com/dns, respectively.

you to have the newest version from the get-go and then upgrade whenever an update is released. If you picked a hosting service that's aimed at Word-Press, you'll be able to install it by following the service's specific instructions.

The overwhelming majority of shared hosting companies already provide a compatible LAMP (Linux, Apache, MySQL, PHP) stack—or some variation of it—for you. If you opted for a VPS, dedicated server, or cloud solution, you'll need to ensure that all these components are installed, configured, and working properly.

WordPress requires a recent version of PHP, MySQL, and the mod_rewrite module if you're using Apache as your web server. Requirements rarely change, but you can always find an updated list of them at wordpress.org/about/requirements/. Apache and Nginx are the recommended web servers, with Nginx being significantly faster and less memory hungry than Apache. In fact, my preferred combo for WordPress is Nginx and PHP-FPM, a FastCGI process manager.

Follow the instructions provided at codex.wordpress.org/Installing_WordPress to install WordPress on your server.

Configure WordPress

With WordPress correctly installed, it's time for us to start configuring the default installation. Log in to your admin section again by appending /wp-admin to the URL of your blog and by using the credentials for the WordPress account you created during the setup stage.

Once logged in, feel free to explore the dashboard to see the wealth of options available to you. In this section, I'll simply point out some key configuration options that will affect your blogging experience. For everything else, use the defaults or adjust to taste.

Pages Menu

Within your WordPress dashboard, you should find a Pages menu in the sidebar. Click on it and you'll see a sample page. Delete it. Pages are different from posts. They don't appear in your site's RSS feed, nor do they have categories. They also tend to be linked to from the navigation menu. As such, they should be used for *sticky* information you want people to see (much like forums often have sticky posts).

While you're in the Pages tab, go ahead and create an About page. This should contain information about who you are and what your blog is about, and it should definitely include some of the results of the exercise we did in the past chapter with regard to why readers should stick around on your site.

If you can, include a photograph of yourself, your office, or your whole team if you're running a team blog (use the buttons above the editing area to upload and insert media content). Remember that a picture truly is worth a thousand words and that it can give a very human and relatable element to your blog.

When putting this page together, your tone should reflect how you want to come across on your site. In general, being friendly, approachable, and thankful to readers for their time and interest in your blog is definitely a safe bet in even the most professional contexts. Avoid boring, official biographies that are written in the third person (unless you're doing so for comedic effect).

Don't forget to include information on how you can be reached: include your full name (or pseudonym) and email address. As a successful blogger, you'll be approached and pitched to by a variety of people. In addition to the emails you'll likely consider a waste of your time, you'll also receive heartfelt notes and concrete opportunities, so if you're open to that, ensure you offer an easy way for readers to reach you. (Some people have a dedicated Contact page for this purpose and even embed a contact form through one of the many plugins available in WordPress.)

Users Menu

In the sidebar, skip Comments, as well as Appearance and Plugins (we'll come back to the last two later). Click Users instead, where you should see the user account you used to log in. Click on your username. Here you'll be able to fill in more details about yourself. Depending on the blog theme you're using, some of this info may be shown publicly as well, typically at the bottom of your posts, so you may want to pay attention to what you share here.

The only option you should really be careful with is the Visual Editor. Disabling the Visual Editor will remove the WYSIWYG editor when editing posts and leave you with only the HTML code editor. The Visual Editor is convenient but it can affect the formatting of your posts, particularly regarding images and code. Switching from Visual to Code view in the editor also has a habit of changing and rearranging your posts' HTML code. This can break the post's code at times. If you wish, start with the Visual Editor and disable it only if you find its behavior to be problematic.

Finally, ensure that your full name is shown via the "Display name publicly as" option. Even if you're using a pen name for your blog, it's worth including a full name as opposed to "admin" or a nickname. This helps to give your readers the perception that you stand behind your writing and your blog (as I'm sure you genuinely do).

Blogger Settings

Many of the WordPress settings described in this chapter exist for Blogger as well and are located under the various menus within Settings.

For example, you can specify the blog author(s) in Settings > Basic. The author name that appears in your posts will automatically be picked up from the Google account associated with your blog.

Look within Settings > Basic and Settings > "Language and formatting" to set your blog title, tagline, and time zone settings.

Settings > Email enables you to define options for posting by email, as well as defining the email address that should receive a notification when a new comment is posted. Settings > "Posts, comments and sharing" allows you to define your comment policy as well as the number of posts that should be shown on your home page.

Your feed options are available in Settings > Other. There you'll also be able to specify your Google Analytics tracking code (more on this in Chapter 4, Customizing and Fine-Tuning Your Blog, on page 57).

Take a look at the various options available. Most are sensible defaults, but there's room for you to customize them to your liking. Just as in WordPress, ensure that your blog's privacy is set to "Listed on Blogger. Visible to search engines." in Settings > Basic.

Edit Your Blog's Settings

Skip everything else in the sidebar and jump to Settings. When you click it, you should see General Settings in the main area and a series of submenu items in the sidebar. This is where most of your configuration lives. Let's take a moment to dissect it.

General Settings

In General Settings, you should ensure that the title of the blog is set exactly as you want it to appear. Eliminate the default tagline (i.e., "Just another WordPress site") and define your own in its place. Once again, refer to the exercise you did when we discussed finding the purpose of your blog to help create a good tagline. Your tagline is your motto and should reflect what your blog is all about. Or if nothing else, it should at least be funny or witty. (Not every WordPress theme will display the tagline; some opt instead to have their own control panel where you can specify such options.)

Change the time zone if necessary, and pick the date and time formats that your target audience is most accustomed to (the default will work for most people).

Writing Settings

Click the Writing submenu under Settings. Here you can customize a few details that relate to posting. The only sections that are really worth your attention are "Post via e-mail," "Remote Publishing," and "Update Services."

The first two are useful if you want to publish posts directly by email (I don't generally recommend that you do this, though) or through a client (for example a desktop client like Open Live Writer for Windows or MarsEdit for Mac). The third one, Update Services, is crucial if you wish to notify a series of so-called ping services about your blog's updates. These services will, in turn, inform search engines of your updates so that your new posts will be indexed quickly. You should see the default rpc.pingomatic.com, which is more than good enough. If you don't see it, add it for SEO reasons.

Reading Settings

Reading Settings is where you define how many posts you'd like to see featured on your home page and how many of your entries should appear in a new sub-scriber's feed reader. It's up to you to decide what numbers you'd like to input here. Ten is a healthy compromise that pushes your content without overwhelm-ing new visitors and subscribers. Start with the defaults and adjust as needed when these defaults fail to work well for a particular situation. Above all, remember not to sweat the small stuff. You can always fine-tune later.

A bigger and more contested issue is the debate of full vs. partial feed. An overwhelming majority of people will want a full feed in order to read your articles in the feed reader of their choice. However, a minority might be annoyed by the wealth of content you share with them if you opt for a full feed. You can't win this one or make everyone happy, so there's no sense in trying. I'd just leave all these settings on their defaults.

Discussion Settings

In the Discussion Settings tab, you can customize your commenting policy and notifications. Personally, I like to leave everything set to the defaults here as well, with the following exceptions:

- Uncheck "Anyone posts a comment" and "Comment author must have a previously approved comment" and instead go with "Comment must be manually approved." This enables comment moderation, with a single email notification to you when a new comment has been posted and is being held for approval.

- Switch the default avatar to one of the generated choices (e.g., Identicon). Doing so will help make it more obvious if someone is using sock puppets (i.e., commenting multiple times while pretending to be different people) to amplify a viewpoint with multiple comments in the same thread. It's not foolproof—changing IP via a VPN service will change the generated avatar image—but it makes the job a bit harder and may discourage a few overzealous commenters in the process.

No doubt the most controversial statement in this chapter is my recommendation that you moderate comments. Moderation may slightly lower the overall number of comments you receive and the level of engagement seen in the comments your posts bring in, but doing so has several advantages when dealing with trolls, spammers, and the flame wars that can arise from time to time in the comment section of your blog.

If you are ideologically opposed to the idea, simply uncheck the option and instead check off that you want to be notified when "Anyone posts a comment." This way you'll at least know about new comments that are being posted and can then reply or remove them (if they're not appropriate) as needed.

Enable Akismet Antispam

Akismet is a must-have plugin for dealing with spam, unless you're using a third-party commenting system that already includes some form of spam control. The current settings that we have in place now should guarantee that no spam is going to end up on your blog. The problem is that you'll still receive numerous email messages for spam comments that you need to manually reject.

Akismet, which ships with WordPress but is inactive by default, can take care of this for us. Click the Plugins menu item and activate Akismet. Once activated, this plugin will ask you for an API key that can be obtained by signing up for an account.

You may be unsure which plan is right for you. If your blog is for a small company, you should go for the premium plans. Otherwise, you can safely opt for the free plan and upgrade later if you start making some serious cash from your blog.

Akismet tends to do a pretty good job. You won't have to sort through thousands of spam comments and trackbacks.

Trackbacks or pingbacks are link notifications from other blogs that have mentioned your post. In most themes they appear just above the comment section. They are so widely abused by spammers looking for free links to their sites that many people prefer to disable trackbacks in Discussion Settings. In the early days of blogging, trackbacks were a defining feature. As blogging became a more mainstream way of publishing content online, the cliquey blogosphere element waned, and people started linking to each other a whole lot less. I'm not suggesting disabling them, but it won't be a big loss if you do.

The occasional false positive (genuine comments that are flagged as spam) or more commonly false negative (spam comments that reach your inbox for approval) will still crop up with Akismet, but using their service/plugin will make your life so much easier.

Alternative Commenting Systems

Over the past few years, a new breed of alternative commenting systems has been emerging. The basic idea behind these new systems is that you can embed a new comment system in place of the native one. These commenting systems tend to have some bells and whistles that make them attractive, such as the ability for your readers to log in via Twitter or Facebook before leaving a comment, as well as good built-in spam control. Their popularity also implies that many users, particularly technical ones, will already have an account with the major players in this field. If they don't, they can register at one blog that uses them and then reuse that account on any other blog that adopts the same commenting system. (In fairness, Jetpack itself now offers the ability to enable a commenting system that includes social logins as well.

Disqus and Facebook Comments are probably the most popular options.[21] Facebook, in particular, is ubiquitous with users, be they technical or not, and would in theory make for an excellent choice. BuzzFeed, one of the most popular blogs on the Internet, uses them.

Facebook Comments are arranged by popularity (i.e., the number of Likes) or chronologically, and enable you to see the real names of most of your commenters. Users' comments will automatically be associated with their Facebook profiles.

When people comment with their real name, they tend to be slightly more civil and careful in what they say (well, some at least). Commenters who opt to do so will also share their comments on your post with their friends on Facebook, further spreading your post via the social network.

---

21. disqus.com and developers.facebook.com/docs/reference/plugins/comments, respectively.

However, there are negative aspects to be considered before installing and activating a plugin for an alternative commenting system such as Disqus or Facebook:

- Dynamically loading the content from a third-party site tends to slow down your pages' loading time. This has a negative impact from both a UX and an SEO standpoint.

- Customization to match the rest of your site's design is somewhat limited.

- Some people might be hesitant to comment if doing so requires attaching their comment to their real name. This could potentially affect the degree of engagement.

- A few of these services will serve ads on your blog, ads whose revenue is not shared with you.

- Third-party commenting systems are usually not "crawlable" by search engines (though Facebook Comments now are). Their content might not be indexed, so you may miss out on showing up in the SERP for quite a few keywords that were organically included in the comment section by your commenters.

- A third party will own your comments. Should this party change its policies or go out of business, you may or may not be able to revert back to the regular built-in WordPress comment system without data loss. As usual when dealing with third parties, there is a risk for vendor lock-in, so ensure that you carefully read the conditions and export options before committing.

If you want to switch to an alternative commenting system, you can do so in WordPress by searching for the specific name (e.g., Facebook Comments) after clicking the "Add new" button in the Plugins area of your dashboard. Pay attention to the number of installations, the rating, and how recently they were updated to quickly assess the likely quality of a given plugin.

Permalinks Settings

Click Permalinks and you'll be presented with Permalinks Settings. What we'll change in this section is going to be absolutely crucial from an SEO standpoint, so don't skip this important step.

The term *permalink* is used to indicate the permanent URL of your posts. By default, WordPress will generate permalinks that have the following structure: yoursitename.com/?p=ID, where ID is the numeric identifier of your post. The problem with this URL structure is that search engines give a great deal of weight to the content of your URL.

For example, if a user is searching for "TypeScript tips" in Google, a post with a permalink including /ten-typescript-tips will appear highly relevant to the user's query. In fact, it contains the target keywords and little else. If the post were to be located at /?p=42, Google would determine your post's relevance based solely on other factors, such as content and incoming links.

Regardless of your permalink structure, search engines will use plenty of other indicators to figure out the relevance and authority of your pages. It just so happens that the keyword density of your URLs is very important, so leaving this out would be foolish. (The portion of the permalink that comes after the domain name is also known as the slug.)

Plenty of blogs, even commercial ones, make this mistake. Since it's such low-hanging fruit, change the permalink structure right away. To do so, you can select "Day and name" or "Month and name" or simply opt for "Post name." These will create permalinks that include the title of your post in the URL.

Most SEO experts would opt for the last choice. Doing so has the advantage of increasing the density of the keywords by removing unnecessary date-related characters. It also makes the URL shorter and cleaner and can positively impact the perception of your content by sneakily hiding the date of your old content.

Go for the Post name slug, which is nice-looking and SEO-friendly. Just ensure that your theme takes care of showing the date and time of your posts and therefore doesn't trick your users into thinking that obsolete content is actually more recent material.

When you click Save Changes, WordPress will update your .htaccess file if the web server has write permissions on the file to do so and if you're using Apache. If WordPress is unable to write to the file, you'll be advised to manually copy a snippet of code for mod_rewrite into your .htaccess file yourself. Keep in mind that .htaccess is a hidden file on *nix systems such as Linux and MacOS, so it may not show up in your FTP program unless you show hidden files. (Cyberduck and FileZilla are good FTP clients that you can use for free.)

Finally, .htaccess is not required if you're using Nginx.

Privacy Settings

Skip or customize Media as you wish (its defaults are generally fine), and click Privacy instead.

Here you'll be able to generate a Privacy Policy page. It's not only a good idea to do so, it is a legal requirement to serve European visitors. (To learn more about the actual laws, search for GDPR in Google.)

Do You Need a Blogroll?

Blogrolls are lists of links recommended by a blogger. They are typically placed in the sidebar and link to somewhat related blogs (and friends of the blogger). They used to be a permanent fixture in the early days of blogging; but much like trackbacks, they have become less common over time as the community element of blogging waned.

Unless you have a large network of friends you want to link to, I think you can skip this feature. Some people believe that it can help with SEO, while others claim that site-wide links can hurt your SEO efforts. Regardless of SEO implications, you have to ask whether this really helps your readers. I think that real estate has better uses. But definitely feel free to link to my blogs if you decide to add one to your site. :-P

Steps Not Needed for Blogger

As you read through the WordPress instructions, you'll find plenty of information that's universally valid, regardless of your blogging platform of choice. However, a few suggestions don't apply to Blogger users.

- You can ignore update/ping services because such features are built into Blogger.

- Blogger comes with a built-in spam filtering system. You don't need any external service such as Akismet.

- You can't use a third-party commenting system. Thankfully the built-in commenting system is excellent and integrates with visitors' Google accounts.

- Permalinks are SEO-friendly by default.

- You aren't able to, nor do you need to, install any of the other WordPress plugins listed in this and the next chapter. This includes SEO, caching, and security plugins mentioned later on. If you want to see how extensible your platform is, you can check out the list of gadgets in the Layout menu area.

Enhance WordPress with Plugins

A myriad of plugins are available for WordPress blogs that can be found at wordpress.org/plugins or by searching from the Plugins section of your dashboard.

Install Plugins

To install plugins, you can download, unzip, and upload them to your wp-content/plugins folder on the server, then activate them in the Plugins section of your WordPress administrative interface.

Alternatively, if your web server has write access to the wp-content/plugins folder, you can install them by following these simple steps:

1. Click the Plugins menu and then the "Add new" button or submenu link. There you can search for plugins by term or related keywords.

2. Click the Install Now button for the desired plugin to install it. Once the installation is complete, you'll be offered an Activate button to actually enable the plugin.

Most plugins add their own menu entry in the admin section so that you can configure their specific options, if applicable.

> Tip 13   Only install plugins that you strictly need.

Recommended Plugins

It would be impossible for me to recommend a list of plugins that won't inevitably become obsolete. My recommendation is to install what you need and incrementally add plugins as the need arises. If one fails to meet expectations, try a different option instead.

Nevertheless, I'm going to list three staples every WordPress blog should use (my blogs all take advantage of these options). You can find them by simply searching in the Plugin section of your site's dashboard.

- *Jetpack*: A collection of common, useful features provided directly by the makers of WordPress.com. At the time of writing, Jetpack offers features that are organized in a few tabs, including Writing, Sharing, Discussion, Traffic, and Security. Quite the broad scope, as you can see. It's a bit heavy, but I recommend installing it because it allows you to skip many smaller plugins that you'd likely want in its place. You'll be asked to register a WordPress.com account to enable all these features (doing so doesn't imply that you'll blog at WordPress.com).

- *Yoast SEO*: An essential plugin for on-page SEO optimization. There are many SEO plugins, but Yoast SEO is flat out the best in my opinion. We'll discuss the SEO concepts you'll need to configure it in Chapter 4, Customizing and Fine-Tuning Your Blog, on page 57.

- *A caching plugin*: WordPress without a good caching plugin is quite heavy on your web server and it won't be able to sustain, all things being equal, a good spike of traffic. A caching plugin is a must-have. You have many choices to choose from and you can't really go wrong. The most popular free options are WP Super Cache and W3 Total Cache. Among premium options, WP Fastest Cache and WP Rocket stand out.

Regardless of which plugins you end up installing, ensure you keep them up-to-date to avoid security vulnerabilities. The same goes for WordPress itself, though recent versions will self-update, provided your web server is configured with the right permission to do so (a balance has to be struck, as this can be a security concern unto itself).

> Tip 14   Promptly update WordPress and its plugins.

Take Action

1. Choose a blogging platform.

2. Associate your domain name to your blog (served on HTTPS).

3. Set up your blog.

4. Perform a preliminary configuration of your blog's key settings as offered by your platform.

5. Create a compelling About page and link it to your primary navigation menu.

6. Create a Privacy Policy page.

What's Next

We covered a lot of ground in this chapter, from platform and hosting choices all the way to a basic configuration of your blog.

In the next chapter, we'll take things a step further by fine-tuning the blog to optimize its behavior.

After the next chapter, we'll promptly head toward discussing content, which is, after all, the real reason your readers will want to visit your blog.

Visualize this thing that you want. See it, feel it, believe in it.
Make your mental blueprint, and begin to build.

    Robert Collier

CHAPTER 4

Customizing and Fine-Tuning Your Blog

By following the instructions so far, you should have a preliminary but well-configured installation of WordPress or a roughly equivalent setup for the blog platform of your choice.

In this chapter, we'll kick it up a notch by fine-tuning and customizing your new blog. We'll take your basic blog and turn it into a full-fledged publication platform that's carefully tailored to your needs and goals.

Pick a Professional Theme

If you opted for WordPress, you'll find that the default WordPress look is clean and minimalist. Depending on your aesthetic preferences, you may like that look a lot. But it would be a mistake to settle for this default theme for three reasons:

1. Most new blogs use the default theme. Sticking with it will not help your blog stand out from the crowd.

2. Visitors value eye candy. A beautiful design will greatly help your blog succeed, even if you settle for a minimalist one that focuses on content.

3. The default theme has very limited features and customization options.

This is true whether you opted for WordPress or not. Sticking to the default theme offered by your blog engine is rarely a good idea.

Spend some time evaluating other themes until you find one that fits your style and the type of blog you intend to create. For example, if you're running a team blog that will be updated on a daily basis, a magazine or newspaper-style theme may be a good idea.

For WordPress, free themes can be found at wordpress.org/extend/themes/ and on other sites easily found on the web via search engines. If you opted for a different platform, your choice might be more limited, but you should still be able to find plenty of themes. I generally don't recommend that you opt for a free theme unless your budget is extremely tight. Premium themes generally offer the following advantages over free ones:

- There is an economic incentive for the developers to keep their themes up-to-date. If nothing else, this is good from a security standpoint. Such themes also tend to be (further) enhanced by their respective designers as time goes on.

- Purchased themes tend to offer all sorts of options and features that are not available with the average free theme, given that premium themes have to justify their price tag. Some premium WordPress themes, for example, include a full-fledged framework built on top of WordPress, which greatly extends its capabilities.

- They don't require you to advertise that you're using a free theme and credit the designer in the footer (which then appears on every single page of your blog) or include affiliate links to dubious sponsors. Now, not all free themes do these sorts of things, but you'll find not having to worry about such licensing conditions quite refreshing.

Buying a well-designed theme is a worthwhile investment that won't cost you too much (think something in the $50–$100 USD range). Premium themes tend to be sold a lá carte or as part of a yearly subscription. MyThemeShop and Elegant Themes are two examples of the latter, where your subscription grants you access to dozens of themes as well as a few premium plugins.[1] Other good providers can be found at wordpress.org/extend/themes/commercial.

Aside from sites that charge a yearly fee for access to a buffet of themes, some marketplaces allow you to buy an individual theme from a variety of designers and companies. ThemeForest.net might be the most popular among them. In fact, ThemeForest has themes for other blogging engines as well, including Ghost, Blogger, Jekyll, and so on.

Take the time to get to know your theme and read its documentation, if available. Common perks of premium themes include the ability to feature posts at the top of your blog, display the home page as a newspaper with clickable summaries and icons rather than as full posts, easy customization via drag and drop, and many other useful features. If you can't afford or don't want to commit funds to the project quite yet, you can certainly find a free theme that looks good and offers some customization options.

---

1. mythemeshop.com and elegantthemes.com, respectively.

If you're creating this blog for a company, you don't have to mimic the look of your main site and integrate your blog with the company's site in a visually seamless manner, but it's a good idea to do so.

> Tip 15   If you run a company blog, prominently link to your main site from it.

Given that company budgets (even startup ones) are usually larger than what your typical solo blogger has at his or her disposal, you may even consider having a designer create a custom theme for your company blog. Another appealing option for those on a slightly tighter budget is to commission someone to heavily customize a premium theme that you've already purchased.

Customizing Blogger's Look and Feel

If you're using Blogger, you can select a variety of themes from the Template menu. This page also allows you to visually customize the template of your choice through a template designer.

If you require further flexibility, you can use HTML, CSS, and JavaScript to edit the template directly. For example, the navigation bar at the top can be hidden via CSS. This doesn't violate Google's terms of service (contrary to popular belief). You can also edit any component of your blog (e.g., your sidebar) from the Layout page by adding and removing gadgets.

Blogger is quite popular, so searching for "blogger premium themes" should give you enough options to find something you'll like. The aforementioned ThemeForest (aka Envato Market) currently offers over a hundred Blogger options.

Enable Stats

Being able to understand who your visitors are and what they do when they arrive on your site is a fundamental part of running a successful blog. To accomplish this goal, we need to set up a traffic analytics suite. In Chapter 9, Understanding Traffic Statistics, on page 169, we'll discuss how to analyze the data you collect in greater detail, but for now let's start by choosing and installing a specific traffic analysis tool.

A multitude of such tools has been created over the years. Some work by analyzing your web server logs, while others avail themselves of a JavaScript tracker that you embed in each page of your site. I strongly recommend that you opt for the latter.

Third-party web-based analytics will, in fact, keep track of your traffic stats for years to come. They won't be impacted if you move your blog to a different server. More importantly, the most prominent hosted analytics suites tend to be very sophisticated and can provide you with highly customized reports.

In particular, you should consider the following two analytics services. I use both for my WordPress blogs. If you don't opt for WordPress, the second one doesn't apply to you.

Google Analytics

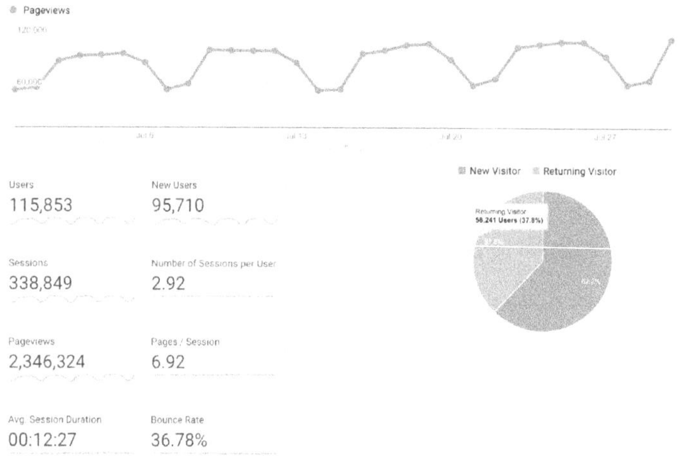

Figure 6—Key metrics in Google Analytics

Regardless of what other traffic suites you decide to install, you really should use Google Analytics,[2] which has become the de facto standard. It's free and extremely rich in features (entire books have been written about it). It also integrates well with Google's other services, such as Google Search Console (a useful service for webmasters) and Google Ads (formerly AdWords), which is great for keeping track of your return on investment if you were to ever run an ad campaign.

Google Analytics makes it really easy to share statistics with colleagues or prospective buyers as well. This is particularly useful for team sites or as proof of your traffic claims if you ever decide to sell your blog.

Once you've signed up for the service, you'll be provided with a snippet of JavaScript that needs to be embedded in your pages. That's the individual

---

2.   google.com/analytics

tracking code that identifies the collected data and associates it with your personal Analytics account. The quick and easy way to accomplish this is to install one of the many plugins that adds Google Analytics for you.

If you'd prefer not to install yet another plugin for such a small task, you'll need to edit the footer of your blog. Some WordPress themes, particularly premium ones, offer the ability to enter footer or analytics codes that will be dynamically added at the bottom of each page. If that's the case for your theme, add your tracking code there.

Finally, you have the option of editing your theme directly, placing it just above the </body> closing tag. In WordPress, the file you're looking for is footer.php, which is located in your theme folder and modifiable through the WordPress file editor under Appearance (or with an editor like Vim). This is, generally speaking, a bad idea as it can lead to you losing your changes when the theme is updated (child themes are a way to solve this particular problem, but I would just avoid the issue altogether).

The tracking code will look similar to the snippet below:

```
<!-- Global site tag (gtag.js) - Google Analytics -->
<script async src="https://www.googletagmanager.com/gtag/js?id=UA-XXXXXXX-XX">
</script>
<script>
        window.dataLayer = window.dataLayer || [];

        function gtag() {
                dataLayer.push(arguments);
        }
        gtag('js', new Date());

        gtag('config', 'UA-XXXXXXX-XX');
</script>
```

Of course, you'll need to replace the code with the tracking code that Google Analytics provided you with. Once that code is installed, load your blog's home page once, then double-check its status in Google Analytics.

Google Analytics is an amazing tool for Internet marketers and bloggers. Historically, the only downside has been that your statistics didn't appear in real time, but rather they reflected data that had been acquired several hours beforehand. This meant that very often you weren't able to study a spike in blog traffic as it was actually happening in real time. Instead you had to settle for a postmortem analysis a few hours later.

These days they offer some real-time capabilities that enable you to investigate traffic spikes and check how many people are on your site at a given moment.

An example of the Google Analytics interface can be seen in Figure 6, Key metrics in Google Analytics, on page 60.

A plethora of other web analytics tools are out there, but it's not worth worrying about them at this stage. Should you manage to outgrow Google Analytics, you'll be advanced enough in web marketing to know the specific analytics tools you'll need to supplement it with.

WordPress.com Stats

Unlike Google Analytics, which can be installed on any site, WordPress.com statistics are provided for WordPress blogs only (self-hosted blogs or the ones hosted by WordPress.com) and can be enabled by installing the Jetpack plugin. You'll then be able to see simple statistics about your blog directly from your dashboard (in a Site Stats submenu of Jetpack) or enhanced statistics directly on your connected WordPress.com account.

> Tip 16   Android users can glance at stats on their home screen via the handy WordPress widget.

WordPress statistics give you a nice snapshot of where your traffic is coming from, what search engine keywords people (who are not logged in their Google accounts) used to find you, which of your articles and pages are popular at the moment, and what links are being clicked, but not a whole lot more than that. Google Analytics is a significantly more powerful tool. Nevertheless, I like the simplicity and focus on key metrics that WordPress.com Stats provides. If you use WordPress, having both is a good idea.

If you're using a different blog engine, Google Analytics on its own will do.

Customize Your Sidebar

Your main sidebar is a crucial component of your blog. In fact, it'll be shown prominently on virtually every page of your blog. Its position, usually on the right of your article's content, makes it prime blog real estate that should be allocated wisely.

As you learn more from this book and gather real-world experience as a blogger, you can revisit your sidebar to customize its components however you like.

What Should You Include in Your Sidebar?

Your sidebar, particularly the area above the fold at common screen resolutions, should include your *calls to action*. Think about the most important goals you have and what you want your visitors to do, and then adapt the sidebar accordingly.

In the beginning, you shouldn't be overly concerned with making money from your blog: your main challenge is blogging regularly and attracting readers. So while at some point you might have sponsors, affiliate links, or even good ol' ads, don't start with them. You won't (yet) have enough traffic to make their presence worthwhile, anyway.

Instead, focus on your number one priority. What is that, you ask? Getting people to join your newsletter (or otherwise subscribe to you). Given that your audience will be at least somewhat technical, an RSS feed icon would also be beneficial. Aside from subscription options, you should include a one-paragraph blurb about you and your blog that links to your main About page where readers can learn more.

Include a nice portrait of yourself (unless you're running a team or company blog) on the About page. You can also include a smaller version in the sidebar unless your blog theme allows you to show the author picture and a short biography at the bottom of your posts, in which case you can skip the photo and blurb in the sidebar. The photo will help people connect with you at a human level. Thanks to the *halo effect* cognitive bias, this is particularly effective if you're conventionally attractive. (Conventionally or not, you're unique and beautiful anyway, so consider doing it no matter what.)

You'll also want to include some social media widgets that invite people to like or follow you on the social networks that you tend to use. Aside from Twitter, LinkedIn, and similar mainstream options, programmers will want to include a link to GitHub.com or an equivalent code-based platform.

> **Tip 17** Feature your newsletter sign-up form near the top of your sidebar.

You'll have a fairly long sidebar because it runs parallel to your articles or to your home page (which is also long, since it'll eventually have, at the very least, a summary of five to ten recent posts). As a result, unlike the top of the sidebar, which is prime real estate, you'll have plenty of room for less critical components further down the sidebar. For example, you could include your categories, tags (called *labels* on Blogger), disclaimers, and so on. Keep in mind that the further down the sidebar an element is, the less visibility it'll generally have (except perhaps for the very last element, which will fare better than the penultimate one).

If your theme doesn't include a search box already, make sure you add one at, or near, the top of your sidebar. Likewise, if your pages, categories, or other important elements are not available elsewhere in the theme, ensure that you add them to your sidebar.

Heatmaps can be employed to help you better understand where users focus their attention on a given page. A service such as crazyegg.com or hotjar.com makes it easy to experiment and adjust elements on a theme or specific page to ensure that users are focusing on the things you want them to pay the most attention to. If you try it on your own blog, you'll quickly see how the human eye scans pages in an F-shaped pattern, which tends to favor the top of your page and the top of your sidebar above all else.

To give you a better idea of what to include, I'm going to propose the following starting template for your sidebar:

• Search

• About picture and small paragraph with link to full About page

• Newsletter sign-up form

• RSS feed and social media icons linking to your profiles

• Automatically generated list of top articles (Depending on your theme, you might need to install a plugin to obtain such a functionality.)

• Automatically generated list of recent articles

• Categories

• Tags cloud (unless you dislike the look of it)

• Earning disclaimer (more on this later)

Adjust to taste. While you begin to think about which widgets you'd like to display in your sidebar, let's take a quick look at how to add them.

How to Edit Your Sidebar

Each theme blog engine will have its own way to edit the sidebar, but for WordPress, you can head over to the Widgets link under the Appearance menu inside your WordPress dashboard. You should see a scene similar to the one shown in Figure 7, WordPress widgets, on page 65.

All you have to do is drag and drop widgets that are available or inactive onto the main sidebar on the right side. Each widget may have configuration options that will be presented to you. For example, the Categories widget will

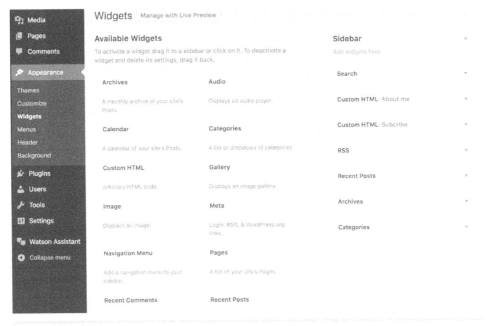

Figure 7—WordPress widgets

ask you to name the resulting div section in your sidebar (you'd typically call it Categories or Topics), as well as other options, such as whether you wish to display the post count for each category. If you've installed a plugin to aid with displaying your top posts or offering up an email subscription form to visitors, for example, you'll have the corresponding widgets to drag and drop from as well.

Text and Custom HTML are very flexible widgets that allow you to heavily customize your sidebar without having to edit the sidebar.php file from within your theme folder (which is generally a bad idea, as previously stressed).

If the sidebar is for a company blog, remember to include a short description of your business and a link to more information on your company site. I often find great technical articles on company blogs and leave not knowing what the company itself even does in the first place (which defeats the purpose to some extent).

Again, if you're not using WordPress, your blog engine will also allow you to customize your sidebar. The same principles outlined here fully apply to you as well.

A sizable percentage of your visitors will read your blog from their smartphones. In the case of my programming blog, that's 25% or so. If your theme is responsive, visitors will be able to comfortably read your content and navigate your site on small screens. Ensure that such is the case by testing your site with a mobile phone or through an emulator (or at the least using the testing tools included in Google Chrome and Firefox).

Many responsive themes will place the sidebar at the bottom of your content or opt not to include it at all on screens with smaller resolutions. It's important to test what happens to your sidebar on mobile because this can affect your calls to action for, say, a quarter of your visitors. You placed them at the top of your sidebar to give them visibility, and ironically they end up being invisible to your mobile traffic instead.

This might be an acceptable compromise to you, or you may wish to do some theme customizations (if you dabble in web design) to ensure that your main call to action (your newsletter sign-up form) is prominent at the top of your page on mobile devices as well.

Encourage Social Media Sharing

One of the quickest ways to market your content is to have your readers do the marketing for you. If all of the readers who found your content useful were to share your site with their friends online, you'd quickly have more traffic than you could handle.

In practice, very few readers bother sharing your articles even if they found them to be exceptional. Depending on how explicit you are with your request and how much you solicit social media sharing, you'll likely only receive a few mentions from other people.

For example, my article "15 Sites for Programming Exercises" that I published on ProgrammingZen.com has received 55,199 visits to date, but only a few dozen tweets at the time of writing. In general, don't be surprised to see a mere 1%, or less, of your visitors sharing your post in some capacity.

That's OK. It's still worth it, as these mentions are essentially free publicity that helps increase your reach. You put your signal out there and never know who might pick it up. Occasionally that might include influencers with massive followings who will, in turn, introduce you and your article to a larger crowd. Don't bank on this happening, but be open to the possibility of random positive events like this striking at any time.

Facebook, Twitter, and LinkedIn Counters

If you read many blogs, you may have seen people showcasing more than a dozen social media icons at the bottom of their posts. Don't bother doing this.

In my experience, adding so many buttons is a waste of time. It's the paradox of choice at work. If you ask me to take one, two, or a maximum of three actions, I may do so. If you offer me fifteen options, I might not know which one to take and I'll feel less obligated to do anything at all.

If you want to provide these buttons as a service to your readers, you can use compact widgets from sites such as AddThis or ShareThis.[3] Some WordPress themes and alternative blogging platforms will already include integration for either service or implement their own social widget. For WordPress, you can also enable the sharing feature that's available in the Jetpack plugin instead.

If you're using Blogger, it already provides you with a social toolbar that includes Facebook, and Twitter, among others. You also have the option of adding sharing tools like AddThis to your blog by pasting the code in an HTML/JavaScript gadget on Blogger.

I would suggest that you start by including Facebook (Share rather than Like, if given the option), Twitter, and LinkedIn buttons in your articles via AddThis. These buttons can provide social proof,[4] because they show a counter of how many people have already shared your post.

On the flip side, if you are struggling to attract traffic, counters may unintentionally end up providing negative social proof (of how few fans you have), and in turn tell new visitors that nobody is reading and sharing your content. That said, you need to start somewhere, and if you don't include these buttons (perhaps initially disabling the option to show the counters), you certainly stand to have fewer people sharing your work on social media.

Contrary to common belief, with a few exceptions, you will receive relatively little traffic from social media sites like Facebook, Twitter, and LinkedIn. In the example about my article above, out of 55,144 pageviews, less than a thousand came from Twitter and Facebook combined, as shown in Figure 8, Traffic sources for my article on programming exercises, on page 68. We will delve further into the reasons for this in Chapter 8, Promoting Your Blog, on page 141.

Why bother with buttons that promote social sharing then? Aside from the argument that every little bit helps, Google takes into account popularity on social media as a ranking factor. In fact, if your article is popular on social media, chances are its content is appealing to users and that's a positive signal (that's the theory, at least).

---

3. addthis.com or sharethis.com, respectively.
4. en.wikipedia.org/wiki/Social_proof

google	39,993	72.52%
(direct)	7,136	12.94%
reddit.com	4,280	7.76%
getpocket.com	710	1.29%
twitter.com	578	1.05%
feedburner	322	0.58%
facebook.com	237	0.43%
duckduckgo.com	130	0.24%
vk.com	123	0.22%
bing	119	0.22%

Figure 8—Traffic sources for my article on programming exercises

Reddit and Hacker News

For technical blogs, there are two large communities for which it may be worth having sharing buttons: Reddit, with its extensive list of subcommunities known as subreddits, and Hacker News.

In the previous section, I mentioned how less than a thousand visits to my article came from Facebook and Twitter combined. Take a close look at Figure 8, Traffic sources for my article on programming exercises, on page 68, and you'll see that more than four thousand came from Reddit, (specifically the Programming subreddit).

If your site is technical in nature (or business oriented), Reddit and Hacker News buttons are worth adding.

Just find the right balance (between too few and too many icons), and focus on the buttons that you care the most about. Don't try to include too many, or their CTR (click-through rate) will quickly approach zero.

Win Over Subscribers

When your blog is starting out, your main goal should be attracting new subscribers. Translating these regular readers into dollars or into the other benefits you may be after is something that you can concern yourself with once your site is already established and has been up and running for a few months.

In the beginning, your goal is to increase your subscriber count. Sure, other metrics such as visitors, pageviews, time on the site, and bounce rate are all interesting and important in their own way, but nothing beats subscribers as an indicator of growth (and that you're doing this whole blogging thing right). If your subscriber count isn't growing, your blog isn't growing and therefore not living up to its full potential.

By subscribers, I mean readers that follow your blog via feed or receive your posts via email.

What About Browser Push Notifications?

I classify web push notifications as an aggressive marketing technique. You might have seen them on sites that immediately prompt you with a dialog to enable browser notifications. If you—accidentally, most often—enable them, you'll start receiving desktop notifications from the site even when you're not on it. Unsubscribing isn't so obvious either.

Push notifications are effective at increasing traffic and reader retention, of course, but they also disrupt people's attention and, quite frankly, are invasive. I suspect most technical readers find them off-putting on a technical blog. They have selected uses (e.g., on apps like Google Calendar), but they're controversial at best on blogs.

If you feel differently, or would like to run an experiment, companies like PushCrew make it trivial to enable this alternative subscription method.

Count RSS Feed Subscribers

As a blogger, you need to know three things about RSS feeds:

1. Readers who add your feed to a client of their choice (e.g., Feedly or Reeder) will receive a notification in their feed "inbox" when you post new articles to your blog. Once a reader subscribes, you can more or less count that person as a regular reader.

2. Despite being a brilliant technology, RSS is increasingly less used among the general public. But many programmers and other highly technical audiences will still use it to some degree, however, so it's worth paying attention to.

3. Virtually all blog engines provide an RSS feed already. In WordPress, you can simply append /feed to your blog URL, to find its feed (e.g., programmingzen.com/feed).

Before discussing how to win over new subscribers, we'll need a system that allows us to count how many RSS subscribers you have at a given time to measure progress. In fact, unlike email, you can't easily count how many people subscribed to your RSS feed.

This problem was solved a long time ago by FeedBurner, a great service (acquired by Google) that allowed you to specify a feed and then provided you with a different feed URL that had analytics capabilities baked in. In a nutshell, it reported how many clients are requesting new posts from your FeedBurner feed, thereby giving you an estimate of how many people were actively subscribing to it.

In the past, I recommended FeedBurner. Today I wouldn't. Google hasn't updated the service since 2012, and the last two updates at the time were, respectively, shutting down the APIs and discontinuing their AdSense integration. Today FeedBurner is a zombie service I wouldn't trust to last. (My full take on this matter is available on my blog at technicalblogging.com/google-killed-the-rss-feed/.)

There are two approaches here: pay for an alternative service like FeedPress,[5] or ignore the feed count and instead focus solely on the number of email subscribers.

It's also possible to accept that we could settle for monitoring progress, and therefore the delta in subscribers, rather than the absolute number per se. So we could use the number of followers displayed by Feedly, a popular web client, to see how our feed subscriber base grows on that site over time. This approach is far from foolproof but can give you a general idea for free.

You Need a Newsletter

Now that you have your feed taken care of, it's time to discuss newsletters. A large portion of your readers will want to follow your blog via email rather than a feed reader. It's imperative that you provide a post-to-email service for those who wish to subscribe via email.

Before you think, as most web-savvy people tend to, that this is a legacy service you just offer for old-fashioned people, allow me to let you in on a secret: newsletters are the most powerful tool an Internet marketer can have. Nothing else comes close. *The money is in the list* is an old adage among web marketers and it couldn't be more true. The most valuable visitor you can have is the one who subscribes to your site via email.

The reason for this is that the relationship you have with email readers, unlike feed readers, is an intimate one. There's an unwritten contract that people will at least consider reading most of the messages that they receive in their inbox. This implicit contract is weaker when dealing with newsletters, but

---

5.   feed.press

you're still in their inboxes every time you publish a new post, and that's a very powerful advantage.

In my experience, the number of people who will open your newsletter will only be a small percentage of your total subscriber count—about 10%–50% (more if you have an exceptional following). However small that number may sound, it still tends to be massively higher than the number of people who will spontaneously revisit your site.

You have two main options when it comes to setting up an RSS-to-email newsletter. You can handle the newsletter yourself through a third-party mailing list management service such as MailChimp or Aweber,[6] or, if you use WordPress, enable the option to "Allow users to subscribe to your posts and comments and receive notifications via email" in the Discussion tab of the Jetpack plugin.

The advantage of Jetpack is that it handles everything automatically for you and it's free. Once enabled, WordPress will take care of the workflow for you, including forwarding your posts automatically, managing unsubscribes, and so on. You'll also receive notifications when people subscribe and will be able to see a list of subscribers on WordPress.com.

The main disadvantage is that the interactions with your list are limited to what you publicly post to your blog. You can't really send messages out for just those on your list, contact subscribers with *autoresponders* (messages sent at set intervals after a user signs up), customize emails with users' names, or add all sorts of other nice touches that are often used by email marketers. In other words, it's extremely easy to set up and accomplishes what it's supposed to do, but it does little more beyond that.

You can see how the option to subscribe is presented at the bottom of the comment form in Figure 9, Jetpack's comment system in WordPress, on page 72. This also shows you what Jetpack's commenting system with social logins looks like. Don't worry if it doesn't look like the option to follow is very visible. You'll still be able to publicize your newsletter in the sidebar by dragging the Blog Subscriptions (Jetpack) widget.

If you choose to go with a service like MailChimp or Aweber, you'll generally have to pay for it, but you'll have full control. MailChimp is freemium and offers a *Forever Free* plan that currently provides a generous free tier for up to 2,000 subscribers. That should cover you for many months at the very

---

6. mailchimp.com or aweber.com, respectively.

least. If you outgrow it sooner than that, you should definitely pay for this service, because your blog is Seabiscuit and you'd better feed that horse.

The main steps involved with emulating what you automatically get with Jetpack would be to create a list and then an RSS feed-to-email campaign with these email providers. You'll need to customize the look of your messages and your sign-up forms and then embed one on your site (or use a plugin that does that for you). You'll also have to provide your own address or a P.O. box in the footer of your emails to respect the CAN-SPAM Act (a funny name for antispam legislation).

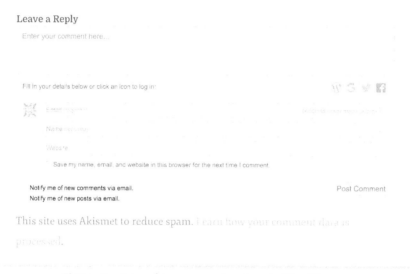

Figure 9—Jetpack's comment system in WordPress

It's worth noting that you could technically export email addresses from Jetpack and then import them via MailChimp at some point, but doing so is a delicate operation that must be handled very carefully due to the high probability of spam reports and complaints from readers who may see your new newsletter as something they didn't technically sign up for. (And some email providers won't even allow the procedure at all because of this.)

Which of the two is right for you? If you don't mind spending some time setting it all up and assuming that the primary intent of your blog is commercial, go with a service like MailChimp. You'll get your money's worth from it. If, on the other hand, you're mostly in it for other, non-monetary reasons and you're using WordPress, then the built-in option in Jetpack is the quick and easy way to go.

Single vs. Double Opt-In

If you choose to operate your own newsletter and currently reside in Canada, you are legally required to make your sign-up process double opt-in. This means that your readers have to enter their email addresses and then confirm their request to join by clicking an activation link that gets sent to them by email.

Even if you are not legally required to do so where you live (e.g., in the United States), it's a good idea to implement double, not single, opt-in. Your list will only contain addresses from people who genuinely signed up for your newsletter (i.e., they proved ownership of the email address). As a result, your subscriber list will be much more valuable than a list of unconfirmed emails.

You'll also get fewer fake emails, misspelled emails, bounce responses, spam reports, and abuse complaints. You may lose a few subscribers who never received your activation email or didn't bother reading it, but that's a small negative compared to the benefits of having such a clean list.

Invite People to Subscribe

When it comes to attracting subscribers, two variables are at play: the number of visitors and your conversion rate. All things being equal, the larger the number of visitors, the higher the number of subscribers. The problem is that if your conversion rate (from visitor to subscriber) is low, most of your effort to attract new visitors will be wasted. These visitors will reach your blog and then leave. The majority of them are unlikely to ever return (especially not on any kind of regular basis).

The real issue then becomes increasing your subscriber conversion rate. Excellent content definitely helps, but that's not enough in and of itself. You need to remind people that the subscription is available. Solicit them to take the action you want.

Create a Lead Magnet

If you want an even greater conversion rate, you may have to take things a step further. Don't just invite people to join your newsletter: (ethically) bribe them. The easiest way to attract new subscribers is to offer them something valuable for free when they sign up for your newsletter. For example, if your blog's niche is TypeScript, you could offer a short collection of TypeScript tips beautifully formatted in a PDF, or a mini-course on the topic via email that will send one lesson per day for two full workweeks.

Use a mini-course for your lead magnet. It'll get people used to receiving and opening emails from you.

This is known as a lead magnet because you're offering an incentive that attracts new leads (in the form of their email address and the authorization to email them). This technique has three caveats:

1. You can't verify feed subscriptions, so you will have to tie this to email sign-ups only.

2. You can't automate this process with the built-in Jetpack email subscription in WordPress. You'll need your own newsletter, and you'll have to create an autoresponder, which will include a link to the download for those who sign up. In MailChimp, you could even include it in the confirmation email sent to new subscribers, without setting up a separate autoresponder for the download.

3. Technical people tend to dislike the idea of having to sign up just to download a file, so you may get a few people complaining about it. Remember, however, that you're not doing anything wrong—you're the one who sets the conditions for your own content. Readers can always subscribe, download, and then unsubscribe if they wish.

Some people go so far as to create so-called *content upgrades*, which are different lead magnets for different articles. This more advanced technique is best reserved for later on, when you already have a list of articles that perform really well. You can then capitalize on the large amount of traffic coming to them, and convert readers into subscribers by offering them a lead magnet that's relevant to the specific article.

Even if you want to ignore freebies, which convert extremely well, you still need to promote your email subscription options throughout your blog. Do so in two spots. The first and most obvious spot is somewhere at the top of your theme or in the sidebar (as mentioned before). The second is at the bottom of your posts.

In WordPress the file that you need to edit to add custom code at the bottom of your posts is single.php, which you can find in your WordPress theme folder. But as usual, this isn't a great idea unless you know what you're doing. Instead, see if your theme offers an option to hook custom code at the bottom of posts, above the comment area. If not, plenty of plugins allow you to inject code in your posts. If you're not using WordPress at all, do some research on what options are available to you to add a snippet of code at the bottom of every post on your blog.

At the bottom of each post you could have a message that says:

> If you enjoyed this post, be sure to subscribe to my newsletter or feed.

Both the words *newsletter* and *feed* should be linked to their respective sign-up pages. (If you opted for a mailing list service like MailChimp, your sign-up form will also be available at a URL that will be provided to you.)

Even better, you could have an entire sign-up form at the bottom of your posts. Within your posts, you'll also want to refer to your subscription options when it's fitting to do so. For example, if you're writing the first article in a series, you can suggest within the body of your article that your readers subscribe so as not to miss future installments.

Optimize Your Sign-Up Form

Whether you opted for a service like MailChimp or go for the built-in Jetpack subscription service, you'll be provided with the ability to customize the look and feel of your newsletter sign-up form. You should take advantage of this ability. You can experiment to see what works best for you, but here are some general recommendations.

Add social proof to your title. *Join 5,312 subscribers* is better than *Join thousands of subscribers*, which in turn is better than *Join my newsletter*. If you're just starting out and don't have large numbers of subscribers yet, you could incorporate your social media followers into the number. For example, *Join 1,257 subscribers and social media followers*. If you don't have social media followers either, skip the social proof for now, and use something like *Never miss a post* or *Be the first to read my new posts*. Later on, including specific numbers will act as proof of your site's popularity and can help convince more people that your blog is well worth following.

If you produced a lead magnet, make sure you incorporate it in your subscription form's text. Include an image of the freebie as well.

Don't integrate your form so well that it becomes almost hidden by matching the theme colors perfectly. This might seem like odd advice, but you don't want to camouflage it on your site. Instead, make it stand out. In particular, ensure the subscribe button is a bold, eye-catching color, such as orange or red.

Along the same lines, skip the boring, default "Subscribe" label for your button. Instead opt for something a little peppier or wittier. *Cool. Let's do this!* or *Sign me up for the goodies!* is definitely better than the forgettable and unremarkable *Subscribe*.

If you are using a mailing list service like MailChimp, collect both the first name and email from your readers. Yes, skipping the first name field would help you sign up a few more people due to the reduced inertia at sign-up. But having the subscriber's first name can be a powerful tool in your future email campaigns to help your messages come across as more personable. It's also less likely that your emails, automatically addressed to the person's first name, will be automatically flagged by spam filters.

All of these simple changes can help your subscription form stand out and in turn increase your rate of conversion from visitor to subscriber.

Are Pop-Ups Evil?

Most people would agree that pop-ups are annoying. Some may consider them downright evil. Yet, pop-up newsletter sign-up forms are also extremely effective at converting traffic into subscribers. Over time, I've seen them become more common even on technical blogs.

My take on this is that it's up to you to decide whether you want to slightly annoy your readers and occasionally argue with them about your pop-up usage, or if the extra sign-ups are not worth it. There are sites, like simpleprogrammer.com, which run full-page modal pop-ups as soon as you arrive on their site. The first time I saw it I thought, *Mad lad*! But it clearly works and has enabled massive growth for that newsletter.

I suspect most of my readers would appreciate a more conservative approach, such as employing overlays that don't take over the full page, like some modal pop-ups do. In the case of MailChimp, I'm referring to what it currently calls the slide and fixed formats, in particular.

Do they work? Absolutely. Should you employ them? It's up to you.

Don't Get in Trouble: Use Disclaimers

Honesty and integrity when dealing with your readers are fundamental principles that will serve you well as a blogger (and in life). Your visitors will no doubt appreciate it.

More importantly, being honest and transparent will also help you stay out of trouble with your employer (if you have one) and even with the authorities.

Include an Employer Disclaimer

If you work for a large corporation, it's likely that your employer has employee guidelines for blogging and social media engagement. You should review and respect these rules to avoid being the *n*th blogger to lose a job because of what he or she wrote online.

These guidelines vary from company to company, but they usually boil down to not revealing company secrets or unannounced products, not being a jerk to other people online, not engaging in slandering your competitors, and similar common-sense advice.

What some people may not be aware of is that most large corporations also require you to disclose your work affiliation. In other words, you're required to include a disclaimer on your blog that identifies what you write as your own opinions and not those of the company that you're presently employed by.

As an example, the About section of my programming blog includes the following disclaimer:

> I'll start with a disclaimer that is required by both my employer and my type of job. It's my personal blog, which is entirely independent of IBM. My articles and comments are my own and don't necessarily represent my employer positions, strategies, or opinions.

For your own blog you could use or adapt the following standard disclaimer:

> Disclaimer: The posts on this site are my own and don't necessarily represent [COMPANY]'s positions, strategies, or opinions.

Disclaimers such as these may appear silly to technical people, but they can help get you out of trouble with your employer should a complaint be filed against you.

Include a disclaimer like this in your sidebar and/or About section if you're employed by a company that requires you do so. On Twitter, where space is limited, a simple "Tweets are my own." should suffice.

Include an Earnings Disclaimer

If you think being fired for blogging is bad, how about being investigated by the feds?

In short, the FTC (Federal Trade Commission) expects U.S.-based bloggers to clearly disclose any commercial affiliations with third-party products they're reviewing or promoting. If your post or review includes a link to an affiliate product, including Amazon affiliate links, you need to disclose that fact to your readers. If the book, game, software, or any other product or service you are reviewing was obtained for free, you need to let your readers know that, because this may affect your judgment of the product. You're also not allowed to make any false, misleading, or deceptive claims.

If you are a U.S.-based blogger, it's worth checking out the latest guidelines on the ftc.gov website to ensure that you're operating within the boundaries of the law. Non-U.S.-based bloggers may or may not have similar rules in place, depending on their country, but it's worth adopting the same standard of transparency that's asked of our peers in the States. You could add the following to your sidebar:

> Some of the links contained within this site have my referral ID, which provides me with a small commission for each sale. Thank you for your support.

Also, include a disclaimer at the bottom of each relevant post to explain your connection to the specific product that's being promoted. This can also help you from a legal standpoint when it comes to readers who subscribe to your posts and may not see your sidebar disclaimer.

If you post a review of a book you received for free from a publisher and are including affiliate links to Amazon, you may want to include the following disclaimer (or a very similar one) at the bottom of your post:

> Disclaimer: I received this book for free from the publisher for reviewing purposes. This doesn't affect my judgment of the book nor influence my review. Furthermore, my site is a participant in the Amazon Services LLC Associates Program, an affiliate advertising program designed to provide a means for sites to earn advertising fees by advertising and linking to Amazon.com. Thank you for your support.

Feel free to copy or adapt this disclaimer accordingly, depending on your specific circumstances and blog post.

If you link to Amazon books and other products often, it might make sense to embed the Amazon relevant portion of the disclaimer permanently in your sidebar. This way you'll automatically be covered if you forget it in a post that just happens to link to Amazon with your affiliate ID.

You might assume that these kinds of disclaimers will kill your click-through rate. In my experience, this isn't the case. It may paradoxically help bolster the number of clicks for the products you mention, possibly because disclaimers increase your perceived trustworthiness.

Set Up Your Blog for On-Page SEO

Search engine optimization is a huge topic and one that we'll dissect throughout this book. You won't need to become an expert, but possessing a solid understanding of the essential notions will have a significant impact on your blog's efforts to attract an audience. This is a key challenge for bloggers.

SEO techniques can be roughly divided into two categories: on-page SEO and off-page SEO. On-page SEO is what you do on your site to ensure that the content you present is properly evaluated and classified by search engine bots (also known as spiders or crawlers). For example, we've already seen how having, say, /better-python-errors as your permalink instead of /?p=123 ensures that search engines have a better understanding of what your post is about and which keywords are relevant to your post. That's part of our on-page SEO efforts.

Off-page SEO is what you do to increase the value of your content outside your own site: for example, link-building efforts, or managing to get backlinks from other sites on the web. You guessed it, we'll thoroughly discuss this topic as well.

We've already covered the importance of SEO-friendly permalinks. What else is there for on-page SEO? Much of what needs to be done for on-page SEO is specific to posts you create, so it's best explained when discussing the subject of your site's content, which we'll do in the next chapter.

As far as the initial setup for on-page SEO goes, there are only three remaining steps we need to take care of:

1. Generating an XML site map for our posts and pages
2. Adding our blog (and sitemaps) to Google Search Console
3. Ensuring our blog is fast and responsive (i.e., it renders well on mobile devices)

Generate an XML Sitemap

Sitemaps are XML representations of the structure of your site. As the name implies, they're literally maps of your site that list every page and post within it. They help search engines properly crawl and discover all of your content.

Your first step is to generate an XML sitemap that's automatically updated every time you post a new article or make some changes to the location of your content. This is blog-engine specific, but most platforms either have a built-in option (like Ghost does at /sitemap.xml), or they provide some form of plugin to accomplish this (e.g., the jekyll-sitemap plugin). If all else fails, searching for <blog engine name> sitemap in Google should yield some tutorials on how to accomplish this task.

If you're using WordPress and have installed Yoast SEO, you're in luck as well. Just check the Features tab to ensure the option has been enabled during the initial setup of the plugin. You can find a list of sitemaps it's generated by appending /sitemap_index.xml to your blog URL. The following figure shows the Yoast SEO's generated sitemaps for my programming blog.

XML Sitemap

Generated by **YoastSEO**, this is an XML Sitemap, meant for consumption by search engines.

You can find more information about XML sitemaps on **sitemaps.org**.

This XML Sitemap Index file contains 5 sitemaps.

Sitemap	Last Modified
https://programmingzen.com/post-sitemap.xml	2018-06-26 09:01 -07:00
https://programmingzen.com/page-sitemap.xml	2018-05-22 18:33 -07:00
https://programmingzen.com/category-sitemap.xml	2018-06-26 09:01 -07:00
https://programmingzen.com/post_tag-sitemap.xml	2018-06-26 09:01 -07:00
https://programmingzen.com/author-sitemap.xml	2018-06-18 22:25 -07:00

Figure 10—Sitemaps generated by Yoast SEO

The ones you'll want to pay attention to, in the case of Yoast SEO, are /post-sitemap.xml and /page-sitemap.xml. In the unlikely event that your blog already has hundreds of posts, you might find more than one XML file for your posts (e.g., /post-sitemap1.xml, /post-sitemap2.xml, etc.) Before a much-needed pruning, anynewbooks.com, my new book notification service, whose front-end uses WordPress, had over 17,000 posts, so many sitemaps were automatically generated for its posts.

Blogger users will also have sitemaps automatically, at /sitemap.xml and /sitemap-pages.xml for posts and pages, respectively.

Add Your Blog to Google Search Console

Google Search Console (available at google.com/webmasters/tools/ and formerly known as Google Webmaster Tools) is a tool for webmasters that allows you to take a peek behind the curtain of how Google sees your site (specifically how your site should be crawled and presented by Google). It can inform you of indexing problems. For example, if you change the structure of your URLs but forget to set up proper HTTP 301 redirects, Google Search Console will alert you that you now have many broken links (also known as 404 links).

Sign up with the tool and add your blog. You'll want to add your site and all of its variations. For example, for programmingzen.com I created the following four variations, even though they all redirect to my main URL, which is https://programmingzen.com:

1. http://programmingzen.com
2. http://www.programmingzen.com
3. https://programmingzen.com
4. https://www.programmingzen.com

This will allow you to catch any problems, including possible domain redirect issues in the future. Google also allows you to specify a preferred domain name, among the available variations, in Site Settings. Our selection will determine how the domain is presented to the users in the search engine result pages (SERP).

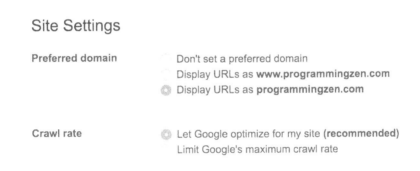

Figure 11—Setting the preferred domain name in the Google Search Console

When you add each variation of your blog URL, Google will ask you to verify your ownership of the site and offer you several ways to do that, including altering your DNS records and embedding a special meta tag in the header of your blog. To take full advantage of what Search Console has to offer, verify the URLs by choosing the verification method that's most convenient for you.

Google Search Console really is a set of invaluable tools that help you to better understand how Google views your blog. Among this tool's many features, you'll be able to diagnose if your site is being properly crawled, which keywords Google thinks are relevant to your blog, what sites link to you, if there are security issues, whether Google has any suggestions for you, and much more.

If you were to ever rename your blog's domain, Search Console will also enable you to inform Google of your change of address (but you'll need to set up the HTTP 301 redirects yourself). Keep in mind that changing your domain name once your domain is already established is generally a bad idea and should be considered only as a last resort.

I invite you to spend some time on your own exploring the many features available in Search Console. Right now, however, we're concerned with adding our blog sitemap(s) to the tool for optimal discoverability.

You can do so by finding the Sitemaps section (currently located under the Crawl section) in Search Console. Here you can add your posts and pages sitemaps if your blog engine organizes them in two different sitemaps. Alternatively, you can submit your index of sitemaps generated by plugins like Yoast SEO (again, located at /sitemap_index.xml), and Google is smart enough to process the information within. This section of the Search Console will also show you information about how many pages and images have been submitted and indexed.

Speaking of Yoast SEO, if you are using the plugin, it's a good idea to connect your Search Console in the Webmaster Tools tab. This way you'll be able to receive notifications from Google Search Console directly from within the plugin for a single-point, seamless experience.

It's worth noting that equivalent webmaster tools to the Search Console exist for other search engines. Bing has one, for example.[7] Perhaps more interestingly, Yandex and Baidu do as well, and you should absolutely add your site if you are blogging in Russian or Chinese, respectively. (And Yoast SEO allows you to connect all of these alternative tools as well in their Webmaster Tools section.)

Performance Considerations

Many good things can be said about WordPress, but speed isn't one them. A default installation connects to the database and dynamically generates content with each request, thus becoming quite demanding on your server's resources.

---

7.   bing.com/toolbox/webmaster/

When you first start blogging, your main challenge is to attract eyeballs, so a slow CMS may not be a huge deal initially. However, by following the roadmap that I've outlined in this book, you may manage to attract hundreds or thousands of visitors in the span of a few hours upon publishing—even in your early days as a blogger.

A vanilla WordPress installation will most likely die under the weight of so many requests, and you certainly don't want to see your site become unresponsive when so many people are eager to read what you've written—what an unattractive, if not uncommon, first impression that would be!

If that's not enough to make you consider the consequences of speed (or lack thereof), consider this: Google is increasingly punishing sites that are slow to load (as well as sites that are not responsive, meaning that they don't render properly on mobile devices) in its result pages.[8] So let's see what we can do to help prevent this situation.

> **Tip 19**   Ensure your theme is responsive.

Depending on the blog engine you're using and how your site is hosted, some or all of these points about performance may not apply to you. However, it won't hurt to read them anyway.

Cache Everything

Server side, if you have control over your server, feel free to optimize the optimizable. Use Nginx instead of Apache, and configure Nginx, PHP, and MySQL to make them speedier than their default configurations (if you're not an expert on these already, you may have to do some Googling and experimentation). More importantly, however, you must install a caching plugin if you are using WordPress. We discussed some recommendations in the previous chapter. If you haven't installed one, please go back and install it now.

Even on shared hosting, a properly cached WordPress installation can handle thousands of visitors. The magic of caching lies in its ability to serve static versions of dynamically generated pages. Once a cached version of a page has been generated, the performance levels aren't far off from those of a static HTML page.

Just ensure you enable caching in the configuration settings of the plugin you installed. Some will be installed with the caching option off by default. Depending on which one you chose, you'll also have different options to speed up your site further, such as compressing your pages with gzip, grouping

---

8.   webmasters.googleblog.com/2018/01/using-page-speed-in-mobile-search.html

multiple JavaScript and CSS files into one .js and .css minified file each to reduce the size and number of requests your pages make upon loading, and so on. In general, you'll want to play a little with these options to see what leads to optimal loading times without breaking your theme.

You may also want to look into what options are available in your blog engine for CDNs (content delivery networks). These can greatly improve performance when serving static content such as images, JavaScript, and CSS files. CDN services are not generally free, but they can be quite affordable. (WordPress users can enable the free image CDN service provided by the Jetpack plugin.)

> Tip 20   Use a CDN to speed up your blog.

Every modern browser offers development tools that you can use to test how the changes you make affect the loading times for your blog, but you might find specialized tools and services to provide a much better experience, along with some insightful recommendations. Two tools worth considering are PageSpeed Insights by Google or the even more informative (and my favorite) GTmetrix.[9]

Jetpack for WordPress offers uptime monitoring that informs you when your site becomes unavailable. If you're not using WordPress, you might want to add your site to one of the many uptime monitoring services available. Uptime Robot and Pingdom are two popular options.[10]

What About AMP pages?

Accelerated Mobile Pages (AMP) is a technology that, by leveraging some constraints on what can be included in a page, allows for lightweight, fast-loading pages on mobile devices, where users are more likely to expect immediate answers. In theory, this is great. In fact, these pages are promoted by Google in a Top Stories carousel or otherwise rewards them with higher mobile ranking. That's why when you search on your smartphone, you'll often see a bolt icon next to top results. Those are AMP pages (yes, Accelerated Mobile Pages pages).

In practice, it's a little more complicated than that. You now have two different versions of your page, a canonical one and an AMP one, that need to be substantially similar. There are some issues related to branding, navigation, analytics, Google providing users with their own cached version to further improve speed, and more. All in all, it's a bit of a headache at the moment,

---

9.   developers.google.com/speed/pagespeed/insights/ and gtmetrix.com, respectively.

10.   uptimerobot.com or pingdom.com, respectively.

even if you use a plugin for WordPress that simplifies their creation. My recommendation is to ignore AMP pages for now and consider them at a later stage, when you'll have more experience with blogging and will be able to decide whether the benefits are worth it to you and your site.

Enable Code Highlighting in Your Posts

Before wrapping up this chapter, let's discuss how to embed highlighted code, a task that most technical bloggers need to do.

By default, you can embed small pieces of code in your paragraphs by using the <code> HTML tag. For snippets of code that span several lines, you can use <pre> instead. Your code will appear in a monospaced font but won't be colored or highlighted.

To make your code more readable and easier on the eyes, I invite you to consider the following alternatives (more or less in order of my own personal preference):

- Use a WordPress plugin. If you're using WordPress, you have many options to choose from. Just search for *syntax highlighter* or *code highlighter* in the plugins catalog.

- Use a JavaScript library. As long as your blogging platform supports JavaScript, you can use a syntax-highlighting library. One common choice is Google Code Prettify. [11]

- Use a snippet-sharing service. gist.github.com is probably one of the best services of its kind, and this too has the advantage of being blog-engine agnostic.

- Use a command-line tool. If you live and breathe the shell, you may want to consider a syntax highlighter tool such as Pygments.[12] Once you've uploaded and linked the CSS theme of your choice, you'll be able to copy the HTML output from the tool directly into your posts. Of course, this method will work regardless of your blog engine as well. The disadvantage of this method is that the marked-up code in the output will be harder to edit compared to some of the other options presented here.

- Use a tool such as Carbon,[13] which converts your code into a beautiful image that will then display your code correctly regardless of the user's

---

11. github.com/google/code-prettify
12. pygments.org
13. carbon.now.sh

browser or mail client. The downsides to this approach are that your code can no longer be discovered by text search and users cannot copy and paste from it (though some will argue this is for the user's own good).

Take Action

I have outlined quite a few steps in this chapter. Let's recap your homework.

- Make your site look good with a nice theme, customizing look and feel to taste.

- Add Google Analytics to your blog.

- Add select social sharing buttons.

- Join a newsletter subscription service and embed your sign-up form.

- Customize the sidebar of your blog, prioritizing your most important calls to action and content.

- (Optional) Create a lead magnet and promote it in your sign-up form and best content.

- Add an employer disclaimer (if applicable), and add an earnings disclaimer as soon as you start monetizing your blog.

- Add your site URL and all of its variations to Google Search Console (or an equivalent webmaster tool). Set up the preferred display URL in the tool.

- Generate sitemaps and add them to Google Search Console.

- Optimize your server (if applicable) and enable caching in your blog engine to improve performance and server availability under load.

- Enable syntax highlighting for your blog to improve the readability of your code snippets and listings.

What's Next

This was admittedly a large chapter, in which we worked through a wealth of topics related to the customization of your blog. At this point, you should have all the tools you need to start cranking out some content.

The next two chapters will be dedicated solely to maximizing your ability to produce great content that attracts readers.

CHAPTER 5

Creating Remarkable Content

You worked hard setting up and customizing your blog. Now we'll bring all your work to fruition as we shift the focus to what your blog is really about: your content.

Content Is King

In the world of Internet marketing, the common adage is, *Content is king.* All your other efforts are useless if your content isn't compelling. No amount of marketing is going to save you.

From an SEO perspective, content certainly is king. Search engines determine when to show your site on their result pages on the basis of its content. If your article isn't relevant to the user's query, Google won't show it to the user.

So the more articles you have, the more opportunities you have to rank for a wide range of matching queries. The length of the content is also a factor. Long content will naturally match a larger number of queries, and Google tends to favor longer articles over short ones.

It's not just about organic search traffic, though (as opposed to paid traffic, such as traffic acquired via paid ad campaigns). Real people will read the words you write. Boring or poorly written content may trick search engines in delivering traffic your way (though, it should be noted, increasingly less so), but it won't please intelligent humans once they're on your site. They won't stick around or remain interested for long. Above all, they won't subscribe, perform your calls to action, or come back to your blog again. It even hurts your SEO, given that Google considers time on page a signal for ranking.

Blogging's many benefits all originate from well-written, original content. Great articles will be linked to more often, be shared more on social media, and receive more positive comments. No matter your primary reason for blogging, great content is the *conditio sine qua non*.

Now to put things in mathematical terms, content is necessary but not sufficient. The quality and quantity of your posts are key; however, you also need to promote your content to have a successful blog. This chapter delves into the quality side of the equation. The next will take a gander at the role that quantity plays in your blogging. Finally, in Chapter 8, Promoting Your Blog, on page 141, you'll master how to go about letting the world in on your writing.

> Tip 21   Write epic content you'd love to read yourself.

Write for the Web

Writing for the web is different from writing a book or a letter. Web visitors skim content rather than reading it word for word. So you need to make the most of their skimming approach. You must lead the user to the essence of your message while arousing their curiosity to read the whole thing.

You only have a few seconds to captivate a visitor, who often has the attention span of a chipmunk on crack. How then do you capture the reader's attention? Let's consider a few do's and don'ts when writing for the web by addressing the three main components of your posts.

Write Killer Headlines

The headline of your posts is what people will notice first. On social media, in Google's result pages, within their feed reader or inbox, most prospective readers will only ever read your headline. It has to be good enough to grab readers' limited attention.

Attention is a precious resource that everyone else on the web is fighting for as well. So it's vital that you write a catchy headline that tells people what the article is about and intrigues them enough to click.

Headlines affect click-through rates more than anything else in your post. All things being equal, a catchy, informative headline will lead to more people checking out your article than if you went with a boring headline.

Inexperienced bloggers will often consider the headline as an afterthought. They'll write their post and then hastily put together a title. That's a mistake. On the other end of the spectrum, you'll have people who write shameless *clickbait* headlines in the format, "X Facts About <TOPIC>; Number Y Will

Shock You!" I call those "BuzzFeed headlines," after the blog that popularized them. I'd stay away from those if you care about your credibility.

> **Tip 22** Write your headline before your post. This will give focus to your writing.

Enticing, factual headlines can help you succeed without misleading your readers with false promises or offending their intelligence with blatantly clickbait-y headlines. Let's see this at work with a practical example.

Assume that you're writing a review of the search engine DuckDuckGo. Within it, you compare DuckDuckGo to Google. What should the headline be?

1. "Review of DuckDuckGo": This is boring and doesn't tell people what DuckDuckGo is within the headline.

2. "Google and DuckDuckGo: A Tale of Two Search Engines": Definitely honest and interesting. It also contains the keywords *search engines*.

3. "DuckDuckGo Review: A Google Alternative You'll Love": It's catchy, apt to grab the reader's eye, and highly likely to pique their curiosity. You're being bold by telling your readers that they'll love the alternative search engine, but you are not being overly sensationalistic.

4. "The Search Engine That Will Put Google Out of Business": There is bold and then there is unnecessarily sensationalistic. This title would attract clicks, but you stand to lose the respect of many of your readers in the process. The content would, in fact, have to be outrageous to try to justify the indefensible position promised by the headline. Or alternatively, the content might not address the issue in the title at all (and thus be misleading).

The degree of catchiness that you can get away with also depends on your audience and where you promote your articles. For example, Hacker News is a community with little tolerance for sensationalism. In fact, it even frowns upon numbers in lists and the use of exclamation marks, so much so that its moderators remove them from submissions when a story becomes popular.

OK, relevant, catchy, honest. You got it. What else should you consider when writing headlines? Quite a few things, as it turns out. Here is a list of tips you can use to write successful headlines.

• Make your titles stand out by using capitalization. For example, "JavaScript Promises Tutorial: Master Asynchronous Programming" looks better than "JavaScript promises tutorial: master asynchronous programming" in the title of a post. Style guides (e.g., *APA*, *AP*, *Chicago Manual of Style*, etc.) differ somewhat about which words should be capitalized, but it doesn't matter which one you opt for, as long as you're consistent. I'd recommend using a tool like headlinecapitalization.com to help with capitalization.

- Your titles are a key on-page SEO factor. You should incorporate your main target keyword near the beginning of the headline. If the focus keyword you intend to rank well for is *javascript promises*, the headline "JavaScript Promises Tutorial: Master Asynchronous Programming" is somewhat better than "Master Asynchronous Programming with JavaScript Promises," and both are better than "Asynchronous Programming in JavaScript," which doesn't even include the target keyword. You'd also want to ensure the slug reflects your focus. In this case, perhaps something like /javascript-promises-tutorial.

- You want an SEO-friendly headline, but that doesn't mean stuffing your headlines with keywords. Your headline is not a turkey at Thanksgiving. Write the headline with the user in mind. Yes, it should include your focus keywords, but it needs to read naturally. "Master JavaScript Promises, JavaScript Futures, JavaScript Async, JavaScript Tutorial" not only won't help you to rank, it might hurt you. Google understands the concept of synonyms and what you are trying to pull. In the early days of the web, keyword stuffing was a widespread problem, so Google got really good at finding and punishing such black hat techniques.

Adopt the mantra, *What's good for the reader is good for my blog.*

- Your headline is typically included in the title tag of your post by your blog engine. It will be the clickable headline shown by search engines and social media sites. It will also be shown by browsers in the title bar or if the reader bookmarks the page. What this means is that you don't have an unlimited amount of characters to work with. If the headline is too long it will be truncated past a certain length. The exact cut-off point varies, because with proportional fonts different letters take a different amount of space, but you should generally aim for headlines that are below 60 characters or so in total. Five- or six-word headlines tend to look good on average. If you use Yoast SEO in WordPress, you'll be able to see if the headline is too short or too long (in orange) or just right (in green). You'll also have a preview of how your post will appear as a result in Google.

- Start your headline with a number. For example, "13 Awesome Features Introduced by ES6." Numbered lists (so-called *listicles*) are always popular among users and quite fun to write as well. Just ensure to intersperse them with posts of other types. A ratio of three regular articles for each listicle you post would be fair.

- Remember to be useful to your readers. Your headline should sell your audience on the benefits of what you're conveying instead of the features within your article. Why should they bother reading it? Why read it now? In fact, consider introducing an element of urgency, if one is applicable. For example, "Free TypeScript Webinar. Sign Up Before the Deadline!" In this particular case, a strong call to action (i.e., needing to sign up) has also been put out to the reader. If you have a post-specific call to action, including it is a good idea (e.g., "Take My Survey <rest of headline>").

- Don't be afraid to craft question headlines. They directly draw in readers, who'll be eager to express their opinion on the topic and start a conversation with you (e.g., "What Minimum Specs Should Your Development Machine Have?").

- Leverage human curiosity. Whether in the form of a question or a statement, it's okay not to give away the punchline right in the headline. Piquing the user's interest will impact your click-through rates for the best.

- If your post provides *statistics* or *trends* in your industry, definitely include those two keywords in the headline. This is particularly powerful when combined with the listicle format (e.g., "33 Chatbot Statistics and Trends in 2019." When journalists (and other bloggers) are writing articles on a topic, they'll often search for statistics and trends (e.g., *chatbot statistics*). If they find you, they might cite you and usually link to you from a site with high *authority*. This will boost the SEO for your article and, to a lesser extent, your whole blog. It's not unusual for other news outlets to follow suit after the first journalist published linking to you. This can be manna from the sky to a blogger. As usual, don't count on it, but it's possible if you publish relevant content.

- Don't include a year in your headline because it will date your content. Would you really be interested in an article about the "Top JavaScript Frameworks to Learn in 2012" if you come across it in 2019? Probably not. *But Antonio,* I hear you thinking, *you just put 2019 in the headline example within the previous point.* So let me rephrase this. You need to handle years in your headlines with special care. Including a year can be useful. In fact, if I see a headline with 2019 in it and it is 2019, I'm more likely to click on it because I know it's going to be current content and not some obsolete article from a few years ago. I might even place 2019 directly in my initial search query. This is particularly true in the tech space, where information becomes obsolete quickly. So you have a choice to make. You can either skip the year altogether or include it and then yearly go back to update the year (and the content) to keep it current. In light of this possible approach, I would keep the year out of the slug for your post (e.g., /33-chatbot-statistics-and-trends rather than /33-chatbot-statistics-and-trends-in-2019).

- Compare these two headlines: "Tips for Writing Headlines" and "17 Scientifically Proven Ways to Write Better Headlines for Your Blog." Which one are you more drawn to? Most people would opt for the latter. Words like, *proof*, *proven*, *fact*, *scientific*, and *established* add credibility to what you are promising to deliver. Include them when applicable.

- Include *you* or *your*. Typically, people care about one thing above everything else: themselves. So popular headlines that are shared and clicked at large tend to include either of those two words. It tells the prospective reader that the usefulness of the content will directly benefit them. "10 Tips to Improve as a Programmer" doesn't resonate with people as much as "10 Tips That Will Make You a Better Programmer."

- Use superlatives and, more in general, words that inject some emotion into your headline. Superlatives like *best* make your headlines bolder, a positive provided you can justify the claims. Emotional words like *inspiring* or *joy* also can have a positive effect.

- If your post contains an infographic image, a cheat sheet, a video, or other special resources, you'll want to include that in the headline. You could even highlight it by placing it between square brackets (e.g., [VIDEO]).

- Mimic viral headlines with care. Certain partial phrases are common in viral headlines and tend to drive clicks and shares. Examples of these partial phrases are *wait till you see*, *will blow your mind*, *you need to know*, *that will make you*, *what happens when*, and the aforementioned *will shock you*, to name a few. They do work, but in tech circles they'll make your headlines sound like shameless clickbait. Since you're not running a site like BuzzFeed, I would caution you to use them sparingly, if at all.

> Tip 23   Use an odd number for your listicles. They perform better.

A Formula for Your First Paragraph

Immediately after the headline, your first paragraph is your article's most visible component. As mentioned before, visitors often (but not always) follow an F-shaped pattern with their eyes when scanning a web page.[1] Your first paragraph has a significant impact on whether your visitors, who were interested enough to click on your article, are actually going to bother reading it.

It's tempting to provide a lot of background info and slowly work your way up to the essence of your post. I recommend that you don't.

Instead, you should adopt the so-called *inverted pyramid* approach to writing that many journalists use. Put the most important information first, starting with the headline and your first paragraph. Proceed to unravel other important details and background information as the article carries on.

Your goal is to prevent people from losing interest and leaving your blog. You need to hook them right away. The tricky part is how to accomplish that. For many technical posts there's a formula that works quite well:

1. Describe a problem that affects the reader.
2. Empathize with them.
3. Promise a solution in your post.

Let's say that you're writing an article on choosing a JavaScript framework. It's going to be a comparison between React, Angular, and Vue for people who are confused about the fast-moving world of front-end development.

You read my previous section and you might come up with the following headline, "React vs. Angular vs. Vue: Which JavaScript Framework Is Right for You?" Great, it even rhymes. Now, let's compare a first paragraph that doesn't use the formula above with one that does.

No formula:

> Modern JavaScript frameworks allow us to build incredible web applications. The common choices are React, Angular, and Vue, though obviously many other choices are available. React was created by Facebook in 2013 to make it painless to create interactive UIs. Angular was created by Google...

With the formula:

> Modern JavaScript frameworks allow us to build incredible web applications. React, Angular, and Vue are all popular options. The problem is deciding which one to learn. It's a process that can feel overwhelming and frustrating. Having worked with all three of them on several projects, I felt I could offer some guidance

---

1. nngroup.com/articles/f-shaped-pattern-reading-web-content/

on the issue. In this article, I'll compare the three JavaScript frameworks and discuss the main differences, advantages, and disadvantages of each. I also included sample code for you to toy with.

You'll notice how it describes the problem (i.e., deciding on a framework), empathizes with the reader (i.e., acknowledging the frustration), and finally promises a solution (i.e., guidance and a thorough comparison). In the process, it also establishes your expertise on the topic and some degree of credibility (i.e., "Having worked with all three of them on several projects").

> Tip 24 — When possible, establish credibility in the first paragraph.

If readers have experienced the frustration of choosing a modern JavaScript framework before and are trying to decide where to invest their limited time, this first paragraph should sell them on the idea of sticking around to read the rest of the post.

From an SEO standpoint, you'll want to include your focus/target keyword in the first paragraph. This further signals to search engines that your post is relevant to that particular search query. In our case, there are a couple of obvious focus keywords: *React vs Angular vs Vue* and *JavaScript frameworks*. Note that Google is smart enough to ignore punctuation, so your properly punctuated use of versus (i.e., *vs.*) will not impact your ranking even if the user is more likely to search *vs* without the period.

Write a Skimmable Post

You have a catchy, bold headline. You have a great first paragraph that connects with users and informs them about how the article will fix whatever it is they are looking to fix. Now it's time to deliver with the rest of your post.

Our goal is to keep readers interested enough to stay with us paragraph after paragraph. But the reality is that most readers will skim the rest of the post at first. So, we need to make the post *skimmable* and effortless.

Your post should not look, especially from the onset, as though it's going to be hard work to read all the way through. Err on the side of larger fonts. If you don't, not only will your post look harder to read, but it will be painful to do so for older or visually impaired readers (who don't use a screen reader).

> Tip 25 — Ensure your font size is large enough to be read comfortably.

Divide your text into short paragraphs. Nothing bounces visitors away like a huge wall of text. You can make your posts look more effortless if you have paragraphs that display as three or four lines at most on a laptop screen with full HD resolution.

Even using relatively short paragraphs, you'll need more visual elements to break up your post. This is not always possible, but in general you'll want to incorporate a few of the following elements:

- *Headers*: Divide your long posts into sections through the use of heading tags such as <h2>. These sections are sort of mini-posts within your larger post, so you should pay attention to each header as if it were a mini-headline of sorts. In fact, your focus keyword should land in one or more headers (aside from the main headline, which is typically wrapped in <h1></h1> tags). From an SEO standpoint, the words you include in these headers carry a lot of weight when search engines determine what your post is about. As usual, keep things natural, and don't try to key-word-stuff your headers or Google will recognize your antics and penalize you for it.

  Try to kick off each paragraph with useful information. When users scan your article on the left side of your site (assuming it's written in a language read left to right, such as English), they'll find keywords that are of interest and in turn will be more likely to actually read your post.

- *Images*: Include one or more pictures. Strive for at least one image in each post. These images will often be picked up by social media sites when showing a preview of your link on their platforms. Such images increase the CTR from social media sites.

  If you're using WordPress, ensure that you select one image as the Featured Image. It will be used for social media and by most WordPress themes when displaying lists of your posts in summary form. If you're using the Yoast SEO plugin, you'll even be able to customize the look on a per-social media site basis. Other blogging engines may or may not offer this feature. If you want to hack it together yourself, look into Open Graph meta tags.

  You can find images that are free to use without attribution on sites like pixabay.com and with attribution on the Creative Commons site.[2] Using your own images is also an option, whether diagrams (I like draw.io for this), charts, drawings, photos, or screenshots. Aim for an image that fits within the width of your article area. 600px is a common width because it's also a safe size when your content is sent to your email subscribers.

---

2. search.creativecommons.org

Your image content should be reasonably clear at this medium size, and you can always link it to a larger version.

Always provide an alt attribute to your images (and for good measure a title as well). It's the right thing to do to make the web more accessible for everyone, and it can help you SEO-wise as well. In fact, here's another SEO tip: name your first image after your main target keywords. For example, you might write these descriptions:

```
<img src="/media/react-vs-angular-vs-vue.png"
    alt="React vs Angular vs Vue Logos"
    title="React vs Angular vs Vue" />
```

These are further signals to search engines of the relevance of your content for the targeted keywords you're going after. Plus, as a side benefit, it will also help your images rank in Google Images, a de facto search engine in its own right, further increasing the discoverability of your content.

- *Videos*: An embedded video is almost irresistible to readers because it's hard to ignore a play button in the middle of the page. The video you embed doesn't have to be yours either. It can be a relevant video from someone else on YouTube.

- *Code snippets*: We discussed before how to embed code in your blog. Such snippets visually break walls of text with colorful code that's highly appealing to the technically minded reader. These, too, are tricky to ignore and have the side benefit of signaling to the reader that your post has a practical element to it. As a programmer, if I see some code on a blog post I'm skimming and I don't fully understand what it's doing, I usually go back and read the whole post until I do. I might not be alone in this approach.

- *Tables*: Embedding a table in your article provides a structured summary of the information you're presenting. They aren't applicable to every blog post, but when they are, they tend to be appreciated by readers. HTML tables are a bit of a pain to work with, so many plugins exist to simplify editing them and presenting them in a more visually appealing manner.

- *Bullet points and numbered lists*: Both bullet points and numbered lists are a fantastic way to break the content into manageable chunks for your reader.

- *Quotes*: Whether other people's quotes or from your own post, including one or more <blockquote> tags visually breaks up the post and tends to grab the skimming reader's attention. Ensure the tags are meaningful since they're very likely to be read. In fact, if you want to take it to the next level, you could generate an image with a nice background for your quote through tools such as canva.com and Pablo.[3] Such images are also good choices for your social media sharing strategy.

- *Bolding*: Highlighting a few words in bold is a great way to guide your readers as they skim your post from top to bottom. Since their eyes will be drawn to bold statements, you'll want to highlight significant bits of your posts. Italic can be used as well, but it doesn't have the same visual impact. Don't use underlined text for anything but links. (Conversely, do ensure links are underlined.)

  Don't abuse bold or italic text, however. Use font emphasis parsimoniously. They can increase readability, but they also tend to annoy readers if they're employed too often. Think three highlighted partial sentences in a thousand-word post, at most. One such highlight should include your focus keywords because it signals to search engines that the keywords were relevant enough to the post to highlight them for the reader.

All these elements contribute to a post that is skimmable and visually appealing and that offers an easier cognitive load for the reader.

If you are using WordPress with the Yoast SEO plugin, you should definitely set a focus keyword for your post and then follow the guidance provided by the plugin to improve your on-page SEO. Incorporating Yoast's suggestions for both SEO and readability of your post will go a long way in helping you succeed as a blogger.

Other Content Considerations

Although SEO isn't an exact science, there are a few hills I'd be willing to die on as far as my SEO beliefs go. The length of your posts is one of them. Long content is more likely to rank well in Google. It's not just a matter of surface area. More words, more possible matches. Google just loves long articles that extensively cover a topic.

A common recommendation is to write at least 500 words if you want to rank in Google (and absolutely nothing less than 300 words). I don't believe that this is enough in most cases. You should aim to have posts with 2,000 words or more in your blog. It's not sustainable to do so for all your posts (more on this in the next chapter), of course, and there is value in mixing it up, since not everyone appreciates epic long-form posts. These are arbitrary numbers, but I want to give you defined targets to shoot for.

---

3. pablo.buffer.com

To see this for yourself, search for a query like "choosing javascript framework" in Google and see the length of the articles that rank in the top spots. When I did it, the top three results had 3,942, 1,928, and 2,125 words, respectively. These results can vary a lot, depending on the query, but they aren't atypical.

This isn't a high school student's lackluster report, though. You shouldn't be logorrheic for the sake of hitting a word count. You should be able to cover enough material in a somewhat concise manner, without inflating the word count with huge tangents and a gratuitous prosaic style.

Be as clear, direct, and unceremonious as possible. For example, don't use words like *unceremonious*. Always assume that some of your readers will misunderstand what you're saying; clarify ambiguous parts to ensure the concepts are clear to your audience. Don't make big assumptions about the reader's existing background or knowledge, unless you clearly establish the technical level needed (to best grasp what you're discussing) at the beginning of your post. A great tool to keep your writing clear, direct, and confident is Hemingway, a web editor and desktop application available at hemingwayapp.com. I find it quite helpful.

In fact, feel free to run your post through a readability checker to establish what reading level is required to comprehend your writing. A Flesch-Kincaid score of 60 or more is desirable. You want content that's easily understood by most readers (even non-native speakers). Out of curiosity I checked the readability of this chapter. It has about 10,000 words and a Flesch reading score of 80 (equivalent to a 3.6 grade level). If you have a fourth grader, your child could read this book with you!

Readable content is good content for the reader, and good content for the reader is content that ranks well in the SERP. Yoast SEO offers this feature and even helps you improve other readability elements of your writing, like complex sentences and passive voice. (There's a reason why I claimed that Yoast SEO is, flat out, the best SEO plugin for WordPress.)

Be informal in your writing. Your posts start conversations with the community; they aren't peer-reviewed research papers. Also, don't write too defensively. You'll often hear a voice in your head that says, "People are going to take issue with this." Don't answer every possible objection to your post in advance, especially if it leads you to include many parentheses to qualify your statements with exceptions to what you just said. You can always discuss those objections, if actually raised, in the comment section.

Don't be afraid to reference, link, and quote other blog posts. Link to other people's posts when relevant. These days it's less common, but other bloggers may return the favor and do the same with you. Link to high-authority sites (e.g., Wikipedia or Stack Overflow) from your content as well, because doing so helps rather than hurts you SEO-wise.

Acknowledge corrections. If you make corrections to your text after a post has been published and the problems aren't just typos, use the <del> HTML tag to strike through the erroneous content (the <ins> would be the opposite tag for small new additions). For code snippets, you can simply correct them and acknowledge the correction in your text. Doing so conveys a sense of honesty to your readers.

Add updates. If you publish small updates to existing articles, disclose that you did so at the bottom of your post (with a timestamp stating when the changes occurred). In particular, credit the updates if they're the results of corrections or comments left by your readers.

Proofread. Web readers are often quite forgiving of typos and mistakes, but to be taken seriously you must try to be grammatically correct and make sure to proofread your content before sending it live. From time to time, you may run into a so-called "grammar Nazi," who will point out every typo you make. Most readers, however, understand that your blog is not *The New Yorker* and will rarely, if ever, point out small typos. To help you out, I recommend using an advanced spellchecker tool like Grammarly,[4] which will catch more than just misspelled words. It'll also take into consideration the context and spot misused words and expressions. For example, it might suggest replacing *my roll* with *my role*, assuming you're not talking about your sushi dinner or your belly.

> **Tip 26** Have your computer read your post to you. If something is off, you'll immediately catch it when you hear it.

It goes without saying, but don't engage in *blogspam*. Blogspam is the act of republishing someone else's original content without adding much (or any) of your own commentary. Quoting and crediting others as you add your own ideas is OK (though less common than in the early days of blogging). Scraping, republishing, or even rephrasing without adding much (also known as spinning) is not. As a rule of thumb, your posts should primarily contain your own original writing.

"Natify" your content as well. If you're not a native English speaker and plan to write your content in English, disclosing this point in your About section

---

4. grammarly.com

will cut you some slack with your readers. If possible, you could also get some help from a native English reviewer, either through friends or colleagues or by paying a native speaker to be your virtual assistant. Draft,[5] an excellent collaborative online editor, even offers a premium editing service that they describe as "Uber for copyediting." It might be worth considering, particularly if you're blogging for business.

Another option you have is to blog in your own native language. You'll likely have less competition and you might have an easier time establishing yourself as an authority in your field among the speakers of your language.

I fully understand if you're hesitant to put yourself out there knowing that your English is less than perfect. It can be emotionally difficult to do so. How do I know? I left Italy at the age of 23 and I didn't grow up speaking English. The first time I walked into a McDonald's in Ireland, I had to gesture my way to some napkins, because I didn't know the English word for them yet. (Yes, even more gesturing than is normal for an Italian!) So I understand your possible insecurities if English is your second or third language. I invite you to give it a shot all the same. Your English will get better and your writing skills will improve quickly. That, in itself, is a massive reward and a good enough reason to pick up blogging.

Develop Your Own Voice

If you do a good job with the headline, people will click and check out the actual content of your article. When they do so, what they expect to read is useful, interesting, unique content. Above all else though, your regular readers expect to find your familiar voice.

Your style and approach to writing, your selection of topics, your personality, and your way of interacting with your audience is what makes your blog truly unique. These elements work together to create your voice and are what you need to hone and develop as you start blogging.

You could be caring, friendly, witty, funny, clever, enlightening, bold, controversial, pretentious, off-putting, vulgar, or a downright bully. It's up to you and the content of your character. In my experience, it pays to be humble and avoid trying to come across as someone who knows everything or is better than everyone else. Revealing an element of vulnerability can be quite powerful in establishing a genuine connection with the reader.

---

5. draftin.com

Whatever opinions you hold now, they may change over time. There are plenty of articles I wrote a decade ago that make me cringe—not so much due to technical details but because of my attitude, ego, and (occasional) overenthusiasm at the time. I learned that compassion and kindness are great filters to future-proof your writing against changes in morality (yours or those of society).

> **Tip 27**   Don't ever belittle or mock others in your posts.

Still, if you have strong beliefs, don't be afraid to be controversial. Nothing you do or write will ever please everyone, so don't try to impress or appease the whole world. Write what you really think and on topics you're passionate about. Controversy works extremely well not when it's done for the sake of stirring the pot but when it stems from real conviction. Convey passion in your writing and you're bound to garner a following.

Adjust your tone and content to match the blogging goals you defined and the audience you hope to attract. If you have a business blog, you might want to avoid swear words for emphasis, for example. If you're a freelancer, try to come across as approachable and someone people would want to work with (this is something that's applicable to all bloggers, really).

Whatever voice you develop, become a bit of a storyteller. People love stories that go with useful information. Even if you are writing a very technical post, your articles should have an arc. You need to tell a story. Who is the hero in your story? It can be you or JavaScript itself. (A Byronic hero, but hey.)

So rather than putting just the bare facts out there, try to give your writing a more human element by expressing why you were facing a certain problem, how you felt, what you learned in the process, what could have been done differently, what you're still unsure about, and similar points. Provide some background and context for what you're writing about. Derek Sivers attracted a huge following to his blog at sivers.org thanks to this technique. Read a few of his posts to see how powerful storytelling can be.

On that note, check out other bloggers you admire. Whenever you come across a post that you enjoy, make a mental note of what worked and what aspects of their style of writing resonated with you. Then apply them to your own writing. (Emailing them to express your appreciation will open doors and pay great dividends.)

Where to Find Ideas for Your Posts

Before writing a post, you should ask yourself if your idea for an article satisfies any of the following criteria:

- Do I care about this topic?
- Will some readers find it useful?
- Does it tell a compelling story?
- Is the post in line with the goals of my blog?
- Does it solve a specific problem?
- Do I have any fresh insight to provide?
- Does it add any value to my field?
- Does it start a conversation with the community that's worth having?
- Is it newsworthy in the context of my niche?

If the answer is no to most of these points, you shouldn't write that post. Instead, search for a topic that qualifies with a resounding *yes* to one or more of the questions above.

Finding ideas for your posts is not too difficult when you expose your brain to other people's writing. I highly recommend you use a feed reader such as Feedly to subscribe to blogs you find useful, inspiring, and entertaining. Spending as little as thirty minutes a day reading other blogs will fill your mind with new ideas.

Personally, I use an iPad and an app called Reeder for my casual blog reading at night. It's given me a workflow that separates work (actual productivity-related tasks on my laptop) and play (casual reading at night). You don't need an iPad just for this, of course, but if you own a similar device, you may consider taking the same approach.

Ask Your Readers What They Want

The easiest way to figure out what your readers want is to ask them. Don't be shy in your posts. Feel free to ask your readers how you're doing (in regard to your site) and what they'd like to see next.

You can also run a survey once in a while to learn more about how regular readers see your blog and what they think can be improved upon. Don't take everything at face value; instead, consider the overall feedback you receive.

To run surveys for free, you can use Google Forms. Alternatively, you can avail yourself of more sophisticated premium solutions such as Typeform, SurveyMonkey, or Wufoo.

Keep an Idea File

I like to keep an idea file. I used to keep it in a Dropbox folder synchronized across all my devices. These days I keep it in my to-do system under an Article Ideas project. It doesn't matter whether it's a file, a note app like Google Keep or Evernote, or a physical notebook: you should keep a list of ideas for your posts. Whenever an idea for an article comes to mind, add it there. Personally, I like to keep at least ten prospective headlines for each of my currently maintained blogs.

You can use some of the SEO keyword tools we discussed in the chapter on niche validation to find further headline ideas from some initial keywords you can think of. Even the Google autocomplete feature can be useful to come up with ideas with vast appeal.

Here are some types of posts to consider:

- Write about what you've been working on lately (just be sure that it's not confidential information that your employer doesn't want you to share).

- Write hands-on guides or tutorials for subjects that you're an expert on. Spread these guides across multiple posts to create an engaging series that keeps people coming back.

- Write about tools you use or even your entire setup.

- Tell a story about your past failures or successes.

- Run some benchmarks and post your findings. When I used to run them, my Ruby shootout benchmark posts were very popular.

- Quote and link to an interesting idea found elsewhere on the web, but be sure to add your own commentary. Disagree if that's truly how you feel about the issue.

- Write an essay or even a rant about a subject you care about. It could be something that grinds your gears or simply a topic you believe more readers should know about.

- Interview popular people in your field (more on this in the next chapter).

- Review books, services, gadgets, or products that are relevant to your niche.

- Collect, organize, and present links to relevant resources all in a single post (e.g., a collection of white papers on web scalability).

- Create cheat sheets (e.g., a CSS3 cheat sheet). If possible, include both an HTML version and a PDF version for printing. As mentioned before, these make for great lead magnets or content upgrades as well.

- Collect interesting data about your industry and compile it into a useful infographic. If you're not a designer, you can usually commission designers who specialize in creating infographics of the sort that tend to go viral online. Many designers on gig sites like upwork.com offer such a service.

- Collect statistics about your industry and compile them in a listicle.

- If you run a business, particularly B2B, consider writing about your social media campaigns, A/B testing experiments, growth-hacking strategies, and sales figures. Traditionally this would be considered bad advice, but being open and frank in posts on such topics has allowed several companies to become the center of attention.

With this system in place, the real bottleneck is not finding ideas but rather finding the time to sit down and actually write out the content that's in your head.

Use Blogging Clients

Many advanced bloggers tend to prefer desktop blogging clients over the default web interface that's available for WordPress, Blogger, or equivalent blogging engines.

Hacker types may enjoy blogging directly from Visual Studio Code, Sublime Text, or Vim, given that these text editors can be configured to post directly to your blog either through a blog generator, such as Jekyll, or via the remote API that's available for WordPress, Blogger, and other blogging platforms.

These three programs excel at editing text, but other, more user-friendly GUI-based solutions are out there that were designed specifically for bloggers who want some help with their workflow to maintain multiple blogs, create drafts, take notes, and so on.

For Mac, I recommend MarsEdit. For Windows, it's hard to beat Open Live Writer.

Mobile devices and tablets have blogging clients too, particularly for Word-Press. Explore some of these options before committing to one client.

Get Readers to Discover More of Your Content

In the previous chapter, I briefly addressed the issue of getting your visitors to explore more of your content. In particular, we covered how certain sidebar widgets can encourage your readers to visit popular or recent posts on your site.

You can turbocharge your efforts and guide your readers to more of your content by taking the following steps:

1. Install a plugin that allows you to automatically display a few related posts at the bottom of each new post (Jetpack for WordPress offers this feature, but many similar plugins are available for WordPress). In my experience, the CTR (click-through rate) of related posts is decent when people liked the post they just read and the related posts are, in fact, actually relevant to it.

2. Create a sticky Start Here page that guides newcomers through your blog. Organize a collection of introductory posts you've already written as well as information about how to subscribe, join the newsletter, participate in the comments, share your content, and other similar topics. Make this page a useful guide to getting started with your blog and then promote it within your own blog as much as you can. You should invite your readers to check out this page in your welcome message to subscribers (if you use a third-party mailing list service like MailChimp).

3. Do the same with a "Best of" page. Unlike the Start Here page, this should just link to your best posts, perhaps organized by category or some other logical criteria. This too should be promoted within your blog as much as you can (definitely link to it from your Home and About pages, for example).

4. Create a Table of Contents page. WordPress already has archives, but these aren't as nice as having a list of clickable headlines organized by month all included on the same page. For my blogs, I use the WordPress plugin called Clean Archives Reloaded. Unfortunately, the plugin hasn't been updated in years, so you might want to consider some of the newer alternatives.[6] Blogger doesn't offer this capability so you may have to settle for its Blog Archive gadget in the sidebar or come up with some clever piece of code to showcase such a list within a page. Other blog engines may or may not provide this option, but if you're a programmer, you could create a script that generates one for you.

5. Assign tags to your posts. Through them, users will be able to quickly access similar posts. This is also beneficial from an SEO standpoint because it increases your blog's level of interlinking.

6. Along the same vein, generously link to other posts within your blog, so long as they're relevant to the current post you're sharing.

---

6. wordpress.org/plugins/search/archive/

Copyright Matters

Online content of any kind, much like its printed counterpart, is protected by default by copyright (in most countries, at least). The moment you write something, you own the copyright for it, even if you haven't registered it with a copyright office in the country you reside in.

Unfortunately—or fortunately depending on your ideological stance on copyright law—many people online assume that copyright laws don't really apply. Copying images and other content online is pretty common and there's a certain nonchalance about the practice. As a blogger, however, you need to respect other people's copyrights as well as determine what to do if your own copyrighted work is plagiarized.

Avoid Infringing Copyright Laws

Laws can vary drastically from country to country, so you should check what rules apply where you reside. Generally speaking though, most countries have a doctrine of fair use that enables you to quote other works for the purpose of parody, criticism, and similar uses.

We are entering a giant gray zone, where the legality of certain actions is entirely debatable. You can read the Wikipedia entry for an overview of the topic at en.wikipedia.org/wiki/Fair_use. I'm not a lawyer so I'll skip the legalese and give you some practical advice instead that, while not legal advice, is generally accepted to be good online etiquette.

It's usually considered OK to quote a few paragraphs from other blog posts as long as you credit and link to the original source and use that text to add your own commentary. Often microbloggers on sites like Tumblr and so-called link blogs highlight quotes or links and rebroadcast them further across the web verbatim. It's generally fine; but without your insight, doing so won't add much value to your full-fledged blog.

Try to limit the number of such quotes to keep their use fair in the eyes of your readers and to the blogger you're quoting. This means that you should definitely avoid quoting a full blog post (unless it's a tiny one, where quoting only a part wouldn't make sense).

Be careful even when dealing with mainstream news outlets. AP (Associated Press) made news a decade or so ago by claiming that quoting 5–25 of their words would require a fee of $12.50. Of course, this was entirely contrary to the spirit of the web, and I can't find evidence that AP still does this. Fair use has quite a bit of latitude; but as a blogger, it's in your best interest to respect copyright owners' rules so as not to run into a legal confrontation. It's just not worth fighting over such matters.

Don't use images unless they're in the public domain or they've been released under a license that allows republishing. In particular, use a site like the aforementioned Pixabay or otherwise stick to images released under the CC (Creative Commons) license. Observe which conditions apply in terms of attribution and usage (e.g., is commercial use allowed?).

Alternatively, you can also request permission for their use directly from their respective photographers. Asking nicely usually does the trick when it comes to amateur and enthusiast photographers. I love photography,[7] and I'm sometimes asked for permission to post an image of mine. If it's just a regular blogger posting a low resolution version, I usually oblige without requiring a fee. Using reverse image search tools like TinEye,[8] I have discovered several people who didn't bother asking.

Even if you have permission to use the images, you should never hotlink them. This means that you should serve your users a local or CDN copy of the image rather than using the original image URL directly. Among the reasons not to hotlink is the fact that you don't want to have the photographer incur bandwidth expenses on your behalf. Also, the original site may not be configured to handle high volumes of traffic.

Hosting a local copy also prevents your posts from having missing or broken link images if, in a few months or years down the line, the photographer decides to shut down that site, forgets to renew the domain name, or simply moves the image to a different location.

Following these simple rules should help you stay out of trouble. If a blogger with a stuck-up attitude complains to you about being quoted, you can always promptly remove the quoted portion from your post when asked. After that, stop quoting and linking to that particular blogger. It's entirely that person's loss (who doesn't like free publicity?) and not yours.

In theory, the worst that can happen for copyright infringement is a lawsuit against you. In practice, however, the more likely outcome would be a DMCA (Digital Millennium Copyright Act) takedown notice filed against you with your hosting company. Depending on the legitimacy of the claim and your hosting company's policies, your site may temporarily be taken offline until you remove the supposedly infringing content.

---

7.   tonycangiano.com
8.   tineye.com

Issuing DMCA Notices

By following the preceding guidelines, you're not very likely to be on the receiving end of a DMCA takedown notice. You are, however, likely to have your content illicitly reproduced elsewhere without any credit being given to you. Lazy spammers need posts for their ad-filled content sites, and they'll get it one way or another—even if that means blatantly ripping it off from you.

Plagiarism can easily be spotted with tools such as Copyscape and Google Alerts.[9] Every single one of my blogs has been plagiarized at some point in the past. So how are we supposed to deal with annoyances like these?

The easiest way is to politely but firmly ask any offenders (by email) to remove your content from their site(s). If you can't find the email address of a violator on a site, try the WHOIS register.

Don't insult offenders, and don't be vulgar or threatening. Simply state that you noticed that they reproduced copyrighted content of yours on their site and that you request its prompt removal. Be specific in your request and point out which URLs are infringing on your copyright.

Many times asking is all it takes. The offenders may remove the content to get you off their case as they go about focusing on lower-hanging fruit instead. Other times this approach doesn't work.

What can you do if your precious, precious content gets shamelessly copied and they refuse to take it down? You probably guessed it. You can file a DMCA takedown notice with the hosting company or with the blog provider (e.g., WordPress.com). You can see an example of this procedure at the following URL: hostgator.com/copyright.

Remember that you can always use creative thinking and get to them where it hurts: their wallets. You could, for example, report the offenders to their advertisers or ad networks.

There will be times when copyright violators will appear untouchable. They may reside in a foreign country or host their sites in one, and nobody will cooperate with your request. In such instances, it's up to you to decide if you wish to continue pursuing the case or simply let things be.

Don't overly concern yourself with protecting your content, and choose your battles wisely. Spending too much attention fighting copyright violations tends to be a waste of your valuable time and energy.

---

9. copyscape.com and google.com/alerts, respectively.

One positive aspect of getting copied is that if your content includes products you promote, copyright violators will inadvertently spread your message further, thereby doing you a favor. Unfortunately, search engines penalize duplicate content, so it might hurt you SEO-wise.

Back Up Your Content

You work hard to write your content and it would be a genuine shame if you lost it. I can't stress enough how important it is to back up your blog's content.

Your hosting company may offer you backup solutions for a fee. Take advantage of such options if economically workable. What you're interested in is saving the database that contains your posts as well as the folders where you store images and other files (e.g., wp-content in WordPress).

To save the database, you can perform a dump of the data (e.g., using mysqldump) in a file. You should save this SQL export file and your other key files locally and online in secure, safe places like Dropbox and Amazon S3.

> Tip 20   Have at least three backups in different places.

For WordPress, check out a plugin called WP-DBManager, which will even email you your backups at intervals that you've specified in the plugin's settings. There are also premium solutions that will store the backups for you, or allow you to upload the data on cloud providers of your choice. Jetpack Backups and VaultPress are popular choices.[10] Blog management tools like ManageWP.com will also include, among many other services, a similar backup option for you.

For Blogger you can export your blog from the Other menu of your Settings and then store the exported file locally and in the Cloud.[11] Google is unlikely to lose your blog's data, but should it kick you out (very unlikely) or shut down the service (unlikely but possible), you'd have access to the data you worked so hard to produce.

Other blogging engines might offer similar backup options. If worse comes to worst, you'll have the HTML or Markdown files stored somewhere (if you created your article through an editor). People who opted for a static site generator might want to consider committing their files to GitHub or GitLab as another form of backup.

---

10. jetpack.com/support/backups/ and vaultpress.com, respectively.

11. support.google.com/blogger/answer/41387?hl=en

Take Action

- Create an idea file and place ten article ideas within it. If you've already created ten headlines as part of the second chapter exercises, copy them over and add ten more. Make sure this idea file is accessible from any device you have, including your smartphone. Ideas can strike at any time.

- Write a first article introducing yourself, your blog, and what you plan to write within it. Use the content and SEO guidelines provided within this chapter to craft a great first post.

What's Next

Congratulations. You're now fully equipped to start writing awesome content for your blog. But wait; there are still questions to be answered. How often should you post? On what days? How to keep up the pace? In the next chapter we'll tackle all these issues and discuss scheduling posts as well as when and how much to post.

I worked hard. Anyone who works as hard as I did can achieve the same results.

Johann Sebastian Bach

CHAPTER 6

Producing Content Regularly

In the previous chapter, we discussed how the quality of your content is paramount to achieving blogging success. How often and when you post are also two important factors that will influence the growth of your blog.

What's the Post Frequency, Kenneth?

In theory, you should try to publish as much content as you can. A large body of content helps to attract organic traffic and gives you frequent opportunities to promote new articles.

That's the theory, reality is that producing lots of content takes a toll on you. New bloggers will often start with a bang, adopting an unsustainable publication rate. A few weeks or months later, they give up, discouraged by disappointing readership numbers. Trying to do too much is the surest path to burnout and failure.

The ideal post frequency then becomes one that you can sustain over a long period of time without causing you undue stress.

I can't tell you what your ideal posting frequency should be—not, at least, without knowing your blog goals, the amount of time you can commit, and how long it takes you to write an average post. But I can recommend that you start with one post per week, see how that plays out, and adjust the pace accordingly.

If you're a very busy person, one post every two weeks might be more appropriate. Especially in the beginning, it doesn't make sense to post more sparingly than that. Conversely, a prolific writer with lots of spare time might opt for three posts a week. That would certainly speed up the growth of your blog.

This suggestion assumes that your entries are a mix of medium (e.g., above 500 words) and long (e.g., above 2000 words) content. If you throw in link collections, quotes, and other forms of low-effort posts, you can likely afford to publish even five times a week.

Epic posts win you subscribers and loyal readers. Shorter posts might appeal to people with shorter attention spans or who are in a rush. A mix of both is healthy, but long content pays the biggest dividends in my experience. Think well-written essays, detailed reviews, or longer tutorials.

Albeit rarer, it's also possible to be so prolific that your regular readers end up experiencing fatigue as they try to keep up with you. This is more of an issue for email subscribers than for feed or social media followers. As long as you don't post more than once a day, this shouldn't be a real cause for concern.

While on the subject of content frequency, length, and email subscribers, one option you have is to not link your RSS feed and your mailing list service. This way, instead of automatically sending an email whenever you publish a new article, you could write and send a short email (through a service like MailChimp) to your subscribers letting them know that you've published one or more articles since you last emailed them. You provide the links and an invitation to comment. Derek Sivers uses this approach and it works quite well for him. Here's the latest email I received as his subscriber:

> Hi Antonio -
>
> I just posted this new article I think you might like:
>
> You don't need confidence, just contribution https://sivers.org/contrib
>
> It's a chapter from my next book, *Hell Yeah or No*.
>
> I'd love to hear your thoughts, so please feel free to leave a reply there on the page. I always appreciate the feedback. Everything I write is a rough draft until it's finally printed in a book, so your comments really help me make improvements.
>
> Thanks!

It's a nice personal touch. It feels like a friend just emailed you as opposed to receiving a newsletter. I bet his open and click-through rates are very high. The only downside is having to take the extra step of writing that quick email after you publish a new article (and remembering to do so consistently)!

Consistency Is Queen

When you have chosen—and perhaps even publicly announced—your posting schedule, you should try to stick to it for a period of at least a few months (after which you can change your schedule again, if required).

Interestingly, there's almost a Pavlovian mechanism at play when you start posting on a regular basis, wherein your subscribers get excited and start looking forward to your next post. This, in turn, builds loyalty toward you and your blog.

If your articles stop appearing at their usual time, you may end up breaking this cycle of expectation and as a result, lose a few readers. Imagine reading a given newspaper every day and suddenly not finding it on your doorstep one morning (or perhaps worse, having it show up on random days). Humans are creatures of habit.

What Days Should You Post On?

Unless you choose to post every day, you may be wondering what the best days each week are to post your blog.

This is a conundrum that's well known to marketers who manage large newsletters. What's the best day? What's the best time? The difference an opportune choice of day makes can be measured in many thousands of dollars if a marketer's mailing list is large enough.

Bloggers don't have the luxury of A/B testing the same way email marketers do, because you can't publish the same public post one day for 50 percent of your audience and on a different day for the rest and then compare which day was more successful.

What you can do, though, is publish articles on different days of the week in the beginning and see if over time a clear traffic trend emerges. It's not exactly a scientific approach, but it may give you a better picture of when your specific audience is most receptive.

Tuesday, Wednesday, and Thursday are very effective, then Monday, Friday, and the weekend, in that order. My theory is that people are very focused (or perhaps overwhelmed) by their jobs on Mondays, so they tend to get around to catching up with online news and blogs from Tuesday onward. On Friday they're tired and their mind is already focused on the weekend, therefore they're less likely to seek out new knowledge. It's not unusual for technical bloggers who post three times a week to publish their best content at the beginning of the week (Monday and Wednesday) and then publish something lighthearted on Friday. It's the blogging equivalent of Casual Friday. Just don't overdo it, or you may bring the overall quality of your blog down too much.

Some bloggers opt to run a series of posts on different days. You could, for example, publish a pundit-style essay on Tuesday, a handy HOWTO on Thursday, and a roundup of fresh new links to some of the latest articles from fellow bloggers in your niche on Friday.

When it comes to the specific time of the day, I tend to favor early morning (e.g., 6 a.m. PST) for my English blogs that target a predominantly North

American audience. This time of day still captures part of the afternoon European traffic while welcoming American and Canadian readers as they sip their morning coffee (well, those on the East coast and early birds on the West coast, at least).

Please note that organic traffic coming from search engines is not directly affected by the day or time you publish your content. All the considerations in this section relate to the behavior of *timely* traffic you receive shortly after publishing a blog post. Indirectly, it still has an impact because the more buzz you generate when a post first goes live, the more backlinks and social media sharing you'll receive, which in turn affects long-term organic traffic.

Schedule Time to Blog

Before getting serious about blogging, you should determine how much time you're really willing and able to allocate to researching, writing, and promoting your content.

My recommendation is to set aside no less than four hours per week to your blog. With four hours at your disposal, you should be able to publish at least one blog entry.

Regardless of how much time you allocate to blogging, you'll want to prepare the majority of your posts the week before and schedule them for publication by using the scheduling feature that most modern blogging software includes (see Figure 12, WordPress's scheduling feature, on page 115). By doing so you can write your entries in advance, set them to be published automatically on a certain date and time, and be done for the week. (WordPress users who schedule posts frequently may enjoy one of the many editorial calendar plugins.)

If you can't commit to the same amount of time every week, I would highly encourage you to take advantage of the good weeks and schedule time for writing as many posts in advance as you can. Then you'll be covered during weeks when you're too busy, are traveling, or encounter unexpected situations that deter your ability to devote as much time as you normally would to your blog.

I like to write down ideas (in the idea file mentioned before), notes, and even whole paragraphs in a notepad or on my computer as they come to mind. But in my experience, it's far better to treat blogging as a serious business and schedule time in your calendar for the sole purpose of this activity.

Tip 29   Have 3–5 posts in your blog "savings account."

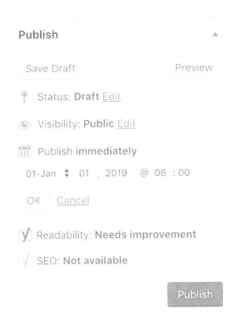

Figure 12—WordPress's scheduling feature

The good news is that as you gain more experience, you'll become faster at preparing new posts and should be able to get more out of your scheduled blogging time, regardless of how long you're able to devote to this area of your life.

Survive Writer's Block

From time to time you may find yourself in an annoying predicament. A new post is due on your blog, but you simply can't seem to bring yourself to write it no matter how much you try. This phenomenon is commonly known as writer's block, and it can be quite serious if your livelihood depends on your ability to produce new content.

I'm not a psychologist or a neurologist, so I won't provide a lengthy explanation of what causes writer's block or how to cure said ailment. Instead, I'll share a few tips that work for me. I hope you'll find them useful as well:

- Check your idea file to see if you can write about a different topic that's less challenging or time-consuming than the one you're having trouble with.

- If the writer's block is there regardless of the post you're attempting to write, consider changing your environment. Go to a local cafe, the library, a park, or somewhere else that's different from where you normally hang out while writing your posts. The key part here is to introduce a change. Switch to writing with pen and paper if you have to.

- Consider taking a break and going offline entirely for a couple of hours. Go for a walk or to the gym; do anything aside from writing or web surfing. Chances are your brain's background processes will continue to work on the post for you, giving you more insight and a fresher outlook when you decide to try writing again.

- Start writing without the intention of publishing your post. Simply write down whatever comes to mind. Nobody will ever see what you write, so you're free to type away without too much concern regarding grammar, sentence structure, paragraph order, and other considerations that make for good writing. You'll quickly realize that polishing these paragraphs and reorganizing them is easier than coming up with the perfect phrasing for each one from the get-go.

- Edit your posts in fullscreen mode to achieve maximum focus. WordPress and several editors offer this feature. The app Cold Turkey Writer will even block everything else on your computer until your writing (up to the specified amount of words) is done.

- If you don't like the draft that came out of the stream-of-consciousness exercise above, try rewriting it from scratch now. Chances are that this time the words will come to you, since you've already mentally addressed some of the points you wanted to discuss. You can now formally articulate them.

- Write the h2 headings for your post and then see if you can write each section as if it were a mini-post.

- Lower your writing expectations and give yourself a break. What you write doesn't have to be perfect. It can simply be a spontaneous thought, a reflection, or a quick consideration. You'll be surprised at how often posts like this end up becoming extremely popular and well liked by your readers. Perfection is the enemy of the good enough.

- Don't write your technical post down. Instead, talk about it with someone else, explaining the subject matter to them in a clear and interesting way. Doing so will help you organize your ideas and express the thoughts you've had tucked away in the back of your mind on a given topic. It doesn't even have to be a person. It can be your cat or dog, though expect puzzled looks from them. If you have a rubber duck that you use for debugging,[1]

---

1. en.wikipedia.org/wiki/Rubber_duck_debugging

the same technique can be applied to get unstuck from writer's block and clarify your thoughts. As you approach the blinking cursor again, you'll probably find it easier to formalize what you discussed verbally.

• Consider having a reserve of unpublished, evergreen posts (content that will still be current and useful in the foreseeable future). That way, if you can't snap out of your writer's block in time for a given week, you can tap into your reserve of prewritten posts to keep up with your usual blogging schedule.

> **Tip 30**   Discuss your post prior to writing it down.

Of course, you're free to decide that you'll simply publish when you feel you have something worth saying, without a set schedule. That's definitely okay. The danger is ending up without having a new post go live for weeks or even months on end, which is particularly damaging in the beginning, when your blog isn't established yet.

Get Others to Write for You

One of the best methods for increasing your blog post frequency is to get help from other people. Having others write content for you as you churn out your own posts will definitely increase the volume of content your blog is able to publish.

In this section, we'll explore four free methods you can use to get others to contribute to your blog:

• Interviews
• Guest bloggers
• Article translations
• Leveraging HARO[2]

We'll cover hiring bloggers in Chapter 13, Scaling Your Blogging Activities, on page 247.

Arrange Email Interviews

The premise behind email interviews is straightforward and only requires that you send out one or two messages. The first asks an expert in your field about doing an email interview with you. Alternatively, you could make contact on social media (e.g., Twitter). It helps if you establish a rapport with the person for a while on social media or by commenting on his or her blog before asking

---

2.   helpareporter.com

outright. If the person says yes, you can then send them an email with a series of interesting questions tailored to that person. You can agree beforehand whether to send all the questions at once or conduct an organic back and forth in which you ask the next question only after reading the previous answer.

Coming up with a series of intelligent questions and handling the email communication back and forth may take a bit of your time, but since your interviewee will be doing most of the writing for you with his or her answers, you'll end up with an interesting post that required relatively little work on your part.

From a promotional standpoint, prominent experts tend to have their own audiences who may discover your blog thanks to the interview, assuming said interviewees mention your post on their blogs or on social media sites (not an unusual occurrence). This type of content also has the advantage of lending credibility to your blog if the people you interview are well liked or respected in your field.

In my experience, you cannot realistically expect to interview Bill Gates or Elon Musk, but if you email enough people and are polite and mindful of their time, you'll find that sometimes even fairly popular folks are willing to answer your questions.

This works particularly well if your intended interview subject has an ulterior motive for participating. For example, I interviewed Giacomo "Peldi" Guilizzoni, founder of Balsamiq Studio, LLC, back in 2009.[3] This interview exposed my readers to his Mockups software, potentially leading to more sales and exposure for him. In fact, if you are a startup owner trying to promote your own products, you should definitely jump at the opportunity to give interviews to fellow bloggers.

I often get approached by companies (and their marketing agencies) that are trying to promote their products for free on my blogs. Replying by suggesting an interview by email has been a great way to get rid of the less earnest ones and has helped me score some great interviews with more serious companies.

Finally, consider the possibility of creating a thematic series of interviews on your blog. For example, I used to have a Startup Interviews series on ProgrammingZen.com. A series tells new readers that similar content is on the horizon and can be a big motivation to subscribe. It may also lead a few experts to contact you to be featured in the series as interviewees.

---

3.   programmingzen.com/2009/04/13/startup-interviews-balsamiq-studio-llc

If you can stand the sound of your own voice, consider getting a decent microphone (e.g., a RØDE Podcaster or Blue Yeti) and conducting audio interviews. You could even start a podcast and then link or embed the audio file in your post whenever a new episode airs. If you want to take it to the next level, you could also embed the transcript of your episodes as they air. Depending on how much time you have on your hands, you might consider outsourcing the job or relying on automated transcription software (before manually fixing the inevitable mistakes).

Find Guest Bloggers

Guest blogging is the act of publishing posts on a blog that you don't own. This is typically done in order to obtain some form of free publicity and backlinks to the guest blogger's own blog or site.

Later in the book, we'll discuss how you can effectively use this technique to promote your site on other blogs, thereby reaching a wider audience. In this section, however, we'll focus on ways you can leverage eager promoters in order to score some free posts for your own blog.

The easiest way to attract guest bloggers is to advertise that you're accepting content submissions. You can write a post on your blog that welcomes contributions from your existing audience, a Write for Us page, or an invitation to do guest blogging below each guest post you publish.

Before I sold MathBlog.com, I constantly received emails from prospective guest bloggers and authors simply because my Write for Us page did a good job at selling the benefits of contributing to the blog (it also clarified what type of content I was interested in publishing).

Thanks to that page, I found John F. McGowan, Ph.D., a scientist and consultant who became a regular writer for the blog on a volunteer basis. My blog received high-quality content for free, and he had a platform to advertise his technical expertise and consultancy business. It was a win-win situation that truly benefited both of us.

Another easy way to find guest writers is to email bloggers you respect, asking them if they're interested in guest blogging for you or in doing an exchange in which you guest-blog on their sites and they do the same on yours.

You'll want to have established your blog a bit already before attempting to solicit other people to write for you, but tasks like this take little time and can often lead to symbiotic relationships and new connections with other bloggers.

> **Tip 31**   Contact people who guest-blog on blogs that you follow.

If you're reasonable with your request (don't expect them to write a 10,000-word guide that gets spread out across five posts) and persuasive enough with your pitch, you may also be able to create guest bloggers out of people who have never blogged before in their lives.

Insightful commenters who are already hanging out in the comment section of your blog, valuable technical mailing list contributors that you approach privately, and experts you know from the offline world may gladly take you up on this sort of offer. Going to technical meetups and conferences is a great way to befriend potential guest bloggers, as well.

The only downside to being open to guest bloggers is that you'll have to sort through some terrible proposals to find the quality authors you're seeking. Internet marketers are quite aware of the effectiveness of guest blogging, so you'll likely receive requests from people who are solely interested in getting a backlink to their unrelated—and often less than reputable—sites that were MFA (Made for AdSense) or created for the sole purpose of pushing affiliate offers.

I consider these emails to be little more than spam and tend to reply to them with a polite but candid response about not being interested. Alternatively, you may simply ignore them, if you'd prefer.

Once your blog is established, they might even offer to pay a small amount of money to publish an article on your blog. Generally speaking, they'll insist on dofollow links and you'll receive poor content from them. Unless you publish the links as nofollow links, you're also in violation of Google's linking recommendations and you can be seriously penalized for it from an SEO standpoint.

Translate Other Bloggers' Content

If you speak more than one language, you can easily score great content by translating articles that were originally written by other people in a language that you know.

The key is to ask for permission before you jump headfirst into translating. In your comment or email to the original content creator, explain that you appreciate what they wrote and that you'd like to make their work available to people who speak the language your blog appears in. Reassure them that you'll credit the post back to them and link to the original article(s). Only proceed with translating the post if the original creator grants you permission to do so.

Depending on your mastery of the given language and your skill as a translator, you may find the process to be rather easy. In going this route, you'll be offering a valuable service and providing high-quality content to your readers. I would not advocate publishing only translations on your blog, but I certainly wouldn't ignore such a valuable opportunity to create worthwhile content either.

If a blogger agrees that it's OK for you to translate a particular article, ask if it's also all right to translate other content from the blog into your language under the same set of conditions (or if you need to ask for permission explicitly each time). This way you'll have another easy pool to draw from should you find yourself temporarily out of good ideas for posts.

Let the blogger know when you've published a translation by commenting with, or emailing them, the link. They may link back to the translation from the original post or mention the translation to their circle of followers.

My programming blog has been occasionally translated by other bloggers (Brazilian bloggers in particular, for some reason). And if you blog in a language other than English, you are officially authorized to translate any of my blogs' content under the same conditions described above. Namely, credit the original post and link back to it from your post (since you're not getting paid for it, you'd use a regular link and not a nofollow link).

Leverage HARO

Help a Reporter Out is a site where you can register as a journalist or as a source. Let's say that I'm an expert on AI. I can sign up as a source and receive emails from the service whenever a journalist is looking to write a story on the topic. I can then be the AI expert who gets quoted in the article the person is writing.

I haven't personally done it, but I've seen some bloggers take advantage of the service to produce content for their blogs. They registered as a journalist and then asked experts on the subject matter to provide their specific opinion on a given subject for their blog (specifying a deadline). Once they collected all the opinions from the experts, they simply proceeded to compile them in a large article that didn't require much content of their own (e.g., "13 Deep Learning Experts on the Future of AI").

If your blog is not already well established, I think this technique is a bit of a stretch. I've never felt the need to use it myself. But it can work, so I've included it for the sake of completeness.

Take Action

- Decide on what day of the week you're going to post and how often (e.g., weekly or biweekly).

- Schedule some time in your calendar each week to blog.

- Find one person in your field to interview by email.

- (Optional) Create a Write for Us page for guest bloggers on your site.

What's Next

Having worked through this and the previous chapter, you should have a clearer picture of what to blog about, when, how often to post, and even how to score some high-quality content through the help of others.

In the next chapter, which is brand-new to this second edition of the book, I address an important topic that I hope will justify the price of admission on its own—namely, where to find time to blog. More specifically, I talk about how to organize your (no doubt) busy life so that you can carve out the time and energy needed to blog.

It could be argued that the following chapter is not specific to blogging. Nevertheless, I was compelled to include it after seeing many readers struggle with this time management element. I myself lead a very busy life and have fallen offtrack many times before. Still, every time I follow my own advice, which I lay out in the next chapter, I've been extremely productive and, dare I say, happier.

So my sincere hope is that you'll find the insight useful for you as well—both in terms of blogging and in other areas of your life as well.

Either you run the day or the day runs you.

　　Jim Rohn

CHAPTER 7

Finding Time to Blog

In this chapter, we're going to discuss how to find time to blog. My hope is that some of the suggestions will not only benefit your blogging but also make you a more productive and organized person in general.

It's easy to be productive in the early days of a project. This is true whether considering a new blog or a software project. There's no stopping you when everything is new and enthusiasm abounds. Over time, however, the initial interest wanes and motivation alone isn't enough to keep going. It takes discipline and ideally a system that can keep us on track when our fallible nature inevitably rears its ugly head.

Master Your To-Do List

The human brain is great at processing information but not at storing it. A to-do list can be a helpful tool to assist us in remembering all that needs to be done. Have an idea for an article? Dump it in your idea file or add it to your to-do list. Remembered that you need to add a privacy policy to your blog? Add it to your blog to-do list.

Whether you use pen and paper, a text file synchronized across your devices, or a proper to-do application, you're definitely less likely to forget important tasks if you add them to a to-do system whenever they come to mind. Another benefit of this approach is that you don't ever have to worry about remembering what to do since you systematically added ideas and tasks to your to-do list as they came to you.

This, in turn, can reduce your stress and the sensation of forgetting something important. Not to mention the feeling of being overwhelmed that we all experience at some point in our lives. In the aftermath of the arson fire I mentioned before, I got to practice my time management skills as I literally rebuilt many aspects of my life from scratch. I don't think I could have made it without the help of a solid to-do system and the belief that it could be done.

Define Your Goals

Before you start an initial brain dump of all the things you need to do, I recommend that you dedicate some time to setting goals.

Goals give you direction and allow you to devise a proactive plan of actions to reach them. They also offer a much-needed moment in our busy lives to reflect on what you really want from your life. They are not as important as the actual system of actions you'll adopt, but they're an important catalyst.

Like Jim Rohn, the father of the modern self-improvement movement used to say, you cannot change your destination overnight, but you can change your direction overnight. Goals are a first step toward changing your direction. It might all be about the journey and not the destination, but it helps if you're headed somewhere pleasant rather than nowhere—or worse, in a bad place that's rife with stress, worry, and depression.

You want to set a couple of goals for each area that matters to you. Blogging may be one such area, so you would create a couple of goals for your blog. If you decide to take a broader look at your life, you can include other areas and define one or two key goals for each area. If possible, make them SMART goals: Specific, Measurable, Achievable, Relevant, and Time-bound.

> Tip 32   For each goal you set, write down WHY it matters to you.

The areas I use to identify goals to improve myself are health (including mental health), spirituality (religious or not), growth/learning, career, finances, relationships, and leisure.

It's perfectly okay to limit your to-do list to the professional sphere if you wish. The advice I provide here is not revolutionary, but it can be helpful, regardless of the scope you apply it to.

Define Your Projects

Just as there are countless project management apps, you'll find a plethora of to-do apps available on the market. I'll suggest a few options I've personally found to be effective. Fellow productivity enthusiasts reading this book might prefer a different app, but the key take-home message here is that you should quickly try some of these options and then start with one that works well enough for you.

There is no perfect to-do system, and searching for one can become a distraction and time waste in and of itself (second only to the temptation of creating your own to-do app).

I can personally recommend the following to-do applications, having used each of them at one point or another over the years:

- *TickTick*: Overall the best cross-platform choice I've found to date

- *Todoist*: A much more popular alternative to TickTick and also quite good

- *TaskWarrior*: If you live and breathe the command line

- *Things*: Gorgeous minimalist GTD (Getting Things Done[1]) option for Mac/iOS users

- *OmniFocus*: Powerful option for Mac/iOS—steeper learning curve, but worth it

- *Trello*: If you prefer a kanban approach to to-do list management

- *KanbanFlow*: An alternative to Trello that I've found to be better suited for a GTD-like to-do system

- *Dynalist*: Not a traditional to-do list, but the outliner approach allows you to create highly organized hierarchies of lists

I have been an avid user of TickTick because I needed a cross-platform option for having a Mac but also an Android phone. It's not as slick as the Mac-only options, but it gets the job done. Recently I made the decision to switch back to iOS, so I've been using Things in anticipation. It lacks a few advanced features of TickTick, but it provides a very polished user experience. My go-to choice might change in the future, but the general principles of how I go about my to-do stay more or less the same.

Once you have decided on a particular to-do list app (even if it's just pen and paper), I suggest that you do an initial brain dump. Write down every task that comes to mind and enter them in your to-do app (typically in an Inbox list/project). You'll definitely forget things, but that's okay because you'll be able to add them later when they come to mind. If you follow David Allen's GTD system strictly, you won't add tasks that you can accomplish in just two minutes. You'll just do them right then and there. But everything else can be added to the pile as it pops into your brain.

---

1. en.wikipedia.org/wiki/Getting_Things_Done

Next, you'll want to look at the list of goals you created in the previous section and extract actions that will get you closer to these goals. Keep in mind that the most powerful actions are the small routines you repeat frequently. These end up becoming your habits. But your system will certainly contain a mix of both one-off tasks and routines.

An example of two financial goals might be paying off your student loan by a set date and saving enough money to retire at the age of 65. From these desired outcomes you can derive, in some instances by literally doing the math, the system of one-offs and routines, respectively, that you need to adopt. Dump those into your to-do app.

 Keep track of appointments in your calendar, not in your to-do list.

For tasks that have a set date, like a meeting with a financial advisor, I like to use my calendar rather than the to-do list. I then have two calendar reminders set, one for a day and one for an hour before. This way I won't forget and my to-do app shows me my calendar from within the UI, so I don't need to replicate it there.

At the moment, I have four areas in Things (think of them as folders in other to-do apps): personal, work, business, and miscellaneous. I then categorize my to-do tasks further in lists/projects within those areas. These lists roughly correspond to areas of my life, plus specific projects. For example, for personal I have the following to-do lists:

- Self-Growth
- Health
- Relationships
- Finances
- Learning
- Photography
- Leisure

Some people adopt Stephen Covey's style of organization, where they group to-do tasks by life role instead (e.g., Husband, Employee, Blogger, etc). There is no right or wrong approach here, just what works best for your way of thinking.

My blogs are listed under the Business area, each with their own list. Writing this second edition is its own project, also under Business.

It's worth noting that not everything can be neatly categorized, so don't obsess too much. Some tasks are just miscellaneous or errands. Under Miscellaneous I have the following lists:

- Household
- Errands
- Miscellaneous
- Groceries
- Wish list
- Meta

Meta is an important one. It's where I put maintenance tasks like cleaning the to-do inbox, devising a daily plan from my to-do list, and reviewing all the tasks in my to-do lists weekly, for example, not to mention measuring progress monthly or quarterly to make the required adjustments. It's important to do this sort of maintenance to stay on top of your overall list and your progress.

Assign Priorities to Tasks

A lot of people feel overwhelmed by to-do lists. I think it comes down to a common misconception: the idea that you need to do everything on the list. This is generally not possible and not the point of having a list.

The real point of having a to-do list is dual in nature: 1) to dump tasks out of your brain; 2) to quickly determine what you should be working on at a given time. A to-do list system should enable you to accomplish those two steps, which are crucial for high productivity.

For a to-do list system to help you with the latter point, you'll need to know what's important and what's not, as well as what's urgent and what isn't. Effective people prioritize ruthlessly when allocating how they spend their time. For each task in my to-do inbox, I like to assign it a specific project, a priority, and if a deadline exists, a deadline.

These are the priorities I like to use:

1. *Must do*: Your most important tasks. The ones that will have the biggest impact on your future, have serious consequences if ignored, or simply give you the most anxiety. Tasks that offer a significant contribution toward the given goal you've defined belong to this priority. They are the big seeds you plant in the garden of your life.

2. *Should do*: Somewhat important tasks that have similar outcomes to must-do tasks, only to a much lesser degree. So although there are consequences if you ignore them, their ramifications are not apt to be life-altering or

goal derailing. You really *should* complete them, but they aren't as high in priority.

3. *Nice to do*: Actions with little impact and virtually no consequences. Most tasks in people's to-do lists tend to be of the should-do and nice-to-do kind when examined closely. You can delete them or keep them in your system (perhaps in a Someday list); just don't feel bad if you never get around to executing them. They don't really matter.

If your software supports priorities, you might opt to simply use high priority, medium priority, and low priority, respectively. In Things, I have them as tags with an appropriate emoji prefixed to their name. This way it's even easier to visually distinguish important tasks from not-so-important ones.

I will occasionally have doubts regarding whether a task belongs to one priority or another. In such a scenario, I assign the lower priority one to the task. If I don't, it's very easy to end up with everything being important on the list. Be selective and only assign *Must do* to tasks that are genuinely important.

> TIP 34   Do not assign artificial due dates to tasks.

I'll note here that I don't add artificial deadlines, because it can quickly become stressful to have countless due dates that aren't really due dates become overdue. Instead, I only assign a due date/deadline if one genuinely exists. I leverage priorities and trust that important things will be done as quickly and efficiently as possible.

Some productivity experts like to use the Eisenhower matrix, popularized by the aforementioned Stephen Covey. So instead of having those three categories, we assign tasks to one of four possible quadrants of priority:

1. *Quadrant I*: Urgent and important tasks
2. *Quadrant II*: Important but not urgent
3. *Quadrant III*: Urgent but not important
4. *Quadrant IV*: Not urgent and not important

Covey suggested to tackle those things housed in Quadrant I if you have any, but really focus in a proactive manner on tasks in the second quadrant: tasks that are important before they become urgent. This way you'll be more likely to lead a proactive, rather than reactive, life. He recommended delegating tasks from the third quadrant (after all, they aren't important) as much as possible and completely deleting or disregarding Quadrant IV tasks.

This is certainly a valid alternative approach I've used with success in the past. If you choose to go for the simpler must-do, should-do, nice-to-do system instead, the presence of deadlines on selected tasks will still allow tasks that are urgent and important or conversely urgent but not important to emerge on a daily basis.

Your Daily Plan

We now have a huge list of tasks, assigned to the right projects/lists with the right degree of importance, and deadlines (if any exist). That's great, but what should you work on next? That's the question your to-do system should help you answer. So our next step is to have one meta task that repeats daily called *Plan next day*. You can also simply add it to your calendar as a reminder instead. But the idea is to dedicate some time each evening to plan for the next day.

The night before is ideal, as it gives your brain time to mentally prepare while you sleep, but the morning of can also work. Whenever you do it, on a daily basis you should select items from your to-do program and add them to your Today view. Depending on the program you are using, there might be a Today view available or you might have to use a custom list, star the tasks, or something else. Printing a sheet or writing them down with pen and paper works too. Essentially, create a daily plan that contains just the actions you intend to tackle on a given day.

In practice, this day plan should mostly have urgent tasks (of various degrees of importance) that can't be delegated and must-do actions. Depending on how many must-do tasks you have in your system, should-do actions will also appear here frequently. Nice-to-do tasks shouldn't appear too frequently, but you might find yourself in the mood to tackle a specific task even if it's not that important. Flexibility is worthwhile, so don't be afraid to include a few of those as well.

If you're consistent, focusing on important tasks before they reach the point of becoming urgent will lead to far fewer urgent tasks down the road.

When it's time to execute your tasks, focus on nothing else until urgent and must-do actions have been completed. I like the approach suggested by Brian Tracy in *Eat That Frog!* Give your most important task your full attention. In fact, reserve the most productive time of your day to it (whenever that is; for many people it's during the morning hours, but there are plenty of night owls out there).

If your program allows you to do so, sort your Today view manually in the order of desired execution of the tasks, from most important to least important. In some cases, your context, such as where you find yourself at a given time, will affect your ability to execute certain tasks. So your order might not be precisely sorted by order of importance, but shoot for it.

> **Tip 35** To-do programs have many advanced options. To keep your overhead to a minimum, err on the side of simplicity.

Don't touch should-do and nice-to-do items that might be on your daily plan until all urgent and must-do items for the day have been executed.

Stephen Covey had a great analogy for this concept. If you try to fill a jar with big rocks, pebbles, and sand, the order you choose matters. If you start with the sand (nice to do) and then the pebbles (should do) and only add the big rocks (must do) last, you may not be able to fit everything in the jar. Instead, if you start with the big rocks—what really matters in your life—you'll find yourself able to jam in the pebbles and sand. And even if some sand is left out, it's just nice-to-do stuff, so it won't really matter.[2]

Looking at every list in your to-do program every day as you plan your next day can be a lot of work if you have many tasks across a couple of dozen lists/projects. One way to solve this problem is to establish a weekly list as well (I tag such tasks as *Sprint*, to borrow from the SCRUM methodology nomenclature). Then, each day you select tasks from the shorter weekly list, rather than your entire huge to-do list. Every week, on Sunday, I review the tasks that were completed and assign new ones to the new sprint. Ideally, you should pull into this weekly list tasks from several projects so you can make consistent progress in various areas of your life.

Figure 13, Creating a to-do item in Things, on page 131, shows what a to-do item might look like in Things when adopting the Eisenhower matrix and this sprint approach.

And speaking of reviews, I like to schedule a daily review as well, to reflect on the day, ensure tasks that were accomplished have been marked off as completed, journal, and so on. It's basic maintenance that keeps the system up-to-date and something I can trust. In fact, I find that trusting the process is vital for this personal productivity approach to work.

---

2. youtube.com/watch?v=zV3gMTOEWt8

Figure 13—Creating a to-do item in Things

That was a lot, but I found it to be a very good system to stay organized and keep up with the many responsibilities and demands in my life. On that note, I'd like to place the emphasis on the *I*. It's what works for me. Feel free to adapt this system to your needs, your way of thinking, and the specific program you choose, if you don't already have a system in place. Keep useful suggestions; discard the rest.

Figure Out Where Your Time Goes

At this point, you might have a solid system in place that helps you keep track of what you've done (and the sweet, sweet endorphin release that comes from checking off items), as well as what you should focus on in a given day. Unfortunately, we're only halfway there. Depending on how much you have on your plate, you might still find yourself overwhelmed. Many folks are selective, perhaps even ruthless in how much they tackle each day, but they still don't seem to have enough time.

If that's you, there are a few hacks that can definitely help improve the situation. Generally speaking, people aren't as busy and productive as they think they are. The truth is, they waste a ton of time each day. Not intentionally, perhaps, but we all do to some extent. Now, I'm not talking about well-deserved rest, sleep, or planned fun activities. Those are all sacred. I'm referring to the time that gets stolen from us and is genuinely wasted.

Before attempting any strategy to find more time, we should look into how our time is actually spent. You could set up an alarm that goes off every 30 minutes and write down what you're doing when it goes off; but assuming your work is mostly carried out on a computer, there are better methods.

RescueTime is a great option for analyzing which apps and sites you spend most of your time using.[3] It allows you to easily separate productive time from unfocused casual browsing. There are some inevitable privacy concerns when using such a monitoring tool, but I think it might be worth running it for a spell to gain an initial understanding of how you spend your time at the computer. If privacy is not a huge concern for you and you find the gamification element motivating, you may even decide to run it permanently.

You can also monitor how you're spending time on your mobile phone, since that's essentially a computer in your pocket that you've come increasingly to rely on. At the time of writing, RescueTime offers an app for Android but not iOS. Thankfully, Apple shipped a built-in tool called Screen Time directly in iOS 12. So if you have a modern iPhone or iPad, you won't even need to install a third-party app.

I don't know you personally (feel free to say hi on Twitter at @acangiano), but chances are this type of analysis will reveal that a few hours a day (or at least a week) are unintentionally wasted. If you could recoup some of them, you might be able to make faster progress on your goals (and find more time to blog). Who knows what we could all become if we actually stopped wasting so much time.

On that note, don't commit to too many things that don't directly advance your progress toward your goals. No matter how many minutes or hours you recoup, your time (and energy) are a scarce resource that must be protected. Focus on what makes your life (and yourself) better.

Limit Distractions

Many of us are addicted to the Internet and can't resist its siren song. It's not that we set out to waste time on it. It just happens organically if we let it. You start looking for an answer as to why you're getting an error and you somehow end up watching a vaguely related video. From there, YouTube will recommend entirely unrelated clickbait-y videos. Two hours later you'll wonder where the time went.

OK, YouTube videos might not be your vice. Perhaps, it's Hacker News, Reddit, or insightful articles that enrich your cultural understanding of the world but ultimately hinder your ability to get as much done as you should.

Deep down we all face distractions, regardless of their specific nature. So how do we go about wasting less time? Since technology is the source of much of

---

3. rescuetime.com

our distraction, I like to leverage technology so that it works for, not just against, us.

I block distractions as much as possible. I can't rely on my willpower to always be ready to resist, so I use the digital equivalent of Ulysses's crew, who placed wax in their ears to avoid the sirens' temptation.

Deep work requires focus and undivided attention. It's hard to achieve flow in your work when you are constantly pinged by notifications. So the first thing I do is strictly limit notifications on my phone. I disable badges that show unread counts (a trigger for my curious mind) and only allow a handful of apps to provide me notifications. This way I get virtually no interruptions from my phone and I'm still able to receive important calls. When I'm really trying to focus, I might even put my phone on Do Not Disturb mode altogether.

> Tip 36   Avoid installing known time-waster apps on your phone.

The same discipline applies to my laptops. I allow very few notifications (e.g., Slack messages) at work. If you work in an office and are often interrupted by colleagues for trivial reasons, you might want to find socially acceptable ways to guard yourself against such human distractions. Depending on your environment and colleagues, a pair of headphones might just do the trick. In less receptive places, a polite request to limit interruptions when you are wearing headphones might be in order.

Once you've tamed the giant dragon that is notifications, I'd look for ways to block distractions that you voluntarily walk into. I'm a fan of tools like FocusTime (by the same company that makes RescueTime) and Cold Turkey Blocker. These programs allow you to block distracting sites automatically. You can customize the list of sites, when they should be blocked, and whether you should have an allowance (say, 30 minutes a day).

On iOS, where the operating system is more restrictive, you'll want to use the aforementioned Screen Time to allocate usage limits to time wasters like social media apps.

Automatically blocking or limiting sites and apps really works and you'll be amazed by how much you get done when you're not getting lost in the meanders of the web (or gaming, watching TV, or whatever it is that makes you waste time). If the source of your distraction is offline, adapt the recommendations accordingly by altering your environment or setting boundaries.

If you're a programmer or a highly technical user, you'll also want to look for opportunities to automate. Automate anything that can be automated. Start by paying attention to what you do repeatedly and ask whether the task could be accomplished by a script, a service like IFTTT or Zapier, or delegated to one of the many inexpensive virtual assistant services available online.

Nobody is advocating for productivity 100% of the time here, but these suggestions, if applied, will likely yield a non-negligible amount of time that can be used instead for focused writing (and other priorities in your life, of course, including spending time with the people you care about).

Schedule Productive Time

You have a daily plan of important tasks to accomplish and a system in place that blocks distractions as much as possible. You're in a good spot, planning-wise, and can now get down to work. The best approach I know to ensure a consistent outcome is scheduling.

I'm a big fan of reserving time in my calendar. A meeting with myself, if you will. I don't trust that things, even on a list, will get done if there isn't dedicated time allotted for them. Inspiration might strike some of the time, calendar alarms every single time. What gets scheduled does indeed get done (or at least has a higher chance of getting accomplished).

So I recommend that you schedule blocks of time in your calendar to work on tasks. To keep the overhead low, don't assign specific tasks to your calendar. Just reserve blocks of one, two, or more hours for specific categories of tasks, like work, exercise, blogging, and so on. Have an alarm go off when the new block starts so that you can quickly wrap up what you're doing and switch to the next block.

Don't forget to include padding in your schedule. If you exercise for an hour at the gym, you have to factor in the time to get there, change, actually exercise, shower, come back, and so on. So don't block just one hour for gym time. It's likely going to be 90 minutes or even two hours all total, if you plan to work out for a solid hour.

You might be tempted to add breaks as well, and generally speaking, you should, if you wish to make your schedule realistic. However, I'll show you a technique that bakes in breaks within your blocks, so I don't recommend that you schedule breaks between blocks. Though going for a daily walk in the park can easily be promoted to its own block, and an important one at that!

> Tip 37 Take at least one day off to recharge each week.

If you have the authority to do so, schedule less important actions (e.g., appointments and certain meetings) during less productive slots of your day. Assign your most productive time to the most important blocks in your calendar, if feasible.

In the beginning, you might fight this structured approach, finding it very limiting (especially if you have a naturally rebellious streak). However, over time you might find it freeing. You won't feel as overwhelmed and stressed, and if you stick with it, you'll get tons of important tasks accomplished. It turns out to be empowering for most.

If you really find it too constricting, you can always relax the rules to make it more manageable and less intense on yourself. The key takeaway here is to not just wait for inspiration to strike out of the blue. Do the work with consistency, because consistency beats the hell out of intensity.

Focus with the Pomodoro Technique

Whatever technique or method you adopt to manage your time (whether the approach I outlined, which is heavily inspired by Getting Things Done, or something else entirely), you'll get to the point where your calendar says "Blogging." Now what? You actually have to do the work. And maybe, on that day, you're not overly inspired or are feeling tired.

Don't let procrastination win. You want to gather as much focus as possible so as to make productive use of the time you've allocated for blogging.

Enter the Pomodoro technique. The Pomodoro technique gets its intriguing name from kitchen timers, which are often shaped like tomatoes (*pomodoro* means "tomato" in Italian). This productivity hack is extremely simple and can be used when writing for your blog, doing marketing on social media, or for any task that's important to you.

The basic idea is that each of us can only focus on a given task for so long before we become distracted or too fatigued. This time management technique also weaves in the fact that it's important to take regular breaks as you work (both for the sake of helping you stay focused and for your overall health and mental well-being). The Pomodoro technique regulates when you are to diligently focus on a task and when you should take a breather.

This technique is centered on breaking your time down into *pomodori* (plural for pomodoro). You start your tomato-shaped timer (or one of the many apps for it), and then sprint your way through that pomodoro, focusing on one single task on your to-do list. After 25 minutes of dedicated work, the timer goes off and you take a nice five-minute break from your work.

Once your break is over, you start another 25-minute-long pomodoro. This new pomodoro can be dedicated to the same task as before (if you didn't complete it during the previous pomodoro) or to a new one. If you are seriously interrupted during a pomodoro session, you'll have to cancel it and start from scratch. Make sure you are dedicating twenty-five solid minutes of focus to the given task.

Most people, understandably, have a hard time intensely focusing for hours on end, but they can muster 25 minutes of attention. After every four pomodori, you can take a longer break (usually between 15 and 30 minutes, depending on your needs).

It's important not to ignore breaks, since they help you refresh before you jump into your next 25-minute pomodoro sprint.

Armed with the Pomodoro technique, you'll start to think in terms of the number of pomodori that a given post or task might require. Thus instead of mentally allocating four hours to blogging, you may start to think of it in terms of eight pomodori per week. As you gain experience, you'll soon discover how many pomodori you need for your average post.

> Tip 38　　If you find 25-minute dashes to be too short, set your pomodoro length to 50 minutes, with 10-minute breaks.

If you're new to this technique, chances are that you'll be amazed by how much you can accomplish in 25 minutes of unadulterated focus. Over time, you might even train your "focus muscle" enough to start feeling that breaks at 25-minute intervals interrupt your flow too much. I personally use long pomodori instead (San Marzano tomatoes, if you will), setting the pomodoro length to 50 minutes and taking 10-minute breaks instead of 5. Every four long pomodori, I take a 30-minute break. I find taking a walk during breaks (especially outside, when possible) to be very beneficial for restoring my energy levels.

For the record, my average blog post is on the longer side, and it usually takes me just one long pomodoro (or two at most) to write it. I find longer pomodoro lengths allow me to really get in a state of flow without drifting away into distraction.

Even if you decide not to use the Pomodoro technique for all of your work, consider performing one pomodoro to kick-start your work. This approach will allow you to overcome the initial inertia, and momentum will carry you forward once you start.

There are applications for virtually every platform (including Android and iOS) out there. Shoot for one that allows you to customize the length of the pomodoro and ideally allows you to log how you spent those pomodori. Pomodoro logs can be helpful in becoming better at assessing how long tasks actually take you (and therefore allocating your time, or just deciding how much to take on). My bet is that you'll find that procrastination might have skewed your perception of how long things actually take (unless procrastination isn't a problem for you).

Some to-do apps (e.g., TickTick) even have built-in pomodoro timers, which are quite handy. This way you can assign your to-do task to specific pomodori and review how many were logged for a specific task right within your to-do app. Other to-do apps don't have built-in pomodoro options, but some allow third-party apps to sync pomodoro data with your to-do lists. For example, PomoDoneApp supports many popular to-do and productivity tools,[4] including Todoist, Trello, Asana, Wunderlist, and so on.

As a reminder, don't get too caught up looking for apps and the optimal tools. It's important to remember that even a simple timer application and a text editor would essentially accomplish the same result without all the bells and whistles. They're nice, and I enjoy them, but the key value lies in the technique itself.

For an in-depth look at this technique and its subtleties, I recommend the book *Pomodoro Technique Illustrated [Nöt09]*, also published by The Pragmatic Bookshelf.

Take Action

If you haven't taken action yet, now it's your turn to put the advice into practice.

1. Write down your goals.

2. Set up your to-do system by leveraging one of the many available applications.

3. Create a daily plan with your most important actions for the day.

4. Schedule blocks of time for blogging (and other important activities) in your calendar.

5. Adopt the Pomodoro technique to focus and sprint through your work while still getting enough breaks.

---

4. pomodoneapp.com

What's Next

Some readers might see this as an odd chapter, perhaps even an optional one. After all, you might already be way more organized and productive than I am. But I hope the approach I outlined here makes sense to you and you can incorporate some of the suggestions into your own customized productivity and time management system.

We're all different, and it would be myopic to expect every reader to find my method, as it's written, to be a perfect match for your way of thinking and—more importantly—of doing. So follow along verbatim, discard the whole chapter, or find a great middle ground that works for you—whatever it takes to find enough time to blog and do the things that really matter in your life.

So what's left to do? Plenty. You've planned it, you've built it, and now it's time to promote it.

Part III

Promote It

Marketing is too important to be left to the marketing department.

  David Packard

CHAPTER 8

Promoting Your Blog

This chapter kick-starts the third part of the book, which is dedicated to the marketing side of your life as a blogger.

Self-promotion and marketing can be touchy subjects among technical audiences, so we'll start by considering why these activities matter, before delving into what you need to do in order to promote your blog.

Market It and They Will Come

The 1989 dramatic film *Field of Dreams* popularized the expression "If you build it, he will come" and its variations. When it comes to blogging, the opposite is often true: "Build it, and they still won't come."

The truth is that once you've built your shiny blog and published some content, traffic will roll in very slowly unless you actively promote your site. In other words, building is necessary but not sufficient to ensure your blog gets the attention it deserves.

Most bloggers skip this promotional step, and as a result they end up receiving only a handful of visitors. At that point, a vicious cycle starts in which seeing so few visitors demotivates the blogger, who in turn publishes less frequently and consequently attracts fewer visitors (which discourages the blogger further). The end result is a blog abandoned in a matter of weeks, or months at best.

This disastrous outcome can be prevented. First, you've done your homework regarding subject matter, niche size, on-page SEO, headlines, calls to action, and the type, quality, and frequency of content. These actions alone put you miles ahead of many bloggers and also partially vaccinate you against a complete lack of readership.

However, there are millions of active blogs in the wild; standing out and attracting a serious following will require a conscious effort on your part.

Another way to look at this situation is that you've got the first part of the equation right. Now you need to get your marketing efforts right as well. Don't skip this or the following chapters; they're absolutely some of the most valuable ways to make your blog a success.

Correct a Self-Sabotaging Mindset

Marketing is bullshit. Marketing is evil. Marketing is everything that's wrong with this world. Marketing is the root of all evil. Marketers should be shot.

Believe it or not, I've heard all these statements—and plenty more like them.

If you agree with any of them (hopefully not the last), you're not alone in your dislike of marketing. I've found that technical people, particularly programmers, tend to have a strong hatred of marketing.

Anti-marketing stances stem partly from bad experiences with manipulative marketers and partly from a misunderstanding of what marketing actually is.

Wikipedia defines marketing this way:

> Marketing is the process used to determine what products or services may be of interest to customers and what strategy to use in sales, communications, and business development.

At its core, marketing is about connecting people to solutions. For example, some people may have an interest in buying an environmentally friendly car. Good marketing involves identifying this segment of the population and then devising a strategy to let that portion of the population know about the existence of your brand-new electric car and its benefits (in a style and manner that will appeal to them).

Though the ultimate goal is to sell a car, marketing isn't about convincing people who aren't interested in your product to buy it. Instead, it's about exposing the right product to the right audience. Done correctly and in an ethical manner, it's possible to promote without deceiving, manipulating, or forcing people to spend their hard-earned money on goods they don't want or need.

It's important to understand that marketing is so much more than just advertising. Marketing encompasses countless aspects of your product, including what you name it before it even exists.

If you still feel that marketing is mostly evil, I encourage you to reflect on the forms of marketing you already do, perhaps without even realizing. Ever applied for a new job? Or dated someone? While you probably didn't misrepresent yourself with your future employer or partner by blatantly lying, you still wore nice clothes and tried to showcase your favorable traits.

In doing so you were marketing yourself.

In blogging, the aim of your marketing is to reach as many people who are potentially interested in your content as possible and who will benefit from such content. As we'll see in future chapters, this promotion will end up providing you with many benefits as well, including promoting yourself professionally, marketing your services and products (if you have any), and so on.

Like all tools, marketing can be used for good or in unethical, obnoxious ways. In this book, I advocate only white-hat marketing techniques that will get your content in front of the people who need to see it. So if you're the stereotypical antimarketing developer, please approach the rest of this chapter with an open mind. I promise that you won't have to sell your soul to do well with your blog.

Perform On-Page and Off-Page SEO

As discussed before, the goal of your on-page SEO efforts is to present your content in the best light possible in the eyes of search engines. You're trying to provide Google and others with positive signals of the relevance of your content to the search queries provided by end users.

Let's recap some of the most prominent *on-page* SEO actions you can take.

- Create plenty of well-researched, nicely written original content.
- Favor long (1000 words or more) content that's genuinely useful to your audience.
- Write catchy headlines containing target keywords.
- Have a keyword-dense slug for your articles.
- Use headings in your posts (and include desirable keywords in your headings).
- Interlink within your site by using tags, categories, related article plugins, and so on.
- Ensure your site loads quickly and is mobile friendly.
- Have an XML sitemap.

On-page SEO is all about what you can do on your site to better your chances of ranking well with search engines. *Off-page SEO* is the promotional work you do outside of your site to generate backlinks from relevant and high-authority websites.

Historically, search engine optimization specialists (aka SEOs) have used Google's PageRank, a score between 0 and 10, to judge the authority of a site (or a specific page). This score is calculated on the basis of the quantity and quality of backlinks a given domain (or specific page) receives.

Although not entirely irrelevant today,[1] Google hasn't published new public PageRank scores in years. As a result, most SEOs have switched over to other metrics to assess the authority of a site. Moz's DA (domain authority) and Ahrefs' UR (URL rating) are popular among modern SEOs. If you don't pay for such premium tools, you can search for *domain authority checker* in Google to find a few web tools that will provide you with Moz's DA (and PA—page authority) for free.

It's worth noting that an internal page on a high authority site won't generally have the same authority as its home page. Nevertheless, even internal pages of popular sites offer massive SEO benefits.

Link building is so fundamental because quality backlinks are one of the strongest signals used by Google's algorithm to determine the authority and relevance of your site. The premise is that if a variety of authority sites trusted by Google link to your site with related anchor texts (i.e., the linked words), then your URL must be important and trustworthy for that particular set of keywords. The same is true for sites that are less authoritative but highly relevant to your niche.

Because of this, always use meaningful anchor text in your links. Don't use "Click here" or similar generic text when linking to other pages (as a courtesy to them and your readers) or, if you have control over it, in your link-building efforts as you point links to your site.

Link building will help you get found, indexed, and ranked higher by Google. To help Google discover you quickly, you should also submit your blog directly at google.com/addurl when you first launch your blog.

The rest of this chapter is dedicated to techniques to perform link building as well as social media promotion. This chapter is really all about techniques

---

1.   ahrefs.com/blog/google-pagerank/

that will lead to more traffic for your blog, whether through organic searches, referrals, or social media.

> Tip 39   Check your blog with website.grader.com.

Not All Links Are Created Equal

Remember that not all links are created equal. A link to your blog from the home page of *The New York Times* will far outweigh a link from an unknown blog. You should not only strive to build a lot of backlinks but also try to receive them from authoritative sites and highly relevant sites. These will, in fact, increase your PageRank value and ranking and possibly send you a stream of referral traffic as well.

The PageRank of a blog correlates with the domain authority and actual popularity of that site. The whole point of link building, however, isn't to increase this magic number (especially now that it's no longer available to the public). The point is to rank well for your target keywords and for as many "long tail" keywords as possible.

Although an important one, the PageRank of your home page (and internal pages) is only one of many signals that are used by Google to determine the rank of a given URL for a certain query. And they continue to tweak this algorithm to provide better results and stay ahead of unscrupulous SEO techniques.

> Tip 40   Install an SEO extension for your browser (e.g., SEOquake).

SEO isn't an exact science, so there isn't complete agreement on every factor that determines the value of the backlinks you receive. The ranking algorithm changes frequently as a means of combatting spam, Google bombing,[2] and other such abuses, so that doesn't help matters either.

Nevertheless, here are some common characteristics of the ideal backlink that can help your ranking for a variety of keywords you value.

- Pages that link to you have a high level of authority and are hosted on sites with high domain authority.

- The domain linking to you is an .edu or a .gov. Google values university and government sites.

---

2. en.wikipedia.org/wiki/Google_bomb

- The backlink anchor text contains keywords that you're targeting. Some variety is good here, because it's unnatural for every site to link to you with the exact same anchor text.

- The page that links to your blog contains few other external links. In other words, your URL is one of the main links on that page.

- The page linking to you is relevant to the topic of your blog, and your link occurs toward the top of the page (as opposed to a footer link or on the bottom of the sidebar).

- Other links on the same page are relevant to yours. In other words, the page linking to you is not just a collection of random links.

Remember that you can't expect the perfect link to your site every time. Most blogs will naturally attract backlinks from a variety of sites with varying degrees of authority. Google would consider a site that only had high-authority backlinks to be quite odd and may suspect foul play. (Some people will, in fact, purchase backlinks from high-authority sites in bulk, against the Google webmaster guidelines.[3])

> **Tip 41** Read the Google webmaster guidelines in full.

Also, keep in mind that you don't have control over most backlinks. Our discussion about the perfect backlink is meant to help you obtain a few high-quality backlinks. But many backlinks you'll attract will probably not occur as a direct consequence of your link-building efforts. Instead, creating great content that's genuinely useful is likely to attract a variety of organic links from people referencing it.

There are even links from shady sites that can actively hurt your ranking because they mislead Google into thinking you were trying to game the system by, for example, buying backlinks. For this reason, Google even allows you to disavow specific backlinks so that they don't negatively impact your ranking. Generally speaking, you don't need to worry about this unless you have a competitor actively trying to sabotage you or you engaged in some shady practices yourself in the past. In which case, Google Search Console and its disavowing feature will come in handy.

In Chapter 5, Creating Remarkable Content, on page 87, we described how to create (good) linkbait that naturally attracts links. Now let's dive into how to build high-quality backlinks through off-page efforts.

---

3.   support.google.com/webmasters/answer/35769

Guest Blog on Other Blogs

In the previous chapter, we talked about finding guest bloggers as a way of obtaining additional, often free content. In this section, we'll turn the tables. This time around, we're going to use guest blogging as a tool for promoting your blog.

Guest blogging can be an extremely powerful marketing tool. Compelling content and a dose of charisma can latch onto an existing community created by someone else and quickly attract many followers to your own site. You'll also obtain high-quality backlinks, which can be so hard to get.

Here are the three essential ingredients you're going to need to successfully promote your blog via guest blogging:

- A blogger who is willing to accept contributions from guest bloggers

- A great article, typically comprised of original content that hasn't been published elsewhere—you'll want to position yourself as an expert on the subject matter you're covering and provide content that's relevant to both the blog you're guest-posting on and your niche.

- An enticing biography that includes one or two links to your blog—this biographical content, sometimes referred to as a *resource box*, is typically placed at the bottom of your guest post and may include a small picture of you and a description of who you are, as well as a blurb about what you're promoting (e.g., your blog, a book, etc.). The specifics are typically agreed upon in advance with the blog's host. If you can link to the site or page you're trying to gain a backlink for directly from the body of your guest post, even better.

Find Prospective Blogs

As you can probably imagine, the hardest part is finding bloggers who are willing to let you post on their blogs. Guest blogging is a win-win situation. So all you need to do is explain its benefits to prospective hosts. Compile a list of twenty or so blogs in your niche or field. Give priority to those with high authority (use an SEO toolbar to assess it) and especially to blogs that have accepted guest bloggers before. This task will be a lot easier if you're already following many blogs in your niche via a feed reader, as you should be.

> Tip 42   Establish a relationship with a blogger before proposing a guest post.

Learn more about each blog, including its style, its elevator pitch, and so on. Then individually and sequentially approach each of these bloggers by email, starting with what you believe are the most valuable and promising ones. You can use a customized template message for each of them, but don't just copy and paste the same message for dozens of different bloggers. A message that starts with "Dear Webmaster" rightfully belongs in the spam folder.

The key to connecting is being personal and easy to relate to. Address the blogger or editor-in-chief by name. Don't forget some honest praise, including the specifics of what you like about that person's approach to blogging. Even if the creator is very famous and you're just starting out, remember that you're dealing with a colleague and you have a fair proposal. Stress the benefits of your contribution, without sounding boastful, and acknowledge that you'll benefit from this relationship, too.

Before you approach the first blogger, ensure that you have a title and a rough idea of the word count of the post you'd like to write. Briefly explain what the article is going to be about, what angle you plan to take, and how it's a relevant and welcome addition for readers. If you are feeling proactive, you can even write the article beforehand and mention it in your email pitch.

In fact, most bloggers have a hard time asking a stranger to write an article that they might have to reject on the basis of its poor quality. So most guest-blogging requests go unanswered or are rejected outright. Mentioning that you already have the article and asking if they'd like to take a look will engage far more bloggers (at the very least the most curious ones).

> Tip 43   Submit your best content when guest blogging.

Popular bloggers receive a lot of emails, so don't expect an answer in two hours. Give them a couple of weeks before following up with a second email that kindly asks whether they're interested or if you should opt for other blogs instead. If after another week or so you haven't heard back, let them know that you've withdrawn your offer and will now consider other blogs. Thank them for their time. Don't burn bridges with fellow bloggers. If things don't work out, remain as polite, professional, and amicable as possible.

At three weeks or so per blogger, you may assume that it will take you over a year to reach the bottom of that initial list. Thankfully, this is just a worst-case scenario. If your article and proposal are sensible, you'll likely receive a positive answer way before you reach the last name and email on your list. The typical response times will also be much shorter than three weeks.

You can also pitch different articles in parallel to different blogs. Just know that you might find yourself in the position of having to do a lot of writing in a short time span if multiple blogs take you up on the offer. But you can always negotiate deadlines to navigate your way through this sort of situation.

Once someone shows interest, you can agree on the details regarding how the article should be formatted and submitted, what kinds of links are permitted, whose referral code should be used for possible affiliate links, the specifics of your resource/author box, if this is a one-off arrangement or if you plan to guest-blog regularly in the future, and so on.

The survivors from the initial list (those you haven't contacted yet) will come in handy as you proceed to pitch a new article down the road to expand your network of backlinks from other authority blogs. If your niche is very small, you may have to space out your contributions a little or you'll seem to dominate the conversation via multiple blogs.

Repeat the process as many times as you wish. At some point, you may see your returns from guest blogging diminish as your site becomes an established blog in its own right within your online community.

If you're not having any luck with this, let's call it cold-emailing, technique, consider becoming known to your target bloggers with insightful comments on their blog for a while before pitching an article. Likewise, consider connecting with them by interacting on Twitter or whichever social platform they tend to use. (Avoid Facebook personal profiles because they tend to be used for personal purposes, unlike Facebook Pages, Twitter, and LinkedIn.)

Maximize the Effectiveness of Your Resource Box

The resource box is your reward, so you should pay close attention to what you include within it. The main goal should be to sell yourself as an expert on the topic you're blogging about and then get readers to take the action you want (be it buying your product, checking out your blog, signing up for your newsletter, or whatever else).

Don't write a gigantic biography that no one's actually going to read. Include a short, carefully crafted biographical paragraph that highlights your experience without sounding too boastful or coming across as a complete list of everything you've accomplished since junior high.

Your resource box should also include a single, strong call to action. Include many calls, and people will ignore all of them—a pattern we've seen before with regard to social buttons on your pages.

Carefully select anchor text for your backlinks so that they appear organic yet optimized for your target keyword. Typically you'd be choosing your blog title or a variation of it as the anchor text for the link to the home page of your blog.

When you discuss the resource box with the blogger who'll be hosting your guest post, ensure that you're allowed to have regular links and not nofollow links. The nofollow value in the link below tells Google that it shouldn't positively influence the PageRank of the linked site (e.g., *Programming Zen*).

```
<!-- Don't link to your blog this way -->
Check out my <a href="https://programmingzen.com" rel="nofollow">Programming
Blog</a>.
```

Nofollow links were invented as a way of discouraging the rampant comment spam on blogs, so they have a legitimate use (just not for guest blogging purposes). As you work through your link-building efforts, remember that nofollow links are essentially useless for search engines (however, people may still click those links, of course).

I have heard the argument before that people doing massive link building for very competitive keywords should also include nofollow links in the mix to make the link-building process appear more natural over time. We're not taking that approach here, so you shouldn't worry about that. Focus on obtaining high-quality *dofollow links* (i.e., links that don't have the rel="nofollow" attribute), but don't be scared to occasionally link from pages (e.g., certain blog comment systems) that mark all links as nofollow.

Other Forms of Article Marketing

Guest blogging is a specialized form of article marketing. Try it out. When you guest-blog, you're adding value to your community with content that has been reviewed by at least two bloggers (you and the host of the blog you're publishing on). In other words, it's a form of promotion that ends up benefiting everyone involved.

Other forms of article marketing, while still technically white hat, can't truly make that same claim with regard to adding value to a community. I'm referring to the more traditional forms of article marketing that are carried out through article directories and press releases.

Ignore Article Directories

Article directories are sites that accept article submissions on a variety of subjects. In exchange, they usually provide you with a resource box at the bottom of your articles in which one or two links of your choice can be embedded. Most directories review your articles before approving them.

Such sites make money via AdSense and other advertising forms and give you backlinks from high-authority directories. In some cases, they'll ask you to pay to submit your article and receive a backlink from a page with high domain authority. Win-win situation once again, right? In theory, yes; this is very similar to the experience of guest blogging. In practice, though, things are rather different, particularly in the past few years.

The average article quality on the most popular directories leaves a lot to be desired: the articles are full of typos, they're bland, and they're often commissioned for a few dollars from people who know nothing about the subject matter they're writing about. Not only are the approval standards much lower than the average blogger who accepts contributions, but the people reviewing your articles usually have no clue about your subject matter (assuming there's even a review process in place).

The majority of articles, you'll find, are poor, commercial in nature, and published under pen names by people who wouldn't want to be associated with what they've written. I understand that this may come across as elitist, but if you've ever stumbled upon any of the following sites, you'll probably know what I'm talking about and will share similar feelings: EzineArticles, HubPages, or Squidoo (now acquired by HubPages).

Google downgraded the ranking of most of these directories because it, too, perceives them as poor-quality content (i.e., *content farms*) that adds little value to the user. And as far as search goes, usefulness to the searcher is the primary goal for Google.

They used to be quite effective from an SEO perspective, but today these backlinks do not provide SEO benefits despite being hosted on directories with serious PageRanks. They're not considered a black-hat technique, but they won't help you out either.

The audience of these directories is mainly comprised of random people arriving from search engines (increasingly less so) and other fellow article marketers. It's not the cohesive, tight-knit kind of community you can expect from a blog niche that specializes in topics similar to yours. So while you may receive minimal SEO juice from article directories, you won't get all the benefits you can typically expect from posting on the high-quality blog of a fellow expert.

Affiliate marketers loved article directories because they offered an easy way to obtain hundreds of backlinks. In fact, most of these marketers outsourced the creation of a handful of articles (for a few dollars apiece), and then used synonym-based software (i.e., *article spinners*) to automatically rewrite hundreds of combinations of those articles in a way that was difficult for duplicate filters to detect. Other software would then be used to submit a rewritten version of each article to hundreds of directories. Today such an approach would not be effective and would be considered either black or gray hat.

In short, focus on guest blogging and leave article directories as a tool of last resort because today they have a negligible effect on SEO.

Use Press Releases Sparingly

Press releases have traditionally been used to announce news about a company or product launch to members of the media. Much like article directories, there's nothing evil or inherently wrong with using them in the hope of attracting the attention of journalists and other media.

In practice, however, you'll find that most journalists aren't interested in your new blog unless it has a novelty factor that's well suited to attention-grabbing headlines about the hot topic of the moment, or you're announcing something noteworthy.

Historically, however, press releases were used for SEO purposes. In fact, every time you used a PR distribution service, you'd see your press release reprinted across hundreds or even thousands of sites. If you included links to your site in the press release and carefully selected your anchor texts based on your target keywords, you'd magically receive a boost in the SERP. Your story wasn't going to be picked up by AP or Reuters, but you got some nice SEO juice.

Google quickly found out what SEOs were up to and began to penalize the approach. So today, many sites will publish links in press releases as nofollow, de facto neutralizing this technique.

If you are sharing something newsworthy, a press release still makes sense, because journalists noticing it might end up writing about you and link back to you. However, much like article directories, they're no longer an effective SEO tool.

In short, feel free to skip press releases for your blog for now, but be aware of their existence for those times when you have something truly remarkable to share with journalists.

Add Your Blog to Planet Sites

Planets are feed aggregator sites that display a list of posts from a variety of blogs on the same topic on a single page (and in a single RSS feed).

For example, Planet Python (planet.python.org) aggregates a large number of posts from blogs by Python programmers.

If a planet site exists for your niche, you should consider contacting the owners to add your feed to their list. The perks of doing so include greater exposure for your posts and SEO advantages because you're receiving back-links from the planet site.

If you intend to start a planet for your niche yourself (a good idea), take a look at some of the open source software mentioned on the Wikipedia page.[4]

Planet sites are less common than they once were. They're still worth your time, though. After all, a one-time effort of getting added is then rewarded for years to come.

Participate in the Community

One easy way to boost your link-building efforts is to actively and genuinely participate in the blogosphere. Follow blogs that are relevant to your field and actively engage in commenting on the stories they feature. Book fifteen to thirty minutes a day for this activity if doing so doesn't come naturally to you.

Commenting will foster your relationships with other bloggers and provide you with plenty of backlinks. Although some of the backlinks will be nofollow, you'll still receive new visitors because of them.

Most commenting systems allow your name to be linked to a URL of your choice when leaving comments. The key point here is to add value with your comments, though. Don't leave comments just to obtain a backlink. Instead, read what the blogger has to say and then comment with your own insight. Few things will attract readers to your blog like excellent comments from an expert voice.

The difference between comment spam and an active reader who's trying to be useful lies in the words used. Responding to a post with a comment such as "Great post" while filling the URL field of the form with your blog URL is not that different from what comment spammers do (OK, they automate the process to scale, but conceptually it's not that different at all).

---

4.   en.wikipedia.org/wiki/Planet_(software)

Always add value to the topic at hand. Ideally, take the time required to leave an insightful comment that's at least a paragraph or two long. Don't speak solely because you want a backlink. Comment because you have something valuable to say. And by all means, forget SEO when commenting. The name field should include your name, not target keywords.

At times it may be appropriate to link to your blog directly within your comment. In fact, if you're the first or second person to comment with a link, people may click on your link even more than on the links within the post itself.

For example, the following comment would probably be OK with most bloggers:

> Brilliant post, Richard. I expressed very similar thoughts about the behavior of subatomic particles here: <link>. I must say, however, that your diagrams are an extremely clever representation of quantum electrodynamical interactions. They may catch on.

Be very careful with this, as it's easy to come across as a spammer or as an aggressive self-promoter. Step back for a second and think about how you'd react if the same comment were made by another blogger on your own blog. Would you approve it or reject it? Would it upset you?

 Remember the golden rule: treat others as you'd like to be treated.

Leverage Foreign Blogs

When your blog acquires enough visibility, you may be approached by foreign bloggers who'll ask you to translate some of your content into their own language.

Let them publish your translated content (for free). You will get further distribution of your ideas and/or products as well as a backlink from a potentially popular blog or online magazine. The only condition you should have is that the article is credited to you and that it links back to your original post. In fact, you may even go so far as to actively scout for related blogs in other languages and then propose such an arrangement yourself.

Most of the people who approach you and offer to translate your content are genuine bloggers who are interested in propagating your content in other languages.

When a translation is published on someone else's site, you can decide if you want to link back to the translation from your original article or not (e.g.,

"This article is also available in Spanish, Japanese, and Chinese."). You don't have to. Some bloggers opt to do so, however, and this is where scammers see an opportunity.

From time to time you may be approached by scammers who will ask you if they can translate a highly popular article of yours. You'll say it's OK, and they'll supposedly work on a translation. Then they'll send you a link to a page that seemingly includes your translation and in turn, they'll ask you to include a backlink to their translation from your article page that has high authority.

The scam factors in when the page you've been pointed to is not an actual translation of your article. Scammers may keep the title, but the content will have nothing to do with what you wrote. Even if they do translate your content, perhaps badly via Google Translate, don't be afraid of saying no to the request of linking back to the translation.

Link back only when you receive a link to a quality translation of your actual content. Again, Google Translate can help you figure that out, but a friend or reader who speaks the language would be better.

Evaluate the overall quality of their blog and not just the translation. If the foreign site isn't in your niche, contains translated content about all sorts of unrelated topics, or is plastered in ads, an offer to translate your content may have little to do with admiration and a whole lot to do with SEO and link building. Don't be afraid to say no to requests for backlinks to translations from your original article or page.

The Dark Side of Link Building

If you pursue link building and SEO education further on your own, you'll quickly discover what I'd call the dark side of online marketing.

I'll refrain from teaching you black-hat techniques and opt instead to list a series of borderline activities you may come across and be tempted to partake in. Don't. They're not worth your time.

- *Buying high PageRank links*: As mentioned multiple times, buying links will get you blacklisted or penalized by search engines.

- *Renting email addresses*: At best this is a waste of time; at worst you end up spamming people who don't know you or your blog. It also violates privacy laws in many countries.

- *Buying social media votes*: You can artificially boost your popularity on social networks like Reddit by buying votes for $0.10–$1.00 USD each. In many cases, doing so will get your blog banned from or penalized on social networking sites.

- *Three-way link exchanges*: Reciprocal links between two sites don't offer much in the way of SEO benefits, so there are services that take advantage of intermediary sites in the link chain to generate nonreciprocal links among those who participate in their network. Google is well aware of such schemes.

- *Fake blogs*: You can create a series of dummy blogs through free services like Blogger or WordPress.com, and then have all of them point back to your blog. Such services routinely ban fake blogs and accounts in an effort to keep down spam.

- *Link wheels*: This is a linking scheme involving fake blogs and article submissions that are organized to boost the authority of the URLs linking to your "money page" (the URL you want to promote), with the ultimate goal being to greatly boost the PageRank and relevancy of your money page for target keywords.

- *Mass article submissions*: Spun content is submitted not just to article directories but also to networks of low-quality blogs and is set up only to attract the content of other bloggers and to earn money via AdSense and other advertisements.

- *Automated submission to a variety of directories*: This is when you use software to automatically submit your site and feed to hundreds or thousands of crappy directories that no human will ever truly find useful.

You get the gist. While some black-hat SEOs do pretty well with these techniques, even when not technically illegal, they're still trying to game the system and will eventually be caught. Focus on adding value to your readers and your online community. The rewards and efforts will be far greater, and you won't risk being penalized by search engines and social media sites.

Promote Your Articles on Social Networks

In this section (and the next), we'll talk about promoting your articles on a variety of social media sites.

The same principles can be applied to new social networks that will pop up in the future, as well as to specialized social media sites for your particular sector that aren't named here.

General Social Networks for Promoting Your Blog

You should use the following general social media sites:

- Twitter
- Facebook
- LinkedIn
- Instagram
- Pinterest

Consider Instagram and Pinterest as optional, but they can be effective marketing channels. In 2018, Google announced that Google+ would be discontinued for consumers, so you can safely ignore that social network.

Great content of yours might be shared on these sites by people you don't even know. Nevertheless, it's important to get the ball rolling by sharing your own articles yourself. If you opt to promote your articles on Instagram and Pinterest (not a bad idea), make sure you generate images since these social networks are picture-based. These can be diagrams, charts, images of code from your posts, or significant quotes on fancy background images.

The success of your own promotion on Twitter, Facebook, and LinkedIn will largely depend on your network of friends and followers. If you don't have existing accounts on the sites mentioned above, now would be a good time to create them and start adding friends, colleagues, and acquaintances. (More on this in the chapter on social media strategies.)

Your Promotional Workflow

Whenever you publish a new article on your site, you should go ahead and perform some basic initial promotion on social media sites that you're targeting. Don't forget to also do this for articles that you scheduled a while ago that just went live. A calendar reminder might be a good idea if you schedule your posts to be published automatically.

Announcing your new posts on social media can be automated as well. Some services will do this for you from your RSS feed, and it's often even built in within blogging systems like WordPress. An argument could be made that this is very convenient and will ensure that you don't forget to do so yourself. Nevertheless, I tend to prefer and recommend that you perform this workflow manually every time you post.

This approach has three key advantages:

1. You get to decide when the post is shared on social media. You might, after all, publish a post at a time that isn't ideal for promotion on social media (say, at night or very early morning in your target geography).

2. You can customize the message for each social media channel. Your audience on your Facebook personal profile (friends and family) will be different from your Twitter account (followers) or your LinkedIn professional connections. You might want to announce the post differently to each audience, tag specific people, use or not use hashtags as appropriate (e.g., yes on Twitter, no on Facebook), and so on.

3. You have the option to skip promoting a particular post you don't want to broadcast on social media (for whatever reason).

A tool like Buffer simplifies the process of posting customized messages to multiple social accounts you own.[5] It's a time saver and offers some nice features like analytics to track how well your post announcements (and other social media messages you post) perform.

> Tip 45   Install Buffer's browser extension.

After publishing an article, don't forget to send out the newsletter to your mailing list subscribers as well, if you haven't automated that step. Unlike social media rebroadcasting, I tend to automate RSS to mailing list messaging, as the process of sending a manual email each time is a little more time-consuming than posting on social media (especially if using Buffer).

Make sure that Facebook, Twitter, and LinkedIn correctly pick up the title, meta description, and an image before posting on them. Social media posts with a preview of the link, as opposed to just a naked link, tend to perform significantly better. This doesn't apply to Instagram and Pinterest, where the image you post is the key content and there are no link previews. (To learn more about how social media pick up information from your post, research the topic of Open Graph meta tags online.)

Alternatively, use the image you're going to post on Instagram and Pinterest as the preview for your announcements on Facebook, Twitter, and LinkedIn as well (just make sure you still share the actual link to the post in your message).

> Tip 46   Make sure your links are posted on social sites with a preview.

On Instagram, linking is limited. One option you have is to link your latest post to your account bio, adding in the description of your image a reminder that "the link to this article is available in my bio."

---

5.   buffer.com

When promoting your posts on social media, it's important not to get discouraged by the relative lack of engagement. Even if you have ten thousand followers on a given platform, it doesn't mean that all of them will like and share your post. Even worse, it doesn't even mean that all of them will be shown the post in the first place. So adjust your expectations accordingly.

You're broadcasting on social media that you published something new. You're making people aware of your articles, and it might help you SEO-wise because Google takes into consideration popularity on social media in its ranking algorithm. It's perfectly normal to only see a few clicks on your articles unless you luck out (e.g., you get lots of retweets) or someone popular picks it up, spreading your message further.

Stick with it. It will help your blog in the long run and raise your profile on the social media properties where you keep being active and promoting your content.

Promote on Social News Sites

As a blogger who is focused on technical or business topics, you should consider submitting your articles to sites dedicated to topics related to your content, places where you'll find technical audiences interested in hearing what you have to say.

Without knowing the details of your blog, I can only suggest some sites that are broadly applicable to a variety of technical blogs. Namely, I'd recommend promoting your blog on Reddit and Hacker News. On Reddit, you get to choose which subreddit to submit your posts to, depending on their content.

I would recommend Slashdot as well, but only when you've just broken an important or newsworthy story. It's not exactly the kind of place where you'll routinely promote your blog.

Don't be discouraged if only a small percentage of your articles ever receive any love on these platforms. It's nothing personal. Your content might be great, but it competes with a huge number of other submissions—including those that receive unfair promotion through various techniques used to game the ranking algorithm (e.g., a large network of voters).

Other similar sites worth considering are DZone and the emerging Lobsters and Steemit.[6]

Feel free to search for and explore more social news sites on your own, particularly those that specialize in your particular niche or sector.

---

6. dzone.com, lobste.rs, and steemit.com, respectively.

Social news sites tend to operate by accepting stories that have been submitted by their users. Then they sort them so that the "best" ones end up at the top of the home page. *Best* as it's used here is a very relative term, given that each site uses a different algorithm to determine what floats to the top and what will only be shown to people who check the queue of new stories submitted to the site.

The most common factors that influence the popularity and visibility of your links on these sites are the number of upvotes you receive (as opposed to downvotes or other forms of negative flagging/reporting) and how quickly you receive them. Old submissions will not randomly make the front page of these sites, even if they receive a lot of votes all of a sudden. A story either receives a lot of votes shortly after being submitted or it'll never stand a chance of making the home page of that particular social news site.

The majority of stories will only attract one or two votes and never move from the new queue to the home page/popular page. This is simply the nature of such sites. Only the best (or most interesting) stories are supposed to surface. The difference between your story hitting the front page of one of these sites or not can often be measured in the several thousand visitors you'll likely receive. Your objective is definitely to hit the front page of such sites as often as possible.

As part of your blogging workflow, submit your most relevant new articles to these social news sites. If you have a blog that already has numerous articles, don't submit past stories all at once. You'll be seen as a spammer. Instead, pick your three to five best articles and submit them over the course of a week or two. If they are well received, you can submit more existing articles over time.

At any rate, submit your best new posts as soon as you publish them from then on out. Always ask yourself, is my article really a good fit for this particular social news site or online community? Sometimes the answer will be no, even if your article's content will be loved by search engine users.

To speed up the submission process, install site-specific bookmarklets whenever they exist. These will allow you to submit stories by simply clicking on a bookmark in your browser. To find them, search for "reddit bookmarklet" or "hacker news bookmarklet."

> **Tip 47** Submit your stories between 9 a.m. and 1 p.m. eastern time (ET) to maximize votes and exposure.

Submit Your Posts to Reddit

Reddit has one of the largest audiences in the world, so it has many popular subcommunities (called subreddits), with hundreds of thousands of subscribers. Whenever you submit a story, you get to choose which subreddit to submit to. Occasionally you can submit the same story to two or three different subreddits, but doing so too often might make you come across as spammy.

reddit.com/r/programming is the largest community for developers, with well over a million subscribers. /r/webdev is also quite popular, with currently over a quarter million subscribers. Depending on the topic you blog about, there's a good chance you can find relevant subreddits at reddit.com/reddits.

Other large geek subreddits to consider are /r/gaming, /r/technology, /r/science, /r/apple, /r/android, /r/math, and so on.

Always check the number of subscribers a subreddit has before deciding to submit your story there. (You can do so by looking at the number shown in the right sidebar.) A story about GraphQL may as well belong more to /r/graphql than /r/programming, but its current 3.5K subscribers means that you'll receive a limited amount of traffic from it (even if the story hits the customized home page of these subscribers). On the other hand, ranking on that subreddit is significantly easier than the ultracompetitive /r/programming.

You can always try to submit links to your posts to the most popular applicable subreddit (e.g., /r/programming); and if it fails there (likely), then submit it to more specific subreddits where it might have better luck (e.g., /r/graphql). Of course, there are also middle-ground subreddits that are larger than a few thousand subscribers but not quite as huge (and competitive) as /r/programming. These are a valid option as well.

If the most relevant subreddit has 10,000 subscribers or more, it may make sense to submit your story there directly, rather than to a larger, more generic subreddit. For example, a HOWTO about Ruby will most likely be killed instantly on /r/programming, whereas it might receive several upvotes on /r/ruby. Evaluate each case, and if you are truly in doubt, try submitting to both. (Again, as long as you don't do it too often.)

Reddit won't admit to it, but it tends to like a bit of sensationalism. So make your submission headline bold and interesting (it doesn't have to be the same title as your actual blog post title). If you quickly attract a few votes on /r/programming, you may get some ego-killing comments (regardless of your content), but you'll also receive thousands of visitors. In the past, I've received up to 50,000 visits within 48 hours from /r/programming for a single article of mine.

Some users may complain that you submit your own stories there, but it's considered fair play by the admins of the site as long as you do the following:

- Pick relevant subreddits.
- Don't flood the site with your submissions.
- Participate in the community by submitting stories from other sites and by commenting as well.[7]

 Participate in social news sites; don't just submit your own blog entries.

Submit Your Best Posts to Hacker News

Hacker News (HN) is currently my favorite community. It's smaller than Reddit, but it's growing quickly and tends to be a smidge more respectful than communities such as /r/programming. If you hit its front page, you'll still receive several thousand visitors (and quality ones at that).

On Hacker News, you can submit any story that's relevant to programming, technology, business, and the world of startups. War stories about your entrepreneurship or development experiences are particularly loved by this community. The audience tends to be smart, so the standard for your submissions is higher than the average site.

Stories that the community sees as fluff, off-topic, or devoid of real content are routinely killed by users who flag them. Politics and gratuitous controversy also tend to be no-nos.

Take a look at the existing stories on the front page and their comments to help you figure out the type of content and headlines that are appreciated on Hacker News. Then read its guidelines in full at ycombinator.com/newsguidelines.html.

If your link receives enough upvotes, it'll also be converted from nofollow to a regular link that receives SEO juice (though the real value is in the instant referral traffic potential, since it won't stay on the home page permanently). For the record, Hacker News's home page has a domain authority of 91—a staggeringly high number.

It's extremely important that you spend some time understanding the site before you make your first submission. If you submit your blog for the first time and your story is flagged and killed, your blog's submissions will automatically be killed from there on out. Not being able to promote your quality content on Hacker News would be a great shame that translates to the loss of several thousand valuable visitors each month.

Your first submissions from your blog must categorically be very high quality to ensure that the community welcomes your blog and doesn't flag it. If you're even remotely in doubt, don't submit your own blog posts yet. Submit other relevant stories you find interesting.

With this and other social news sites, you should avoid gaming the system by having all your friends upvote your stories. And if you send a link to your submission to a friend on Twitter or elsewhere, know that direct visits to item pages are valued less (or not at all) than organic votes obtained in the "new" page by HN's ranking algorithm.[8] (Yeah, this can be easily worked around by pointing your friends to the new page instead of to your submission. But don't do it.)

Case Study: ProgrammingZen.com's Social Traffic

In order to provide you with a more realistic idea of how much all these social media sites respectively contribute to a blog about programming, I have included the top ten referral traffic social sources over the entire existence of my own programming blog.

The percentages are based on the total social traffic only, and not on organic search traffic or other referral sources.

Rank	Social Site	Percentage (%)
1	Reddit	29.10
2	Hacker News	9.89
3	StumbleUpon	8.67
4	DZone	4.48
5	Digg	3.98
6	Slashdot	3.03
7	RubyFlow	1.52
8	Twitter	1.09
9	Delicious	0.95
10	Facebook	0.81

Note that the social traffic you're likely to experience will be quite different because some of these sites are either no longer operating or are significantly

---

8.   news.ycombinator.com/newest

less popular than they used to be. Namely, don't expect to see much traffic from StumbleUpon, Digg, RubyFlow, or Delicious.

In the past (and certainly when I first authored this book), traffic from Reddit and Hacker News eclipsed traffic from the likes of Twitter and Facebook. However, over time, it's become increasingly hard to obtain visibility on Reddit and Hacker News, while Twitter and Facebook usage has grown exponentially. If we look at my social network referrals limited to the past year, the top ten is quite different from the historic results shown in the table above.

Rank	Social Site	Percentage (%)
1	Twitter	35.38
2	Facebook	32.60
3	Reddit	10.04
4	Pocket	7.88
5	StumbleUpon	4.94
6	Hacker News	2.19
7	YouTube	2.11
8	Blogger	1.83
9	LinkedIn	1.39
10	Google+	0.39

Reddit and Hacker News are more likely to send many thousands of people at once to your blog than Twitter and Facebook, but they're also more likely to send virtually no traffic if your submission doesn't attract votes. Twitter and Facebook are more likely to send some traffic consistently; but unless you go viral (a very rare occurrence), they're not going to send thousands of people at once. Still, over time, they add up, as you can clearly see in the table above.

Promoting on Quora

Quora is a popular question-and-answer site. I suggest using it in a couple of ways. The first one is to fish for article ideas. Search it with keywords relevant to your niche to find questions people have about your topic. Then write articles that answer such questions. If Quora users have a given question, chances are people searching on Google are likely to ask the same question as well. I find it to be an endless source of good ideas for posts.

The second way to use Quora is for promotional purposes. Provide useful answers to questions within your niche, and then link to relevant articles on your blog to further support or enhance your answers. Quora is one of the few sites where it's socially acceptable to blatantly promote yourself, as long as you provide value with your answers.

So, your workflow can consist of searching for a question with no good answers, writing a post that answers it, and then replying with a summary answer that includes a link to the more comprehensive post. Or alternatively, after publishing a post, search Quora for relevant questions to which you can provide an answer (that will embed your link).

Links within your Quora answers are nofollow, but the site is popular enough to send quite a bit of traffic your way if you engage in this promotional technique often enough. You'll also raise your profile there, and that in itself can be a great tool to amplify your online influence and recognition in your field.

Cross-Post to Medium and dev.to

Generally speaking, it's not a good idea to republish your content on other blogs. Google will penalize you for duplicate content. The exception to this rule is if you specify, as you cross-post your content, a canonical URL. This tells Google which article should be considered as the canonical source of the post, preventing the re-publication from hurting your SEO efforts.

Two places worth considering for syndication of your content are Medium and dev.to (a friendly and inclusive community of programmers). As I said before, Medium is too much of a walled garden at this point to use as your main blogging platform. Nevertheless, you can leverage its popularity and built-in community to spread your message further. Unlike social media, where you simply point people to your new article, on Medium you'd republish the whole article by importing it (so that the proper canonical URL is set for you).

If you are using WordPress, you can use the Medium plugin to automatically cross-post your articles to Medium.[9] If you didn't opt for WordPress as your blog engine, you can use Medium's import tool instead.[10]

Using either of these tools will ensure that the canonical URL is set for you, safeguarding your SEO efforts. In Medium's own words, "By using Medium's official import tools, you can reap the benefits of high discoverability on Medium while still crediting all authority toward your own blog using Medium's canonical URLs."

---

9. help.medium.com/hc/en-us/articles/213510158
10. help.medium.com/hc/en-us/articles/214550207-Import-post

If you are publishing articles about programming, you should also cross-post your articles (or at least your best articles) on dev.to. To do so, you'll need to specify the canonical URL yourself. In the front matter of your post, where you specify your title, you'll need to include your canonical_url as well, as shown in the example below:

```
---
title: 25 Pitfalls When Learning to Program
published: true
tags: Programming,how to become a programmer,learning to program
canonical_url: https://programmingzen.com/pitfalls-when-learning-to-program/
---
```

You can also opt to import posts automatically from RSS on dev.to as well (look for the option in Settings while logged in).

It's also perfectly okay to cross-post a week after you first published on your blog, to create some sort of temporary exclusivity for your own blog.

Take Action

This chapter covered a lot of possible actions to promote your blog. The truth is, and this applies to the whole book, you don't need to do everything outlined within it to succeed. Instead, you should pick the key actions you're comfortable doing and then execute on them. Consistent action is far more important than trying to do everything but inconsistently.

So your homework, if you will, is to choose at least some of the actions outlined below. If you can do them all, even better.

- If you do, stop thinking of marketing as evil.

- Perform essential on-page and off-page SEO tasks.

- Comment and guest-blog on other blogs relevant to your niche.

- Add your technical blog to planet sites, or start one for your niche if none exist.

- Leverage foreign blogs.

- Don't engage in black-hat SEO techniques.

- Create social media accounts on Twitter, Facebook, and LinkedIn (if you don't have them already). You can also create a Facebook page for your blog (but we'll cover that in more depth in the chapter on social media growth strategies).

- Consider creating Instagram and Pinterest accounts for your blog.

- Create accounts on Reddit and Hacker News, and start submitting and commenting on the sites to get acquainted with their etiquette and culture.

- Cross-post to Medium and dev.to to rebroadcast your posts.

- Leveraging Buffer, announce your posts on your social media accounts while also submitting them to relevant social news sites.

- Leverage Quora for article ideas and to promote your blog.

What's Next

Use the techniques outlined in this chapter, and you'll no doubt maximize the odds of your blog being successful.

An important step after promoting your content—and submitting your blog to various social media sites—is to measure your results. This way you'll be able to concentrate on what works and ignore or adjust your strategy for what doesn't.

The next short chapter is entirely dedicated to the subject of analyzing the traffic resulting from your efforts.

CHAPTER 9

Understanding Traffic Statistics

After you publish and promote an article, visitors from all over the world will come to your blog. This is a very exciting moment. It's important to understand the traffic figures from your web analytics suite and to track them over time.

When it comes to analytics, it's very easy to fall into the trap of vanity metrics —large numbers that boost your ego but don't really help you create a better site or make better business decisions. Great, your business blog had 50,000 visits this month. How many email sign-ups did you collect? How many sales? Traffic correlates with more meaningful metrics such as sales, but only if the site does a good job at converting traffic into sales; and if your blog doesn't sell anything, converting traffic into whatever call to action you target (e.g., getting people to use your side project).

Analyzing statistics is particularly important because you should strive to take an Agile/Lean approach to blogging. When you try something out—a new type of article, a new style of headline, changes to the layout—anything really—you need to validate the hypothesis you formulated. You assume that a change will be welcome and ultimately end up improving your blog, but you don't know for sure until you try it out and verify the results.

Web analytics can also ensure that you know where traffic is coming from, validating your promotional efforts, to see what's working and what isn't, perhaps leading you to double down on what works best for your blog and its audience.

Baseline vs. Spike Traffic

Whenever you publish a new article and promote it on social media and news sites, you're likely to see a spike in your statistics. These jumps (small or big) of immediate traffic can be very encouraging. Your blog will, in fact, receive a certain amount of traffic (i.e., your *baseline*) and then see jumps around the day you publish on. If your post does particularly well on social media upon publication, the spike can be very significant and tower over the usual baseline traffic you receive, as shown in the following figure.

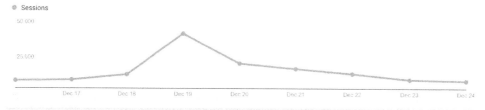

Figure 14—A clear traffic spike, as shown in Google Analytics

If your post does well, the effect usually lasts for a few days. It would be tempting to chase such spikes of immediate traffic. But you can't predict or rely on your posts going viral consistently. So a better and more sustainable strategy for your blog is to actually focus on increasing that baseline of ongoing traffic that you receive.

So what should you do? You continue to publish articles and then aim those articles at sustained traffic over time. In short, you write for readers who'll find you through Google more than social media. You favor articles that will remain relevant for months or years to come (perhaps with the occasional update to keep them relevant). Be patient, since it can take weeks before a post you publish starts ranking in Google.

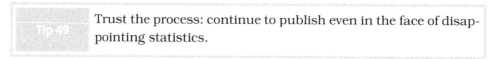

Trust the process: continue to publish even in the face of disappointing statistics.

That's how you ensure that the baseline of traffic grows over time. In the process, you'll also have a few lucky breaks, and some of your posts will indeed receive a big spike when you first publish and promote them as well. You just don't bet or rely on them for the success of your blog.

The greater number of high-quality articles you publish and promote, the more backlinks your site will have. The more backlinks, the higher its authority. The higher its authority, the higher the ranking of all your articles. So every article you publish contributes to the long-term success of your blog, existing content very much included.

If you were to quit blogging for six months, you would still receive most of your baseline traffic every day, thanks to the wealth of existing articles you'll have published. People will find such posts through search engines, links from other blogs, social media citations, and so on.

Of course, ceasing to blog would cause the average number of visitors per day to slowly but surely go down over time. More importantly, your subscribers may begin to vanish as well when they start to notice that you haven't published anything for a very long time.

To grow your baseline traffic, keep publishing, whether your articles cause big or small spikes in your traffic charts.

Key Site Usage Metrics You Need to Consider

Traffic is a generic term. Let's get more specific and consider some of the most common metrics used to describe the number of visitors you receive. (This section also acts as a nonalphabetized glossary.)

- *Pageviews*: the total number of pages viewed by all your visitors. Repeated views of the same page are included in this figure.

- *Sessions*: this concept is harder to define, but it's crucial because it's often used in reports within Google Analytics. When a user first arrives on your site, a session is started within which the user may take many actions, such as visiting multiple pages. After thirty minutes of inactivity, at midnight of the given day, or if the user leaves and comes back from a different site or ad campaign, the session ends.

- *Users*: The total number of people who came to the site—this is calculated by Google by looking at how many people started one or more sessions.

- *New users*: The total number of first-time users (people Google believes to be on your site for the first time [obviously an estimate dependent on browser cookies])

- *Bounce rate*: The percentage of single-page sessions on your site—it's a measure of how many visitors leave after landing somewhere on your site directly from that page versus those who stay and explore other pages before leaving. This number can vary wildly from one analytics suite to another. Since there isn't further action, the session duration for bounce traffic is considered to be 0 seconds long.

- *Average session duration*: Pretty much what it says—how long does the average session last? It can be useful as a metric to determine how engaged your readers are. It's technically more nuanced than that, but you can think of it as the average amount of time spent on the site by your visitors.

The exact implementation of these concepts by your web analytics tool will affect the numbers you see. Google Analytics' figures are generally accepted as a standard of sorts in the industry.

A good analytics solution will show you these site usage details as well as plenty more about the profiles of your visitors (network, country, language), their browser profiles, your site's traffic sources, which search engine keywords were used (for people who weren't logged into Google while performing the search), and so on.

You can learn a lot about your visitors by taking a look at these metrics and by not just focusing on more vanity metrics as a whole (like the total number of pageviews).

Interpret Visit Quantity and Quality

It's important to regularly keep an eye on your site's usage stats. Some of these will tell you how good a job you're doing in attracting visitors to your site. Others will give you a glimpse of how satisfied your visitors are likely to be with what you're providing them.

Sessions, users, and pageviews are *visit quantity* metrics. Average session duration, pages per session, bounce rate, and new users are *visit quality* indicators.

Generally speaking, people pay attention to visit quantity but very little to visit quality. If you were to express the popularity of your site to other people, you would normally list pageviews and users. But do not ignore visit quality parameters. They can give you equally important information about your visitors' behavior.

Visit Quality Statistics

Aim to have high values for *pages per session* and *average session duration*. These numbers correlate to the amount of exploration and reading that your visitors do once they land on your site. If these figures are decreasing over time, you may have to work on the quality of your content and the way you interlink so as to facilitate the discovery of other pages and posts on your blog.

It's fun, for example, to add a Start Here page, prominently feature it on the blog, and then see if these metrics change.

Conversely, aim for a low bounce rate. A high number often correlates to visitors who are disinterested in your content, unless your site is a one-page site by design. For example, the landing page (or entrance page) they reached may not be that relevant to what they came looking for. Or perhaps your layout, eclectic font, unique background choice, ads, and so on are putting your readers off straight out of the gate.

The issue of new versus returning users is a bit complicated. On the one hand, a high percentage of new users indicates you're reaching new audiences. On the other hand, it implies a low number of returning users, which in turn could be a red flag regarding your visitor loyalty or your ability to retain them.

Don't obsess over these general metrics, but be mindful of overall trends.

To help you out, Google has something called Analytics Intelligence, which is a series of insights into your data. Instead of querying the data yourself, this feature monitors your traffic and then alerts you on your analytics home page when a particular anomaly has been detected (both bad and good outliers). For example, Google might notify you that your user loyalty rate has gone down from the previous month (so fewer returning users, percentage-wise) or that a particular post has received an unusual spike in traffic (which in turn can be used to investigate if someone popular linked to you or mentioned you on social media).

> Tip 50   Pay close attention to engagement metrics such as pages per session.

How Social Media Affects Your Stats

As you analyze your statistics, you should always keep the nature of your site and traffic in mind. For example, song lyric sites—which many seem to hate—probably have a pages per session ratio approaching 1.0 and a bounce rate nearing 100 percent.

People come to them in order to read the lyrics to a song and then leave immediately. It's hard to engage users further, due to the very nature of these sites, so their owners opt to be ruthless in their monetization strategy instead. This further alienates users who land on these ad-ridden sites. The one exception to this category is Genius,[1] thanks to its emphasis on comments and lyrics interpretation.

In the case of a technical blog that has been promoted as described in the previous chapter, visit quality metrics will primarily be affected negatively by the fickle nature of social media traffic. Your blog will most likely be relatively

---

1.   genius.com

popular and grow quickly, but you'll also have relatively low pages per session and average session duration figures, as well as a high bounce rate.

For example, ProgrammingZen.com's bounce rate for social media traffic is 84.30 percent, with an average session duration of a little over one minute and 1.30 pages/session. Filtering the statistics for search only shows significantly better results.

In fact, the typical use case for social news users would be to click on your site link, skim the post, and then go back to the social news site they came from to read the comments and perhaps share thoughts of their own there. Or simply to move on to the next story. For social networks, such as Facebook and Twitter, the pattern is not much different.

These low values, affected by the nature of my traffic, aren't cause for concern per se. What really matters is the trend. Are they getting better, worse, or staying about the same over time? If your numbers get significantly worse, then you need to investigate what's causing that problem and what can be done to drive further engagement.

Where Do They All Come From?

OK, you've published a great post and promoted it everywhere you could. Your site usage statistics are now showing a great deal of traffic rolling in. Awesome. But how do you know which promotional channels worked? Was it Reddit or Hacker News that brought in the masses? Perhaps you made it big on Twitter.

And for that matter, how do you even know that all these new visitors are coming for the sake of your latest article and not from an older one that suddenly got popular? (This certainly does happen.)

Any traffic analytics suite worth its salt is going to be able to answer these two important questions for you. You should monitor where your traffic is coming from (i.e., your *traffic sources*) and what it's coming for (i.e., your *top content*). Doing so tells you where it's worth promoting your content and what kind of content and headlines are working for your blog.

Note that with most analytics software it's possible to drill down or filter statistics for a specific URL. In Google Analytics, you could do so from the Content Drilldown report within the Site Content section (which in turn can be found in the Behavior section within the sidebar).

Figure 15, Sources for a specific article in Google Analytics, on page 175, shows the sources for one specific post on my programming blog. Likewise, you could do the reverse from the Source/Medium report within the Acquisition section, drilling down to a specific source (e.g., Reddit) and then selecting Landing Pages as the Primary Dimension. This would tell you which pages on your blog were the most popular among, say, Reddit visitors.

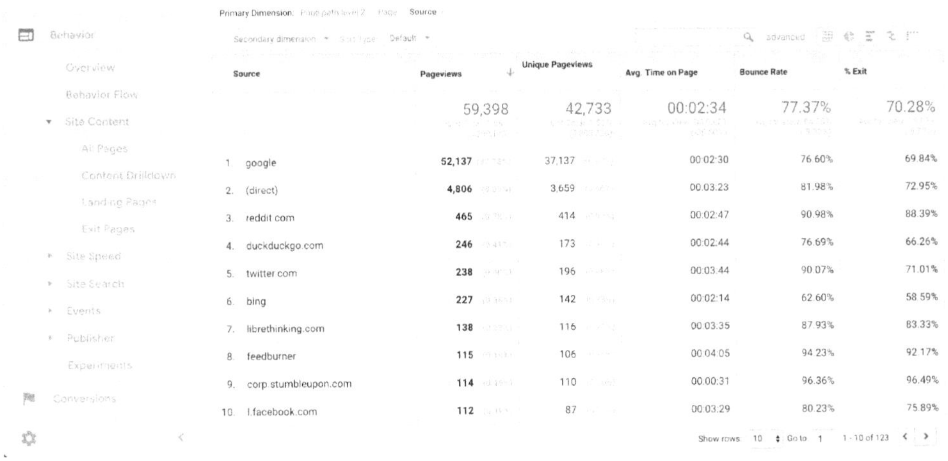

	Source	Pageviews	Unique Pageviews	Avg. Time on Page	Bounce Rate	% Exit
		59,398	42,733	00:02:34	77.37%	70.28%
1.	google	52,137	37,137	00:02:30	76.60%	69.84%
2.	(direct)	4,806	3,659	00:03:23	81.98%	72.95%
3.	reddit.com	465	414	00:02:47	90.98%	88.39%
4.	duckduckgo.com	246	173	00:02:44	76.69%	66.26%
5.	twitter.com	238	196	00:03:44	90.07%	71.01%
6.	bing	227	142	00:02:14	62.60%	58.59%
7.	librethinking.com	138	116	00:03:35	87.93%	83.33%
8.	feedburner	115	106	00:04:05	94.23%	92.17%
9.	corp.stumbleupon.com	114	110	00:00:31	96.36%	96.49%
10.	l.facebook.com	112	87	00:03:29	80.23%	75.89%

Figure 15—Sources for a specific article in Google Analytics

Sources and popular pages are such key statistics that they're even included by WordPress via JetPack. Nevertheless, you should install Google Analytics since it's free (up to 10 million hits per month) and incredibly powerful and can provide you with much more insight into your traffic and your promotional efforts.

Analyzing Traffic with Google Analytics

It's ultimately outside the scope of this book to illustrate how to use Google Analytics to take full advantage of the data it collects from your blog. It's really not hard to figure out the basics, and entire books and courses are dedicated to the subject if you're keen to go in deep.

Nevertheless, I wanted to give you an overview of some of the key features. The UI is subject to changes and improvements, so I'm going to give you general guidance rather than very specific, click-here types of instructions, which are subject to becoming obsolete by the time this book is in print.

If you haven't installed the JavaScript tracker for Google Analytics, as discussed in Chapter 4, Customizing and Fine-Tuning Your Blog, on page 57, please do so now.

When analyzing the statistics for your site in Google Analytics, you'll notice a sidebar with a few options. By default, you'll be in the Home tab, which includes a few default tiles to provide information about your site at a glance. This tab includes the metrics we discussed in the previous section, a real-time tile for people presently on your site, the aforementioned Analytics Intelligence insights, information about user acquisition, geography, time of day, popular pages, and more.

Keeping an eye on your Home tab alone would give you plenty of information about how your site is doing. However, you will also notice a Customization menu. There you will be able to create your own custom dashboards or reports that just include the information you are specifically looking for and nothing more.

This is also where you'll be able to create a custom alert. I set mine to warn me whenever my traffic is five times higher than normal for that given day, a "something got popular" alert, if you will.

Further down in the sidebar of your Google Analytics account, you should see a series of report categories. Currently, they are Real-Time, Audience, Acquisition, Behavior, and Conversions.

Real-Time answers the question, *Who is on the site right now?* Audience, *Who has been on the site?* Acquisition answers, *How did they get on my site?* (including paid advertisement campaigns, if you ran any); and Behavior, *What did they do once they got on my site?*

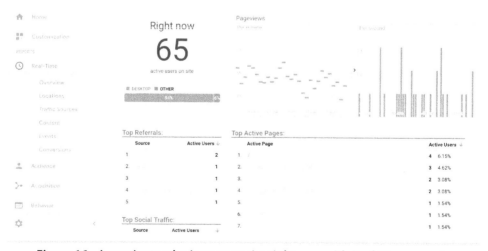

Figure 16—Investigate who is on your site right now with Real-Time reports

Finally, Conversions provide reports for specific goals you set, and this feature essentially answers the question, is my traffic converting to the particular call to action(s) I'm interested in? For example, are people signing up for my newsletter? Are they downloading my product? Are they signing up for my SaaS? And so on, depending on your specific circumstances and goals.

> **Tip 51** Spend some time investigating all the reports available within Google Analytics.

You'll likely find some of these reports more useful than others, and as such it's a good idea to add them to your own dashboard. Likewise, creating custom reports is not a bad idea either. For example, I like to be able to quickly know which content (aka articles and pages) is doing well in a given week as far as referral traffic is concerned. And I like to know the same for organic search traffic, too, to see which articles are ranking well for popular keywords (if any). Hence, I defined two custom reports that provide me with that information at glance.

Understanding what keywords, content, and traffic sources are working for you will give you the edge when deciding what type of content to focus on and how to go about promoting it.

As previously mentioned, searches by logged-in users coming from Google are no longer reported. This means that the keywords shown under Acquisition > Search Console > Queries are only a partial view of the actual queries entered by users. Nevertheless, this is a relevant sample and is quite useful information.

You'll also want to keep in mind that most blogs receive the majority of their traffic from Google. When you check out your statistics, you'll probably learn that you're not one of them, particularly in the beginning. Using the promotional techniques outlined in the previous chapter, you're quite likely to attract a good deal of immediate traffic after publishing a post. It'll take months before traffic from search engines (Google, for the most part for blogs in English) will overtake traffic from social media.

Thankfully, that's not cause for alarm. Keep focusing on attracting search traffic (something that's much more predictable than viral content) and do a little happy dance whenever a post of yours happens to go viral (to some degree, this will usually be within your niche, since you're not breaking news about the Kardashians, after all).

> **Tip 52** Watch out for referral spam.

Occasionally, you might see shady domain names in your top referrals. These aren't genuine sites linking to you; instead, they're an attempt to get you to check out their spammy sites. They're often referred to as referral spam. There are convoluted ways to get rid of such domains from Google Analytics,[2] but unless it's a major problem for you, you can safely just ignore them.

Google Analytics also allows you to set alerts and conversion goals. Alerts are useful for receiving emails (or SMS) when traffic levels reach a certain target or goal. When you're starting out, set your alert to something low, like 500 pageviews per day, depending on your expectations. For my already established blogs, as I mentioned before, I like to get alerted when I get five times the regular traffic. You can see my setup in the following figure. Again, it's essentially a "gone viral" alert. For a brand-new blog, setting the threshold to 500 pageviews per day is quite sensible, however, as five times very little traffic is still very little traffic.

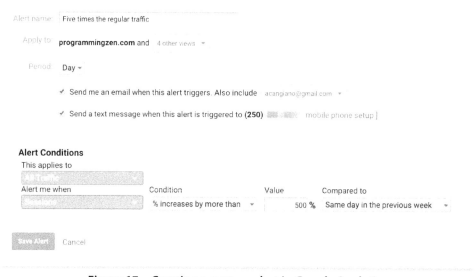

Figure 17—Creating a custom alert in Google Analytics

Conversion goals help you keep track of specific events, such as a reader visiting a particular thank-you page after signing up for your newsletter. These are useful to quickly get conversion statistics on events such as downloads, email subscriptions, sales, and so on directly in your Google Analytics reports.

---

2. neilpatel.com/blog/how-to-remove-referral-spam-in-your-google-analytics/

As we'll see in Chapter 12, Promoting Your Own Business, on page 229, if you run a startup that sells products or service subscriptions, you'll want to keep track of your conversion funnel. This way you'll be able to track the progression from random visitor to actual customer. You can do so through custom reports in Google Analytics or through a specialized (but pricey) solution such as KISSmetrics.[3]

Keep Track of Your Blog's Growth

In the business world, there's a common expression that says that what can be measured can be improved. In my experience, there's a lot of truth to that observation. It's important to assess the current statistics and verify how they evolve over time as a result of your efforts when you start a blog or try to revamp an existing one.

Some entrepreneurs, particularly in startups, like to use a KPI (key performance indicator) dashboard or spreadsheet. As a blogger, regardless if you have a company or not, it's a good idea to do something similar.

Use Excel or Google Sheets to keep track of your blog KPIs. Which ones? The choice is up to you, but definitely include your site usage metrics (as described in this chapter) and your email subscription numbers. Eventually, you may also want to keep track of conversion rates (e.g., from visitor to subscriber), revenue, and so on.

For the time being, you could include a column for the date when you checked your stats, and then have columns for pageviews, users, avg. session duration, bounce rate, the total number of articles on your site, and the number of email subscribers. Update your spreadsheet once a month to see how your site is growing and evolving over time. At some point, you might want to plot some of these metrics to better visualize your progress and trend line.

A final word of advice: don't obsess over statistics. By all means, check your stats for five minutes a few hours after publishing an article. In the beginning, you might even want to schedule 15 minutes each day to check out your statistics. But don't let doing so become an addiction. Checking your global stats once a month to fill your KPI spreadsheet is plenty. It's a fun and useful process. Just remember that checking your stats continually won't help them grow or be a very productive use of your limited time.

---

3. kissmetricshq.com

Other Analytics Tools Worth Considering

Google Analytics is a great analytics suite that allows you to gain deep insight into your traffic. It's all you'll ever really need to analyze how people find out about your site and what they do once they reach it.

That said, there are some specific tools that can work in conjunction with the insight you obtain from Google Analytics. For example, if you use MailChimp or a similar newsletter management system, you'll want to pay close attention to the built-in analytics within that particular web application. Yes, Google Analytics will know when traffic came from an email campaign, but MailChimp Reports will tell or show you these figures:

- How many people the email was sent to
- How many opened the email
- How many clicked on the links within the email
- Which links were clicked the most
- A chart of open rates and click rates over time
- A comparison of your stats against the industry average
- How many people bounced (i.e., the email failed to be delivered), unsubscribed, or complained

And much more. If you have a mailing list handled through a service like MailChimp or Aweber, you should definitely pay attention to this data, especially if you make changes, like updating the layout of the newsletter. How did it affect your results? You can easily compare and see if your changes got you closer to your goals or introduced a regression.

Figure 18—Mailchimp's 24-hour performance chart

Another useful tool is a good A/B testing suite. This enables you to serve different versions of a page to your users to determine which one is more effective.

You're essentially running experiments. For example, you might have a sign-up form in one position on version A of your page, and in a different position or as a pop-up on version B. The suite will show version A to 50 percent of your traffic and show version B to the other 50 percent.

It'll then tell you which one led to a higher number of sign-ups. If the difference is statistically significant, you'll be able to switch your site to the winning version for good. This is a very common tool for optimizing landing pages, where the conversion rate really matters. In fact, if you are selling an e-book on your landing page, doubling your conversion rate means doubling your income without attracting any more traffic than you already were.

Optimizely and VWO are two popular, if somewhat expensive, options.[4] This is a crowded space, however, and many options are available to you should you decided to optimize your site by running experiments.

I mentioned before that I like to use Ahrefs for my advanced SEO needs. Ahrefs, Moz, and similar tools offer many analytics functionalities. A key functionality they offer is to analyze your blog for SEO faux pas, as well as tracking your ranking for desirable keywords.

These, in turn, offer you insight into how well your SEO efforts (or changes you introduce) are performing as far as Google is concerned. Of course, they're also very useful for researching your competitors' performance and new article opportunities.

It's worth noting that there are alternatives to Google Analytics itself. It's hard to compete with such an industry standard, so these suites will often offer some key feature that makes them stand out. For example, Mixpanel allows you to log specific events from within your site or mobile app and log them into their system, integrating with other analytics tools and more.[5] If you have a complex app and want to track complex interactions within your pages, this tool definitely goes further than what you can accomplish with Google Analytics (or at the very least, it makes it significantly easier). You likely don't need it for a blog, however.

In fact, I can think of many other niche analytics tools, but I believe that using too many of them can quickly become overwhelming and a sort of overkill for bloggers. Start with Google Analytics, and add tools only when the need for them genuinely arises.

---

4. optimizely.com and vwo.com, respectively.

5. mixpanel.com

Take Action

Your homework for this chapter is fairly straightforward:

1. Create an account with Google Analytics and add its JavaScript tracker within your blog.

2. Familiarize yourself with Google Analytics and the home tab, and explore all the built-in reports available within the Real-Time, Audience, Acquisition, Behavior, and Conversion sections. If you don't have any data yet, just wait a week before exploring your results.

3. Consider creating a conversion goal for your main call to action (e.g., newsletter sign-up).

4. Under Customization, select Custom Alerts to create a traffic alert. Receiving your first alert will be quite exciting and a validation of your efforts.

What's Next

With this chapter, we have added another piece to the puzzle. At this point in the book, you're ready to go out there and get noticed.

What's missing from your tool belt is one more chapter about user engagement, and then the last two parts of the book, which are dedicated to benefitting from your hard work and further scaling your blogging activities, respectively.

For the time being, wax on, wax off.

Great spirits have always encountered violent opposition from mediocre minds.

  Albert Einstein

CHAPTER 10

Building a Community Around Your Blog

As a blogger, you bother with promotional activities because you want to attract a following. You can then expose this group of readers to your thoughts and writing, amplifying your influence and reaping all sorts of benefits (as we'll see later in the book). Once again, it's all about getting your content in front of the right audience.

The next logical step in this process is to take a closer look at this readership. You aim for a large pool of readers, sure, and that gives you quantity. But what about quality? Ideally, you want a loyal, engaged public who is receptive to your ideas, content, and projects.

You want readers who are fans of your work, who share it with their friends, and who are ready to do word-of-mouth work both on- and offline for you. You want readers who feel like they're part of a like-minded community that they're able to enrich via their active participation, comments, and presence on your site.

In this chapter, we'll focus on how to build precisely that kind of community. The emphasis will be on your blog itself, rather than on social media, because we'll further discuss how to attract fans on sites like Facebook and Twitter in the last section of the book (specifically in Chapter 14, Beyond Blogging: Strategizing for Social Media, on page 257). We'll also spend time discussing some unpleasant aspects of being a successful blogger—chiefly, dealing with criticism and trolls.

Engage Readers

Your main aim is to transform silent spectators (also known as *lurkers*) into active participants of your community. Readers who interact with your site and feel like they're part of a community are far more likely to contribute and promote your site (because they feel it's *their* community).

Below I've listed a variety of effective ways to achieve a greater level of active participation from your readers. You're not expected to do all of these activities at once. Instead, try some and, as usual, measure the response from your community. Then iterate. Each blog is a unique case, so you need to verify what actually works for you and your site.

Keep in mind that your time is limited, so you may not be able to carry out many of these activities on an ongoing basis, even if they've proven to be effective for you.

> **Tip 53** Prioritize and aim for tasks that have a great reward-to-effort ratio.

- Write great content. Remember how it's all about your content? Compelling, interesting, unique, useful, and/or opinionated content will always attract comments, engage readers, and help you build a community. For a good example of how unique, noteworthy content helps you build a community, check out *LessWrong*,[1] a blog that attracts a large community of people who are interested in rationality.

- Ask for comments. As we've touched on before, calls to action are a very powerful tool. In your posts, explicitly ask your readers to share their opinions or ideas in the comments section. Some folks will do just that, simply because you suggested it. The sole inclusion of the word *comment* in your post will statistically increase your blog's commenting rate.

- Reply to questions. If you receive questions or requests for clarification in your comments section, try to be helpful and reply to those queries with a comment of your own. Nobody likes to be ignored. Likewise, thank people who compliment you and your work. Address them by their name, if they provide one. Remember that a person's name is often the sweetest sound to them.

- Credit updates and corrections. We have discussed this before, but always credit commenters when updating or correcting a post thanks to their suggestions.

- Praise insightful comments. Don't just reply to commenters who ask you a question. Instead, take the time to publicly thank insightful commenters for their participation and contribution by replying to them. Acknowledging those who share valuable information will encourage them to continue

---

1. lesswrong.com

contributing (and others to join in). Positive reinforcement can do wonders for your community.

- Don't provide all the answers. In your posts, leave some space for people to add more to the discussion.

- Ask questions in your posts. Get people to interact with you by letting them answer questions you may have. These can be generic ones, such as, "What do you think about this?" or specific ones, such as, "And that's my story. At what age did you start programming?" Aside from asking questions specifically to solicit comments, feel free to ask questions you're genuinely unable to answer yourself (e.g., technical questions for which you don't know the answer). You'll be surprised by the level of expertise shown by some commenters.

- Ask for feedback. This tip has been mentioned before in the book, but it warrants repeating. Engage your readers by asking them for feedback about how you're doing and what sort of material they'd like to see more of. Don't do this weekly, just every once in a while, but it can help bring out lurkers that you haven't heard from before. Don't forget surveys either. (There are many premium web apps for surveys, but I find good ol' free Google Forms to be quite sufficient.)

- Poll your readers. Along the same train of thought, you can poll your readers about topics that they're interested in on a fairly frequent basis. Just remember to share the results of such polls with your community in a new post, adding your own reflections on the results and inviting readers to share theirs.

- Answer commenters' questions in new posts. If a particularly good question has been posted by someone in the comment section, you may want to provide an extensive answer in a new post. Always credit the commenter of the original question and thank them for the question in your post. This will make the commenter feel special, and you may be rewarded with a backlink (if the commenter also has a blog) or a social media mention. Don't forget to reply to the original comment with a link to your extensive answer.

- Showcase commenters. Check to see if your blogging engine has a plugin or feature to showcase your top—and more recent—commenters on your home page or sidebar. People may try to game this for a backlink or "fame," but overall you'll still get an increased level of participation.

- Promote commenters to bloggers. Publicly or privately invite your best regulars to become guest bloggers or to contribute as coauthors for one or more articles on a topic they have shown expertise in.

- Post a collection of the best comments your site has received. Once your blog is well established, consider periodically publishing a digest of the most insightful and informative comments you've received on your blog. Credit the authors and link back to their blogs or sites, if provided with their comments.

- Comment on your commenters' blogs. This can be time-consuming, but you can greatly increase the chances that commenters will be back if you visit their blogs and leave comments there (assuming their blogs are in the same niche). The concept of reciprocity is hardwired in the human brain and it can foment relationships over time.

- Reply to emails. Fans of your blog will feel a personal connection to you. Much like a celebrity, you may not know your fans, but they know you. So do not ignore their emails. Instead, try to be kind, friendly, and appreciative of their enthusiasm for your work.

- Create a serene environment. Use comment moderation and reminders to keep discourse civil and any form of harassment at bay. If your blogging engine doesn't support comment moderation and you're not opposed to it, you can always remove harassing comments immediately after they're posted. (More on these types of comments in Forms of Criticism, on page 189.)

- Help your commenters. If a commenter of yours has a site or product that's particularly relevant to your audience, feel free to mention or review it as a means of showcasing the commenter's work to your readers. Acknowledge that you are mentioning or reviewing—unsolicited—a site or product you found by checking out a commenter and that you'll continue to do the same thing with other people's sites or products in the future. The commenter will no doubt feel appreciated, you may gain a business connection, and this generous act may motivate more people to stop by and comment.

- Challenge your readers. Ask your readers engaging, difficult questions or puzzles for which you have devised an interesting solution. Make such questions relevant to your niche, and they will no doubt generate a series of responses on your blog and elsewhere. (Your readers may also show you a much better solution than the one you came up with yourself.)

- Organize contests and giveaways. Readers love these kinds of posts because they provide them with a chance to benefit directly from your blog. As you'll learn in Chapter 11, Advancing Your Career with Blogging, on page 199, these are easier to organize when the product you're giving away is provided to you for free. Regardless of how you obtain the goods, you can further engage your commenters by selecting judges for your contests among your most valuable commenters.

- Highlight your commenters' expertise. Organize an Ask Me Anything (AMA) or Ask an Expert series of posts with the most insightful experts who hang out on your blog. Once a month or once a quarter, you could solicit questions from your readers on a specific topic that will then be answered in a post by an expert you picked from your commenters or among your professional connections. This encourages commenting all around, but it's best done when you already have a decent following.

- Go where the comments are. By following the promotional workflow described in the previous chapters, you'll sometimes end up attracting more comments on social news sites like Reddit and Hacker News than on your own blog. An article of mine, for example, attracted over four hundred comments on Reddit, but only thirty or so on my blog itself. That's OK. Those are huge communities whose members will have higher loyalty to fellow members than to you and your blog. Read those off-site comments and, if necessary, feel free to occasionally engage commenters on such sites, too. (Just keep in mind that you're now playing a road game, so to speak.)

- Tell readers that they are part of a community. Use words like *we*, *this community*, *participants on this site*, and so on. This will help readers identify more with the community that might form around your blog. Then lead the community by organizing events that help participants bond and feel like they're a part of something meaningful.

Supplement Your Blog with Community Tools

In addition to the suggestions above, you should also consider the following tools and activities that go beyond a regular blog:

- Start a forum. Comment sections limit the discourse to the topic at hand. Having a forum can greatly increase the level of interaction among your visitors, with a much greater degree of freedom when discussing topics within the boundaries of your niche. You may even use the forum's questions and answers as a way of generating more content for the blog itself. Just relentlessly credit people when you do so.

Slack and Facebook Groups are valid alternatives to traditional forums.

Select your most active forum users and commenters as moderators to further reward them, but always keep an eye on their behavior (some people can single-handedly destroy a community by going off on power trips). Finally, don't start a forum until you have a large audience. Dead forums (fora, if you prefer) with very few participants just come across as sad or pathetic to most new visitors.

- Start a wiki. A well-organized and curated wiki for your niche can bring lots of traffic to your blog, provide a useful service to the community at large, and make your readers more prone to produce—and not just consume—content. Encourage your readers to contribute to the wiki and reward them by highlighting the best contributions by your readers in your blog posts and on key spots on your site.

- Hold office hours. In order to further connect with your community, why not have an office hours session once a week during which readers can call you up to discuss whatever they wish for fifteen minutes? Be very clear about the time zone and rules of conduct, and you'll be surprised about the connections you make and the opportunities that may open up for you. Plus, you'll come across as extremely approachable and serious about your site.

- Organize group chats. Using tools like Google Hangouts, Discord, and Slack (or even good old IRC), you can organize monthly chats with and among your readers. Announce such chats in your blog posts well in advance, and again, make the exact time of the chat clear for people in different countries. You can even set a specific, relevant theme for each chat.

- Along the same lines, if you're not camera shy, consider organizing Q&A sessions and live-streaming them on YouTube or Twitch. People will be able to ask you questions in real time through a chat interface, and in turn, you'll be able to answer them live.

- Infiltrate other communities. Without spamming in any way, don't be afraid to mention or link to your blog/community from other forums and communities (particularly in your signature). Before you do this, however, you should contribute value to said communities and become a respected member or you'll be seen as a spammer. Contributing to other communities without hiding the existence of your own is an easy way to increase the size of your community.

Don't spread yourself too thin when it comes to community-building initiatives.

Remember to use this and the previous list about how to engage readers as references to be inspired from and not as a to-do list. You'll quickly become overwhelmed otherwise.

Forms of Criticism

As you work at increasing reader engagement and comments, you'll quickly discover something unpleasant. Almost regardless of what you write, attracting a large audience means being on the receiving end of some criticism.

People are going to take issue with what you say because any content that's worth sharing is worth discussing and debating. Even if you try not to be controversial, you'll inevitably end up being the target of a small percentage of vocal detractors of your content.

The following are some kinds of criticism you may encounter when running a successful blog. For each of them, you may see a rude or a polite version, depending on the mood and attitude of the commenter.

- *Constructive criticism*: The commenter will point out flaws in your reasoning or argument or in the facts you present. It's not pleasant to be wrong, but this is the best kind of criticism because you can deal with it by simply admitting to being mistaken or by rationally and factually defending your position. You may end up "standing corrected," agreeing to disagree, or convincing the commenter that you were right in the first place. The focus of this commenter is the truth and adding value to the discussion, so an intellectually honest debate can be had. It's an occasion to grow that you should cherish.

- *Disagreement criticism*: Particularly for controversial or opinion-based pieces, you may encounter commenters who disagree with your viewpoint or observation. None of you will be objectively right or wrong, because both stances may be valid and defensible. It becomes a matter of opinion, with no objective truth in sight.

- *Nitpick criticism*: The commenters will focus their criticism on marginal issues that don't really affect the validity of your article. Other times they might fixate on minor details you got wrong. This may lead the conversation in unpredictable directions that veer far off the original topic. You might thank them for the minor corrections, but don't overly engage with this type of comment, especially if the commenter isn't polite to you.

- *Misguided criticism*: People don't always pay attention to what you say and may start commenting on articles they haven't read or fully understood. As a result, you'll see comments about points you already addressed in your article or against arguments you never made. Your position will often be misrepresented with this type of commenter, and you'll experience the annoyance of dealing with the straw man logical fallacy.[2] It will also teach you *defensive blogging*, wherein you address the most likely objections as you write the article, and you try to be as clear as possible to make it really hard to miss the point. Some people will still manage to, however.

- *Personal criticism*: Sometimes the focus of the reader's criticism will be you rather than the content itself. This is one of the most annoying types of criticism because it questions you personally as an individual or professional rather than disagreeing with one of your stances. It's also much easier to defend a viewpoint than to try to justify that no, in fact, you are not stupid, evil, a shill for a corporation, an idiot, or an [insert insult of your choice here]. Thanks to these comments, you'll get acquainted with another common logical fallacy known as an ad hominem argument.[3] (Insults are not ad hominem arguments per se, though.)

- *Metacriticism*: This type of criticism won't focus on the actual details of your content or on you personally. Instead, the commenter will question the whole existence of your post or blog. Among technical audiences, this isn't uncommon, because some commenters will take issue with the commercial nature of your blog, your inclusion of affiliate links, the presence of ads, your moderation of comments, or perhaps the fact that you are reviewing a book that was provided to you for free.

- *Trolling*: The sole purpose of these comments is to stir up controversy or intentionally rile you up. They usually lead to drawn-out, pointless debates known as *flame wars*.

Examples of Criticism

Let's see how each of these types of comments pans out with an example. Imagine that you published an article in which you compare your existing Android phone and your new iPhone on your gadget blog.

---

2. en.wikipedia.org/wiki/Straw_man
3. en.wikipedia.org/wiki/Ad_hominem

Constructive Criticism

Here's some constructive criticism:

> I don't think it's fair to draw conclusions about how responsive the two operating systems are when you are using devices that were released two years apart from each other. The brand new iPhone clearly has a hardware advantage here.

Reply to these types of comments and address the issue without getting emotional. Admit when you are wrong and argue back when you aren't. Be aware that this type of justifiable criticism sometimes escalates to other types of unacceptable criticism or overly long discussions, at which point it's no longer worth engaging.

Disagreement Criticism

Disagreement criticism looks like this:

> I don't agree that the two app marketplaces are roughly equivalent at this point. When I switched to Android, I couldn't even find an app to do online banking with my bank!

Generally speaking, don't reply unless you see a gaping hole in the logic or you think you can add more to what you already wrote by addressing the objection. People have a right to disagree with you, as long as they are not complete jackasses about it. It's also fine to sometimes end the argument by simply agreeing to disagree.

Nitpick Criticism

A nitpicker may say this:

> Why would you update a perfectly fine smartphone? That's just wasteful.

Here the aim of the critic isn't relevant to the main point of your article. If your blog is moderated, publish such comments, but generally ignore them. If the comment was posted elsewhere, like Reddit, ignore it as well. Yes, you want commenters, but quality trumps quantity every time. If the nitpick is about a technical detail, feel free to reply to address this minor point.

Misguided Criticism

Misguided criticism may present itself like this:

> How can you say that XYZ has worse battery life than the iPhone? It's a new phone with a new battery; of course it will last longer.

Assume, for the sake of this example, that the article actually explains how a brand-new battery was put inside the Android device and the battery life of both phones was tested over the course of a week in a fair manner. The commenter here would have skimmed the post and posted a knee-jerk reaction to your claim about battery life without reading the details. Feel free to rectify commenter misunderstandings. For example, you could reply by saying, "We actually placed a new battery in the Android phone as well, Scott." Just don't let it escalate into a long argument. Reply once. If they take the hint, good. If they persevere, ignore it.

Personal Criticism

Personal criticism can be very unpleasant and may look like this:

> Color me shocked! An Apple fanboy who just spent two grand on a crappy phone has to justify his purchase by dissing his previous Android phone. News at 11.

You're free not to even let a useless personal attack like this get past the moderation. Unfortunately, when a comment like this is posted on Reddit, you have no control over it. It's extremely tempting to reply, but don't. You don't have to prove yourself to anyone who attacks you (provided you disclose any affiliations you have in your post, of course).

Metacriticism

Metacriticism could be any of the following comments:

> Stop submitting crap like this to Reddit. This is just blogspam.

> This article was written to make money with the affiliate links.

> You're too much of a coward to publish my comments.

If you have control of the channel (e.g., the comment was posted on your blog), you have a choice. You can either approve the comment or opt not to publish it, depending on your stance on moderation. Just know that if you approve such a comment, it rarely makes sense to engage in arguments over it. Sadly, it also creates a less friendly comment section for the rest of your readers if the comment is posted on your blog.

Trolling

Finally, here's an example of trolling:

> Nobody in their right mind would buy an iPhone. Stop being a bunch of sheeple, and get yourself a real phone.

The comment doesn't have a genuine counterpoint to the article. But the end result is that people who have an iPhone will feel personally attacked and will want to reply to this commenter. Don't let such comments through unless you are ideologically opposed to all forms of comment moderation. Above all, ignore them when you see them on social media sites. No good can come from replying to them.

So-called trolls thrive on replies. The good old Usenet mantra was "Don't feed the trolls" for good reason. Ignoring them is the best thing you can do. The most challenging part is figuring out if the person is trolling or is just misguided. The example above is obvious, but successful trolls are subtle and make you think you're dealing with a person who's "wrong on the Internet."[4] When in doubt, let them be wrong.

You'll need a particularly thick skin to stomach the comments on Reddit. It can be a great community (particularly in selected subreddits), but criticism, sarcasm, and cynicism are highly rewarded in most subreddits. From time to time what you write—as well as you, personally—will be shredded to pieces in the Reddit comments. Ignore the negativity as much as you can, and you'll discover that it's worth submitting there for the sheer number of new readers you'll attract. (Don't be surprised if your totally benign programming articles get you likened to Hitler at least once on Reddit.[5])

> Tip 56   Smaller subreddits tend to be friendlier.

Hacker News is friendlier and the average commenter there tends to act with greater maturity. Unfortunately, I must say that in the past few years, it too has become more cynical and negative. So don't be upset if you receive negative comments there as well, should one of your articles hit the home page.

Your Mantras When Dealing with Criticism

The way you handle comments and moderation is highly personal, so you may disagree with some of my suggestions. That's okay. Try to stick to the following principles though, as they will serve you well:

- Welcome constructive criticism as an opportunity for growth.
- Haters gonna hate. Accept it.
- Don't feed the trolls.
- Consider all criticism, but argue only when strictly necessary.
- Moderate comments that poison the conversation and report serious abuses when possible.
- Keep writing.

---

4.   xkcd.com/386
5.   en.wikipedia.org/wiki/Godwin's_law

Remember that in most cases it's not you, it's them. You can't be liked by everyone, and sometimes in life people will act like real jerks. This is particularly true when large audiences and anonymity are involved.

If you receive death threats or have serious concerns about your safety, report such abuse to the authorities. It's rare that you'll have to deal with drastic situations like this, but it does happen occasionally, depending on how controversial you are with your opinions.

As a straight white man I can't speak about much abuse when it comes to attacks to my personal identity online. The worst I get is the occasional remark about me being overweight (though I'm increasingly becoming less so) or somewhat racist comments about the fact that I'm Italian/an immigrant in Canada, neither of which really bothers me, to be honest.

If you're a minority in terms of race, gender, or sexuality, you're more likely to receive real harassment as a blogger. You have my sympathy for that, and I think you should ruthlessly moderate rude comments and, again, report egregious abusers. Take care of yourself, and consider using a pseudonym if you're concerned about being the target of hatred or abuse. Whatever you do, and I know it can be hard, it's especially important that you don't let them silence your voice.

Don't become another victim of criticism. Criticism will ruin your day in the beginning, and it's tempting to give up writing and promoting articles when you're met with such hurtful words. You're not alone in this struggle.

Most readers will love the fact that you share your knowledge and thoughts with them. They'll side with you. Don't deprive 99.99% of your readers because 0.01% is made up of haters, lunatics, harassers, trolls, stalkers, fanatics, racists, homophobes, sexists, people jealous of your success, and other undesirable, sad people. With any large audience comes a small percentage of people who haven't learned about the importance of the golden rule yet.

If you're truly struggling with some members of your personal anti–fan club, consider Googling resources for dealing with harassment, cyberbullying, and stalking. Plenty of help is out there.

Also, if you're at the point of giving up on blogging due to the nasty comments you receive, as a last resort you can consider turning comments off on your blog. This is increasingly more common and acceptable among bloggers. It won't make comments people leave elsewhere disappear, but at least you won't receive notifications of such comments in your inbox to soil your mood.

Tip 57   If you actually wish to be notified of mentions around the web, use Google Alerts.

We'll talk further about preparing for success, including very positive side effects, in Chapter 11, Advancing Your Career with Blogging, on page 199.

Take Action

Using the advice provided in this chapter, think of which specific actions, among the many ones suggested, you'll take to increase commenting activity and create a community around your blog. Specifically, consider the following:

- Will you have comments in your blog?

- Will you moderate comments before publishing them?

- Which techniques will you choose to increase participation?

- Will you want a forum, Slack, or Facebook group for your niche or blog? If so, set it up.

- When facing harsh criticism, reread the relevant section in this chapter before responding.

What's Next

This chapter concludes the part of the book that's dedicated to promoting your blog. Promotion is a never-ending process and something you'll wind up experimenting with throughout your career as a blogger. These chapters, however, should give you the foundation required to get your content out there in front of people and for you to be better equipped to deal with the occasional negativity when some jerks show up.

We'll touch on promotional activities again in the final part of the book, which is dedicated to growing and scaling your blogging endeavors.

Back to the immediate future: turning the page will lead you into the fourth part of the book, which is devoted to reaping the benefits of your work as a blogger. This is the fun part, where you'll learn how to maximize your reward as well as experience the satisfaction of having your content widely read and appreciated.

Part IV

Benefit from It

Success is attaining your dream while helping others to benefit from that dream materializing.

Sugar Ray Leonard

CHAPTER 11

Advancing Your Career with Blogging

In this section of the book, you'll learn all you really need to know to benefit from your blog. By now, you should know how to invest your time and energy to write and promote your content. It's only fair that you learn how to reap the fruits of your labor.

This chapter focuses on career-related benefits, as well as some monetary benefits (if that's of interest to you). The next chapter is aimed at those blogging for a startup or a larger company, or to promote a side project. No matter what your circumstances are, it should give you the right mindset to adapt your approach and take full advantage of what blogging has to offer.

Improve Your Skills

As previously mentioned, blogging is not simply a pulpit but also a conversation starter. Your readers will generally be ruthless about inaccuracy and mistakes in your posts. Likewise, if your thoughts and ideas are flawed or can be stretched further, chances are your visitors will point it out, either on your blog itself or elsewhere online, such as Reddit, Hacker News, or Twitter.

This collaborative, if you will, aspect of blogging has the huge benefit of helping you learn and grow, thanks to the power of constructive criticism and the discussions that will ensue from your posts.

The experience of blogging regularly will enhance your writing and technical skills, help you develop your arguments, and possibly provide you with a thicker skin to handle harsh comments. It could be argued that, overall, you'll become both a better person and a better communicator because of your blog.

The benefits derived from blogging don't end here, though. When you're researching a topic for an article, you'll be doing focused learning for a specific and practical purpose (something that turns out to be very effective).

Teaching others requires a good mastery of the subject at hand. Personally, I find that teaching something highlights any shortcomings in my own knowledge on the topic at hand. If I can't explain a concept or subject simply and effectively to others, it means that I don't know that topic well enough yet myself.

Sometimes you'll have ideas or assumptions in your head that are nebulous because you haven't formalized them or fully thought them out. As soon as you start to make your case in an article, you may find out that those ideas were misguided, flawed, or weak. Or, on the flip side, it may turn out that they are remarkable and worthy of sharing at large.

Either way, blogging can help clarify, streamline, and spread your thoughts further, all with the help of your audience. So not only do you get to be a teacher who helps others, but you grow and learn much in the process as an individual.

Communication and well-defined ideas are at the heart of most professions. So if you're a programmer, blogging really stands to make you a better programmer. If you're a CEO, blogging can make you a better businessperson. Focus your writing on what you want to improve on and not just on what you know best.

> **Tip 58** Blog for the position you want, not the one you have.

Blogging can be a useful way to remember things you've learned but since forgotten, help you look up snippets of code from the past, and/or share technical information with a small group of friends or colleagues. I have occasionally Googled for something and found the answer in an old post of mine—a fun experience were it not for the nagging suspicion that I may have become dumber than my previous self. ;)

Finally, some technical bloggers take a political approach to their blogging. They blog because they feel so strongly about their ideas that they want to convince others to believe in the same principles, with the ultimate goal of improving the field they work in.

Advance Your Career

Blogging can advance your career in multiple ways. Improving your skills, as just discussed, is the first way. But there's much more to it, depending on your current position and ambitions.

As an Employee

Blogging can help you land a better job. It can facilitate the process in two primary ways.

First, your blog advertises to the world that you exist. Prospective employers may come across a particular blog post and be impressed by your depth of knowledge and your personality (remember to have a distinct voice that shines through in your writing).

A post on my programming blog helped me land my current job at IBM, and I often receive job offers from some of the most popular tech companies in the world as a result of my blogs and social media presence.

Second, your blog acts as a sort of résumé/curriculum vitae. A blog can give you a much more detailed outlook on a person's interests, attitudes, and skills. If your blog is highly compelling and you come across as a friendly, approachable expert, your chances of getting hired when you apply for a job or when someone finds your blog are much higher.

> Tip 59   Include a link to your blog on your traditional résumé.

If your main goal is to find a better job, place a LinkedIn button/badge and a link to your printable résumé on your sidebar in a spot that's easy for visitors to quickly notice. If you have other relevant or important presences online, such as on StackOverflow and GitHub, link to those or embed badges for them as well.

In fact, if you're a student or are unemployed at the moment, don't be afraid of placing a call to action, such as "Hire me" or "Give me a job," within your navigation bar, sidebar, and so on. Then link to a *sales page*, where the thing that you're selling effectively is yourself.

If you suddenly become unemployed, you can also consider making a post announcing that you're now available for hire.

Write a nice landing page that details what you are looking for, and be sure to include links to your résumé, projects, open source contributions, and so forth. If prospective employers think you'd be a good match, they can use the contact form and details you provide on the page to get in touch and discuss employment opportunities with you.

> Tip 60   If you're available for hire, mention it in your author box at the bottom of your posts.

I would argue that a compelling, popular tech blog and a solid social media presence are one of the easiest ways to secure a job in today's economy.

As a Freelancer

Blogging can aid you as a freelancer by helping you find more clients and even command higher rates. The way you go about it isn't all that different from the role of a job seeker.

You still need to blog on subjects you intend to be hired for as a freelancer to showcase your expertise in the process. For example, if you're an Android OS freelancer, you'll want to focus on writing about developing Android applications in Java or Kotlin. Don't just talk about it, but show code and HOWTO material that clearly demonstrates your mastery of the subject.

> **Tip 61** As a freelancer, include content that appeals to prospective clients, not just fellow developers.

If you can score a domain such as [TOPIC]freelancer.com or similar, you'll position yourself ahead of the curve. Even if you can't, make sure that your blog does a good job of selling you and your expertise to both humans and search engines. Your theme keyword could be *Android freelancer*, for example. You'll want that same keyword throughout your blog, even if the site is actually located at firstlastname.com.

For example, your home page's title could be "John Smith's Blog—The Adventures of an Android Freelancer," with the latter portion becoming your tagline, even if your site URL doesn't mention Android.

As a freelancer, aside from making it obvious that you are indeed a freelancer, you need your "Hire me" call to action to be very prominent. In particular, the sales page for your services needs to be specific. Don't say vaguely that you'll do anything; instead, try to be specific about what you specialize in and what you're good at.

Above all, don't waste yours and other people's time. Include your rates. You'll spare yourself the grief of dealing with low ballers, and you'll attract qualified prospects who are serious about hiring you for a given assignment. If you don't have a set hourly rate, provide a range or starting price point. For example, a designer may say, "Logo design starts at $2,000." Naturally, the higher your prices, the more impressive your portfolio and services need to be.

Your contact form should have a series of fields to collect information about a project, in case a prospective client wants to get the process started right away. Also include your information, such as your location, (business) phone number, email, and so on.

Another important point for freelancers to remember is to leverage guest blogging on other peoples' sites if your own blog isn't that well known. Guest blogging requires work, but taking advantage of large audiences on other blogs and online magazines can truly make the difference between a continuous stream of clients from the very beginning or a long dry spell as you gradually try to grow your own blog.

Obtain Freebies

A nice benefit of being a popular blogger is that you get contacted by publishers, publicists, and others who will try to give you freebies in the hope that you'll write about them or their products.

Publishers may offer to provide you with free copies of books that are relevant to your blog's subject matter. This is by far the most common type of freebie among tech writers (just like beauty bloggers tend to receive free cosmetics). There are other kinds of offers that may show up in your inbox, too, including mobile apps, desktop software, extended trials, free subscriptions to web applications or publications, the occasional gadget, and so on.

Such offers may look like subtle bribes to your average programmer, but that's the way the PR industry has operated for a long time. You can only review something ethically if you've used, tried, or read it first, and it wouldn't be fair for you to pay out of pocket for a product that a publisher wants you to consider. So the compromise is that you get a free review/media copy, without an obligation to review it if you don't like it.

Take advantage of this unique opportunity to obtain free books and other products you're interested in. Sometimes you may even approach the publisher yourself and ask for a review copy, instead of having one come to you first. Over time you may develop relationships with publishers who'll routinely send you books in an unsolicited fashion.

There are a few ground rules to keep things ethical and fair for everyone involved in these kinds of relationships. I suggest the following:

- Always use a disclaimer in your review, letting readers know when you've received a product for free. This isn't just ethical, it's actually the law (at least it is in the United States).

- Inform the publisher/publicist that you'll only review the product if you find it to be worth recommending. It would be unfair to the publisher for you to bash a book that was given to you for free (though some bloggers opt to do this), and it would be unethical to your readers to promote a book you found to be subpar.

- Only post reviews of books you've read (or products you've tested). Again, if a book or product isn't good, feel free to not review it at all and ideally inform the publisher about your decision not to post a review.

- If you requested the book, find the time to read it and write a review post in a timely manner. Then send the link to the publisher or publicist.

- Don't feel obliged to read books that are sent out by publishers to their list of media contacts if you haven't agreed to read a particular title and it just showed up at your door. Of course, if it's of interest to you, read it. If not, feel free to not review it and perhaps inform the publisher that the books they are posting out to you are not a good fit for you and your blog.

- There will be times when you may build up a backlog of freebies to review, which can become overwhelming. Time is your most valuable asset, so don't overcommit yourself to reviewing too many products during a given period of time.

- If a publisher is making you jump through hoops to get the freebie, consider giving up on the deal. Remember, you're the one doing them a marketing favor.

- Organize contests and sweepstakes in collaboration with publishers, since most publishers and readers alike will love this idea and be eager to go along with it. Giveaways tend to involve social promotion (e.g., participants can get extra tickets for the raffle if they share the post on social media), and these can be good ways to expand your blog's reach as well.

If you follow these rules, you'll enjoy a wealth of great products for free, some of which can earn you money, thanks to affiliate programs such as Amazon Associates.

> Tip 62   Consider Rafflecopter for your giveaways.

Your readers will receive great product recommendations, and the publisher will get some much-wanted exposure for the new product. It's a win-win situation for all the parties involved.

Deal with Opportunities

As a successful blogger, you'll be approached by a variety of people, not just those inquiring whether you'd like to review their products. How you respond to these offers is up to you. In this section, I'll cover some of the most common inquiries and my personal philosophy about how to handle them.

- *Students asking for help with homework*: The response to this should be a no-brainer. Simply don't do other people's homework for them. If you're feeling kind, provide some guidance by pointing them to available resources.

- *People asking for professional advice*: It's up to you to decide if you want to help such people. In general, I tend to—as long as doing so doesn't become a time sink.

- *People trying to connect with you personally*: You'll receive invites on LinkedIn, Facebook, and other social networks from people you've never heard of before. You don't know them, but they know you. Much like with celebrities, they may consider you a friend, even if you don't even know they exist. Ask yourself if you want to connect with everyone or if you're going to be selective. Does your take on this change based on the social network? For example, you could accept connections on LinkedIn but not on Facebook (my approach), or vice versa.

- *Outsourcing companies (or individuals looking for a job)*: If you're in a decent position at a well-known company, you'll be inundated by companies and individuals who are ready to work or consult for you. Depending on your position, you may not even be allowed to hire such people, though you'll still receive plenty of requests. Ignore or reply to them depending on your circumstances and availability.

- *Recruiters looking to hire you or asking you to help them find a candidate*: This is another example of a highly personal choice. Provided the recruiter didn't just mass spam a list of people, but put care to address me personally with a relevant job offer, I tend to foster the relationship rather than burn bridges by ignoring them, or worse—asking them not to bug me. Instead, I freely refer their jobs to friends who are looking for a relevant position. I do not, however, post their job ads on my blog, as some have asked me to do in the past. Not for free, at least.

- *Conference organizers inviting you to speak*: Being a speaker on stage is a fun, challenging experience unless you have stage fright. Unfortunately it often requires you to travel and spend copious amounts of time preparing a world-class presentation. Be very selective about this type of engagement. One remarkable presentation a year that gets everyone psyched about you and your message is far better for your career and blog than five unremarkable ones, in my opinion.

- *Bloggers and members of the media who want to interview you*: Interviews are another activity that can increase your blog's reach and your own visibility. Unlike conferences though, the amount of time required is usually way less substantial, so the trade-off between what you get and what you give is more in your favor. Don't miss out on worthwhile interview opportunities.

- *Publishers inviting you to write for them*: If you've always dreamed of writing a book, by all means take advantage of this opportunity. Just be warned from someone who has written more than one book—being an author takes time and it won't usually make you rich. However, it can be a career-altering move. As usual, figure out what you want and then see if writing a book helps you reach that goal. Sometimes you may be asked to be a technical editor/reviewer rather than an author. The commitment and glory are both drastically lower than when you're writing the book, though this still requires hard work and an ongoing portion of your time.

- *SEO "experts" and link buyers*: People will contact you to tell you how your company (even if you don't have one) isn't doing well with various search engines, and they'll propose all sorts of shady techniques to improve your Google rank. Save your time and money and ignore such emails. Reputable SEO experts don't usually spam people at random and propose their services to bloggers. Other times, such SEOs will want to buy links on your blog. It's not a good idea to do so, even if they link to a reputable source, due to Google's stance on purchased links. Ignore them, reply that you aren't interested, or propose a nofollow sponsorship if you want to see how legitimate they are.

- *People interested in getting an autograph*: OK, this one is much less common, but it can still happen to you. How would you react if someone at a conference were to ask you for an autograph? Or to take a selfie with you for that matter? If you prepare mentally for this occurrence, things should go smoothly and you'll be able to enjoy this type of flattering encounter. (Just remember, it's not an autograph if you're asked to sign a blank check.)

Think about how you want to approach these opportunities so that you can establish a consistent and fair policy before you're required to take action.

Put your blog URL and your Twitter account on your first and last slide when giving a presentation.

Usually such invitations end up benefiting you and your blog in some capacity. For example, an invitation to speak at a conference can further extend your blog's reach and get more people interested in your work. The downside is that it's easy to overcommit and either burn out or deliver poor results.

You must strive to avoid overcommitment. Being selective becomes key. You'll ignore many requests since they're little more than spam, but the day will come that you'll genuinely reject someone with a legitimate offer. So you should also consider what kind of tone you intend to assume when replying to someone that you're not going to work with.

My suggestion is to avoid burning bridges or making people feel rejected. Instead, plainly explain why you aren't interested. More often than not the case will be that you don't have enough time to commit to something new. Opt for kindness. Stating "I appreciate you reaching out with an interesting opportunity, but I'm afraid I don't have the time X would require" is a sincere and gentle way of getting off the hook. If the person doesn't take the hint and insists, then feel free to reply in a firmer—but still polite—manner.

Other Benefits for Startups

Although customer acquisition—the subject of the next chapter—is without a doubt the most common motivation behind why startup and business owners want to blog, there are other benefits for startups, too. Let's review the most typical ones.

- *Providing status updates during outages*: When the service you provide goes down, you may find yourself dealing with a mob of angry customers. As mentioned multiple times before, your blog can be an outlet to communicate with your users and broadcast status updates during crisis situations. If you wish, you could even have a stream of updates at status.your-company.com. You would then echo such brief posts to social media as well (e.g., on Twitter).

- *Customer development*: If you write content that attracts your prospective customers from the very early days of your business, you'll be able to leverage this target audience by surveying them with regard to the urgent questions you have about their needs and the way your business will attempt to meet those needs.

- *Attracting new hires and interns*: Talk about your wonderful offices, the great hardware and perks you provide developers, the state-of-the-art software engineering methodologies you employ, your company culture, your team's bragging rights, and be sure to including lots of photos (particularly of people, not just offices). Paint an accurate picture of how cool it is to work for you and mention that you're hiring and/or looking for interns. You'll attract highly qualified candidates in little time, saving you many thousands of dollars in recruiting efforts.

- *Finding partners and investors*: This one is a little trickier, but business partners and investors can certainly be among your blog readers, too. If you blog about the cool things your company has been doing and the impressive metrics that show substantial growth, you may end up getting noticed by the right person. There's no magic wand that can make this happen; instead, it's all about increasing your "luck surface area."[1]

Make Money from Your Blog

Generally speaking, advancing your position within your organization, finding a better job, amplifying your influence, and establishing yourself as a leader in your field are the most valuable benefits for a technical blogger.

Still, for necessity or inclination, you may want to directly monetize your blog. We'll cover selling your own products, if you're a startup or small business, in the next chapter. Here, we'll consider some approaches to making some side income from your blog.

The following are some of the most common direct monetization strategies for blogs:

- Ads
- Sponsorships
- Affiliate links
- Subscriptions and Patreon supporters
- Donations
- Merchandise
- Selling your own products

Let's review each of them, except for the last one, which will be covered in the next chapter.

---

1. codusoperandi.com/posts/increasing-your-luck-surface-area

Ads

Thanks to ad networks such as Google AdSense,[2] placing ad units on a blog is very straightforward.

Such networks act as intermediaries between advertisers and publishers (i.e., you). The details vary, but essentially ad networks aggregate a series of ad spots on a large number of sites and let advertisers pay to place ads in them. This frees you from the burden of finding advertisers, agreeing on a fair price, collecting payments, and so on.

If you intend to place ads on your blog, you can sign up for free with Google AdSense (the most common choice among bloggers) and then set up one or more ad units. AdSense is the site owner (i.e., publisher) counterpart to the Google Ads program, which is the interface used by advertisers to buy ads on search results and sites that are part of Google's program.

You'll be provided with an embeddable snippet of JavaScript code for each ad unit you create, which you then place in strategic spots on your blog. You could, for example, select a full banner above each of your posts, a vertical skyscraper for your sidebar, and a box ad unit at the bottom of each post.

Ads that are relevant to your content will automatically be displayed inside such spots on your blog, and your account will earn a variable amount of money each time a visitor clicks one of those ads. This is called *contextual advertising* because the ads served vary depending on the content of the page.

The amount of money you receive will be what the advertiser paid in order to have an ad displayed on your site—minus the substantial cut that Google takes. Realistically, this means putting anything between a few cents to a few dollars in your pocket for each click. Such numbers really depend on the competition level and niche you're in, but for technical blogs the CPC (cost per click, meaning the cost to the advertiser) you'll earn tends to be below a dollar.

Google will display a maximum of three ad units regardless of how many units you place on a given page. This means that you shouldn't place more than three ad units on any page of your site. (Each unit may contain a multitude of ads, however, and this is handled automatically by Google.)

WordPress users can include ads in the sidebar by adding a text widget containing the JavaScript ad code provided by AdSense. For other spots, such as below each post, users can choose their theme's ad options (if provided by the theme), use one of the many ad plugins available, or edit the theme's files

---

2.   google.com/adsense

directly (the least preferable option, as explained previously). Common theme files to edit are header.php, footer.php, and single.php (for adding content above or below each post).

Blogger users can configure their ads' strategy under Earnings and take advantage of the AdSense gadget to customize their layout.

Regardless of your blogging engine, you can also add a search box powered by Google AdSense, if you wish. When users search your site with it and end up clicking any ad that's displayed on the results page, you get a cut. Google also enables you to include native in-feed ads within your RSS feed.

Using fonts and colors in your ad units that match your theme will increase your CTR (click-through rate). Squares and wide rectangles also tend to have good CTRs. Likewise, choosing key positions in your template will help you achieve a higher CTR. In my experience, visitors are significantly more likely to ignore AdSense units that are located in the sidebar than those placed before (much more so) or after your posts, as shown in the following figure.

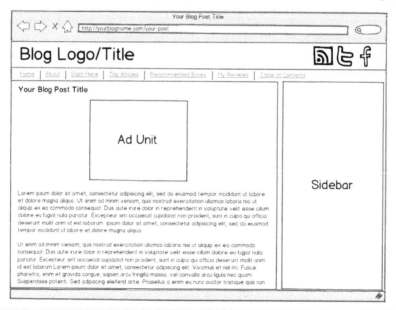

Figure 19—Favor in-post ads over sidebar ads

To increase your revenue you can either bring in more visitors or up the number of clicks you get from the current volume of visitors you receive (your CTR). Ideally, you'll be able to do both.

Avoid positioning your ad units in a way that makes them appear to be actual content, such as horizontal ad units that contain a few links that resemble a list of categories or pages for your blog. Such ads shouldn't be placed where your navigation bar would normally be. Misleading your visitors is never acceptable, and Google will sometimes intervene in situations where such behavior is reported.

Detailed reports will allow you to figure out which ad units and products (e.g., AdSense for content, search, and feed) are performing well. These reports include details such as the number of ad impressions/pageviews you served, the CTR, CPC, RPM (revenue per mille: *mille* is Latin for "one thousand"). RPM is often called CPM elsewhere, where the *C* stands for cost. AdSense will also suggest optimization strategies and recommendations from time to time to help you squeeze more revenue out of your blog.

Don't try to game the system or you'll be banned and all of your unpaid earnings will be frozen. Avoid clicking your own ad units, and never invite your readers (or friends) to click on them either.

Finally, it's important to note that Google requires you to have a privacy policy on your blog (as do many other networks), a subject, you may remember, we discussed in Chapter 3, Setting Up Your Blog, on page 33.

AdSense may be the most common ad provider for bloggers, but it's certainly not the only option available. A wide variety of ad networks exist, and some of them may be good matches for your blog.

Some of these networks pay publishers in the same way AdSense does, on the basis of the actual clicks received (CPC-based), whereas others sell your ad spots at a fixed rate per thousand impressions (CPM-based) or per given time period (e.g., $80 a month). For the latter two types of ad networks, an ad's CTR does not affect your earnings.

Keep in mind that if you opt for an ad network as a technical blogger, you may be better served by niche networks that specialize in the area of your blog, if one is available. For example, for developer and design blogs, Carbon tends to perform better than the more generic AdSense, in my experience.[3]

	Keep an eye on fellow bloggers in your niche to spot niche-specific ad networks.
Tip 64	

---

3. carbonads.net

In the majority of cases, there's an approval process that your site must go through before you can join a network, some of which are by invitation only. The main criteria are always traffic and content quality. If you show up with a brand-new site and little traffic, relatively few ad networks will take you on. Build a following first.

Shortcomings of Ads for Technical Blogs

Placing ads on your blog is a low-effort monetization strategy, particularly if you stick with a network like AdSense, which won't make you jump through hoops in order to have your site accepted. Unfortunately it's not the most profitable way to monetize your blog (as we'll discuss later), and it comes with a series of negative implications. Let's review the most noteworthy shortcomings.

- Ads tend to put visitors off, particularly technical folks. Don't place too many ads, or your blog will end up looking like a spam site and you'll be bouncing visitors like a pinball machine.

- Accept that many technical users will have ad-blocking browser extensions installed, such as AdBlock Plus. Don't try to detect and block these users from viewing your content, as some sites do. It's your right to show ads with your content. It's your visitors' right to decide not to see them.

- Search engines tend to dislike overly commercial sites that are filled with ads and other offers and may penalize your search result ranking if you go overboard. Two to three ad spots are okay.

- Technical audiences tend to ignore ads. This means that your click-through rate will be low, which in turn means that for every thousand impressions of your ad, you'll only get a few clicks and bring in very little revenue. The end result is that your average RPM (again, your revenue per thousand impressions of an ad unit) won't be worth boasting about. In most cases you're looking at the lower end of the US$1–$5 range. In turn, this means that if you manage to attract 10,000 visitors in a given month, that ad unit will only bring you between $10 and $50, and the actual figure will probably fall in the lower end of the range. This is why AdSense is sometimes humorously referred to as "blogging social welfare."

- It can be argued that you're inviting the visitors you worked so hard to attract to leave by clicking ads at the rate of mere pennies per visitor lost, instead of steering them toward calls to actions that are more profitable to you (e.g., signing up for your newsletter or buying your ebook).

- At times, people have been banned from ad networks like AdSense through no fault of their own, simply because foul play has been suspected. Many thousands of dollars have been lost by bloggers in such disputes, where there is little recourse for the innocent. It's unlikely to happen to you, but it's conceivable. Don't depend solely on ads.

Should You Place Ads on Your Blog?

In the beginning, when you're just getting your site off the ground, don't place ads on your blog. Initially you'll have relatively little traffic, so the chances of earning anything substantial from ads are remarkably slim. On the other hand, the chances of putting off your early visitors are substantial.

> Tip 65   Don't place ads on your blog until you have at least 10,000 pageviews per month.

As a general rule of thumb (and depending on the economic goals you've set for your blog, if any), don't place ad units until your site is established and receives at least 10,000 pageviews per month. However, I would think twice before placing ads in your feed even at that point, as they'd be going out to your most valuable readers, the people you want to maintain and not annoy (with ads) the most.

Also keep in mind how well-defined of a niche your blog currently is in. A targeted audience will generally perform better ad-wise than the audience of a general blog. In the case of contextual advertising through programs like AdSense, the ads that are shown will be more relevant and interesting to your audience, who will then be more apt to click and, in turn, generate more revenue for you.

Once you've managed to attract a decent following and have established yourself somewhat in your niche, use a tasteful number of ads (e.g., one or two, three at the very maximum). Don't, initially at least, view ads as your main source of income for your blog, because they likely won't be. Instead, ads can be *one* source of revenue in a diversification strategy that includes multiple sources of income.

> Tip 66   Diversify your sources of blog income.

Finally, don't place ads on your company blog. Your main objective with a company blog shouldn't be to make an extra $50 a month by filling your blog with ads. Your primary product, whatever that is, has far more potential to earn you real money. Putting off readers or sending them away from your site when they click an ad doesn't make sense from a business perspective.

The same applies if you're not an established startup or business but you start selling a digital product like an ebook through your blog.

Sponsorships

Conceptually not far from ads, sponsorships are a good way to make money with your blog. The basic idea is that you find companies that are relevant to your niche and then contact them about sponsoring your blog. In exchange for a monthly fee, you'll provide them with high visibility to your blog's readership.

Before you approach potential sponsors, though, you should have detailed information about your audience, which is easily obtained from Google Analytics. Prepare a page on your blog or as a PDF that you'll send by email with the details of your demographic as well as with details about what you're offering. (Include survey data as well, if you directly surveyed your users recently.)

If you're good with graphic design, make your presentation appealing and be sure to include lots of attractive graphs. Eye candy sells.

Traffic stats aside, what really seals the deal is an appealing offer. You could offer any or all of the following perks to potential sponsors.

- *A banner advertisement in a predefined format and position on your blog* (a so-called "media buy"): Link to the sponsor, of course, but opt for a nofollow link (i.e., `rel="nofollow"`). This way Google won't think that you're selling links for SEO purposes. In your offer, let the sponsor know that such links will be nofollow to comply with Google's policies. Specify if you're limiting the offer to the front page (unusual) or throughout the blog (more common).

- *A thank-you note and backlink at the bottom of your posts*: For example, "This post was sponsored by Acme, the best solution for all your cartoon explosion needs."

- *A periodic thank-you post that includes a shout-out to your sponsors, links to them, and a brief explanation of what they offer your readers:* If your sponsor turnover is not significant, this kind of post can become annoying for your readers, so you'll want to keep them infrequent (e.g., once per quarter).

- *Interviews, guest blogging, and other content-based arrangements that benefit both the sponsor and the readers*: Always disclose your affiliation. Don't hide from your readers the fact that you have a sponsor.

- *Trials, giveaways, and special offers that are useful to your reader and great marketing for your sponsor*

If you don't have any companies in mind, do some research to see if companies in your niche are already sponsoring other blogs. It's far easier to convince them to also sponsor you than it is to approach a company that's never heard of blog sponsorship before.

You can also have an Advertise page in your navigation bar, as well as a Your Ad Here banner or button in a spot that you're offering to sponsors that links to that page. Making a post in which you explain that you're accepting sponsors is also an aggressive but legitimate way to go about it.

There are companies that facilitate the whole process so that it's virtually identical to selling ads through a network, but part of the benefit of sponsorships is that you deal with a handful of companies only, one on one, for months or even years at a time. So once your initial agreement is set up, there isn't much work to do on your part except to collect payments. You may as well cut out the middleman, establish good professional relationships with companies, and keep all the revenue for yourself.

You can set your own price by basing it on an honest CPM. If you require a sensible $3 CPM for a given sponsorship offer, you can divide your average monthly pageviews by 1,000 and then multiply that by $3. So if your blog were to attract 100,000 pageviews per month on average, you can request $300/mo. from your sponsor. Generally speaking, the more prominent your banner and overall sponsorship offer and the narrower the scope of your blog, the higher you can go with your CPM rate.

> **Tip 67** Aim for high-quality, niche-relevant sponsors only.

As usual, respect your readers. Opt for tasteful ads and banners. Don't permit ads that include sounds, and limit the animation level of your banners to a minimum. Likewise, don't feed your readers low-quality, spam-like sponsors just to make a quick buck. I constantly receive offers for sponsorship and to link purchases from companies I don't trust. I always turn them down, and so should you.

For startup or company blogs, sponsorships, just like ads, don't make much business sense.

Affiliate Links

When I was growing up, I set up an arrangement with my local computer store in which I would refer people asking me for computer-buying advice to them and the store would then give me a small percentage commission based on what those people bought. I didn't know it at the time, but the service I was providing to that store was a form of affiliate marketing.

This type of arrangement can be extremely beneficial for both the company and the affiliate. The company receives new business from customers it may not have reached otherwise, and the affiliate gets a commission for each sale that can be directly traced back to the affiliate's site (online, usually through a cookie or coupon).

Typically, online affiliate offers work like this:

1. The affiliate links to an offer with a tracking ID embedded in the link.

2. A visitor visits the link and is redirected to the landing page on the company's site.

3. A browser cookie is stored with a certain expiration date on the computer of the visitor. This cookie associates the visitor with the affiliate that referred them.

4. If the visitor makes a purchase at any time while the cookie is still valid, a commission is provided to the blogger/affiliate by the company.

Depending on the type of goods and the company's approach to affiliate marketing, the commission can be anything between a few percentage points to 100 percent. Yes, you read that right. Some companies will go so far as to give away the entire sale price for a promotional period in order to attract more affiliates and perhaps recurring customers.

More commonly for digital goods such as ebooks and courses, margins are exceedingly high, which means that content producers routinely offer affiliates a 50 percent commission rate for all sales made within a large period of time after the initial referral (e.g., sixty or ninety days, which, again, is often tracked via cookies).

As you can imagine, you can generate a substantial amount of money from affiliate marketing if you have a large-enough audience that you're offering relevant services and products to.

As a blogger, you already have the audience, and as we'll see in a moment, you can find relevant affiliate offers to present to your readers. Affiliate marketing really is an approachable monetization strategy you can't afford to ignore.

Before jumping into key affiliate programs for technical bloggers, I want to provide you with a little background about the stigma associated with affiliates (and affiliate marketing) in general.

The reason affiliate marketing has gained such a bad reputation is that the economic incentives to promote a company's products are very high. Here we're not playing around with a dime a click. Depending on the product and the commission, we could be talking as little as a few dollars or as much as hundreds of dollars (on the higher end of the scale) per referred customer.

Affiliate marketers have gone to great lengths to grab such generous commissions, including spamming, misleading, and downright scamming users.

I really encourage you to look past the negative connotations that are associated with affiliate marketing. In this section we'll take a very ethical approach to this subject, which can reward you handsomely without the need to mislead, spam, or promote crappy offers or products to anyone.

Amazon Associates: A Blogger's Best Friend

Amazon Associates is one of the earliest and most popular affiliate programs on the web.[4] Every time you refer a customer to a given Amazon site (e.g., Amazon.com) with your tracking ID, you'll receive a small percentage of the total cost of whatever that person purchases during the next 24 hours.

Some affiliate marketers and bloggers greatly underestimate the earning potential of Amazon Associates on the basis of the tiny cookie duration (only 24 hours, instead of, say, 60 days) and the small commissions (usually between 4 and 10 percent, depending on the product, instead of the 30 to 75 percent commissions that are common for digital goods elsewhere).

While both counts are true, Amazon Associates provides many benefits that make it a very worthwhile program for reputable bloggers.

- Virtually everyone knows and trusts Amazon as a store. You don't have to convince your visitors that their credit card number won't be stolen when they shop there.

---

4. affiliate-program.amazon.com

- Amazon's inventory of physical products is fantastic. They carry so many items that you can always find something of quality to promote, nearly regardless of your particular blogging niche.

- Amazon spends millions of dollars studying ways to increase the percentage of visitors who end up buying products (i.e., optimizing the conversion rate of their pages). Your main goal is really to send traffic to Amazon by way of your affiliate links, after which Amazon will take care of converting many of these visitors into customers, thus earning you a commission on all of those sales.

- Unlike other referral programs, you get a cut for every sale that's made within a 24-hour period, not just for sales of the product you promoted. My technical blogs have received commissions for goods that I never promoted, including watches, swimming pools, and toys. That's because you may send visitors to check out a book, but once on Amazon they may purchase other books or other products (either instead of or in combination with the original item) within the 24-hour period for which your tracking ID is valid. Those unexpected, additional sales add up quickly.

- Unlike some other affiliate programs, it's considered normal for bloggers to routinely link to Amazon in their posts. This means that your post archives will contain many posts that include Amazon affiliate links, generating you commissions long after you initially posted them.

Amazon also offers Native Shopping Ads,[5] which are a great alternative to Google AdSense (in my experience, certainly a more rewarding one).

Amazon has several associates programs, depending on the locale of the store you're targeting. You don't have to reside in one of these countries to sign up for any of their respective affiliate programs.

Register for each of the programs according to the demographics of your traffic and your blog's language. For example, if most of your traffic arrives from the States, the U.K., and Canada, then apply for each of those three associates programs. (You'll be applying three times.) You can select the locale using the drop-down menu in the top right corner of the Amazon Associates login page.

Amazon even allows you to link these accounts and use a snippet of JavaScript to automatically redirect your readers to the closest store available, maximizing your profits.

---

5. affiliate-program.amazon.com/home/ads

You can also provide links to multiple Amazon locales next to the name of the product by linking the words U.S.A., U.K., and Canada with the correct URLs for each, as follows: "The Passionate Programmer (USA, UK, Canada)." This has the advantage of allowing people to choose the marketplace regardless of their current geographic location (e.g., an American reader currently in Canada for a work trip).

> Tip 68   Review technical and business books you read.

Here is a cheat sheet for getting the best out of the Amazon Affiliates program.

- Be genuine and caring. Don't promote a product simply to make an extra buck. Only endorse the kinds of books and other items you would recommend to your best friends.

- Write reviews of technical books you've read and products you've tried. A recommendation from someone who's perceived as an expert in a given niche can convert to sales like crazy, and people will love reading your thoughts on a given item that's near and dear to their interests.

- Create lists of products (e.g., 5 Books Every Agile Developer Should Read). They can be cheesy or downright good advice. Opt for the latter.

- Announce new books. Let your readers know when an important new industry-related book has been released—even if you haven't read it yet and therefore can't write a full review at that point in time. One time I announced that a new edition of a book was out. I wasn't the first to announce it, so I didn't even promote the post (it was a heads-up for my regular readers); however, someone saw it and submitted it on Slashdot. My announcement made the front page of Slashdot, bringing me a few thousand unexpected dollars. Results like this are not typical, but it can happen from time to time. Besides, you're offering a very valuable service to your readers. (Feel free to use my service, anynewbooks.com, to discover new books in the first place.)

- Mention books and other products. Even if the point of your post is not to review a product, you can still mention it. At times, that innocent mention can lead to awesome rewards if your post ends up getting popular.

- Start linking to Amazon right away. Unlike other forms of monetization, affiliate links aren't as annoying, so you can start using them right off the bat.

- Use images from Amazon in your posts. In fact, take your own pictures and/or videos of products you're blogging about if you happen to own or have access to said items; this will prove that you are promoting something you've tried yourself. When you include book or product images in your posts and pages, link them to Amazon with your Associate ID. Such images will increase your CTR and convert well.

- Don't cloak your URLs (i.e., hide that they're Amazon links) unless the tool you use to generate and track these links does it for you. Even then, use disclaimers and disclose that your posts contain affiliate links. Honesty and transparency are important currencies as a blogger.

- Don't specify an exact price. Prices vary too much over time, plus doing so is against Amazon Associates' terms and conditions. If you wish, say something vague like "which sells for less than $XX at the time of writing." Generally speaking though, steer clear of discussing prices unless the fact that a particular item is on sale is the whole point of your mention.

- Create resource pages. For example, I have a list of recommended Ruby and Rails books on my programming blog. On the math blog that I sold, I used to keep a huge list of recommended mathematical books organized by category. Both brought me thousands of dollars over the years. Stop and think whether such a page can be created for your own niche and, if so, get to work making it. It'll be a useful resource for your readers and an easy moneymaker for you.

- Make your Amazon links nofollow. Google and other search engines will be less likely to penalize you for the presence of commercial links.

- Finally, a counterpoint—if you're a founder who runs a company blog, it's your call as to whether or not you should include Amazon Associates links when linking to products on Amazon. If your main objective is to promote your own product or service, losing Amazon's commissions in exchange for coming across as more genuine and less motivated by money in your recommendations may be a worthwhile trade-off. If you're an indie developer, the revenue such links can generate may help supplement your income, so opting for them can be a good choice. If you're blogging for an established company or a well-funded startup, then don't; you're after far bigger fish.

Where to Find Other Reputable Offers

Keep your eyes peeled for other reputable affiliate offers and networks. For example, an alternative to Amazon Associates (at least for books) is the affiliate program from The Book Depository.[6]

eBay also has a similar program. Although these affiliate programs won't typically make you as much money as Amazon can, they're good alternatives if you were rejected by Amazon, unable to sign up with it, or otherwise opted not to go with Amazon.

Likewise, don't ignore niche-specific programs. For instance, a photography blogger can sign up with stores who offer affiliate programs, such as B&H Photo Video and Adorama.[7]

Depending on your niche, there may be other companies looking for affiliates to promote their products that would be really good fits for your site.

Check out popular affiliate networks that have a huge variety of products and CPA offers. CPA stands for Cost per Action, because the affiliate is paid a fee when the referred visitor takes the desired action, so this applies not just to a product purchase but also to other determined actions, such as signing up for a given newsletter, a trial offer, and so on.

Common players here are CJ Affiliate, ClickBank, and ShareASale.[8]

Particularly with ClickBank, you'll have a majority of low-quality information products, with a few gems here and there. If you can find decent products relevant to your niche and post, there's no shame in promoting ClickBank offers, however.

CJ Affiliate and ShareASale can both have rewarding affiliate offers from more mainstream makers. So apply for all of these programs as a publisher/affiliate, and then promote the offer that makes the most sense, regardless of where it originated.

> Tip 69   Promote only products you'd buy yourself.

With the emergence of self-publishing, you should also keep an eye on new releases of good digital titles within your field. Over the years, I've made decent

---

6. affiliates.bookdepository.com/affiliates/
7. bhphotovideo.com and adorama.com, respectively.
8. cj.com, clickbank.com, and shareasale.com respectively.

money from self-published PDF and video releases created by esteemed colleagues in the STEM field.

Finally, continue looking for possible offers among products you use regularly. Affiliate programs for technical audiences can be found virtually everywhere these days. You can promote hosting, premium blogging templates, domain registrations, email marketing providers, and other similar products simply by using them and then advertising that you do so (and why that's the case).

In fact, I recommend trying to find high-fee, niche-specific affiliate offers. For example, on my Rails Hosting page,[9] I link to affiliate hosting and deployment tool offers. The revenue per referral is much higher than Amazon and the cookie duration is also much longer than 24 hours. In some cases, I'm linking to subscription offers, and the affiliate will reward me with a cut on a monthly basis while the customer I referred stays subscribed. This adds up quickly.

Depending on your niche, you should be able to find similar offers.

Other Common Strategies to Monetization

As listed earlier in this chapter, there are three other commonly adopted strategies to monetize a blog: subscriptions (including Patreon supporters), donations, and merchandise.

Users aren't exactly fond of *paywalls* (sites that require a payment in order to access articles), but if you attract a loyal following you can offer monthly subscriptions in exchange for some form of exclusivity. You could offer extra features to pro users (such as your articles in PDF and audio format), access to exclusive content that's not available to your regular readers (e.g., a screencast section of your site or live chats), or exclusive access to a useful resource (e.g., a private forum where you personally help people).

WordPress users can look into plugins such as WP-Members and WishList Member to obtain membership site features for their blogs.[10] Users of other blogging systems may have to get creative to find similar features for their blogging platform or use third-party scripts/services.

The risk of membership sites is alienating your user base and creating two classes of citizens, so to speak, among your readers (paying and nonpaying). However, over time, it's become a much more accepted idea, thanks to the advent of Patreon.[11]

---

9. programmingzen.com/the-best-ruby-on-rails-hosting-services/

10. wordpress.org/plugins/wp-members/ and member.wishlistproducts.com, respectively.

11. patreon.com

It's now accepted that creators and other online influencers will have special perks and exclusive content for users who support them economically each month. So it's definitely a worthwhile option to increase your blogging revenue.

Receiving donations is much simpler than adding premium membership features to your site or creating exclusive, valuable content for your supporters. You simply add a payment processor button (e.g., PayPal) and invite readers to donate. You can make it cute and ask for a specific amount that would pay for a coffee, a beer, or a slice of pizza rather than having this approach come across as out-and-out panhandling. Add a nice coffee cup icon next to your call to action, and you may get a few donations here and there.

> Tip 70   For one-off donations, consider ko-fi.com.

In my experience, one-off donations aren't a particularly lucrative approach to monetizing your blog. To make them work and be sustainable for you, you'll need a particularly large audience of very loyal readers. The recurring model (for special perks) offered by Patreon is significantly more appealing to your readers.

Merchandise sales can quickly add up and, unlike the early days of the web, you don't have to ship products out of your garage. For using services like CafePress, Spreadshirt, and Zazzle,[12] all you really need is a nice design.

If you did a good job in terms of branding and ensuring that your readers feel part of a community, you may end up selling quite a few T-shirts and other forms of merchandise with your logo or slogan on it. If you have a cute mascot like Reddit or Hipmunk has, for example, selling them will be even easier.

Keep in mind that you don't have to limit merchandise to your logo or mascot. With the help of a good designer, you can very easily create cute, fun, witty T-shirts and other gift shop–like items that are relevant to your niche and make some extra money via that route.

Much of what you'll learn in the next chapter when we discuss selling techniques can be applied to merchandise as well. Keep this monetization strategy in mind as something that's worth exploring later on in your life as a blogger, perhaps a year or two after you've established your blog.

---

12. cafepress.com, spreadshirt.net, and zazzle.com, respectively.

The Wrong Approach to Blogging Income

If you look at the list we just discussed, you might be at ease with the thought of implementing some of these, and intimidated by others. This is pretty common.

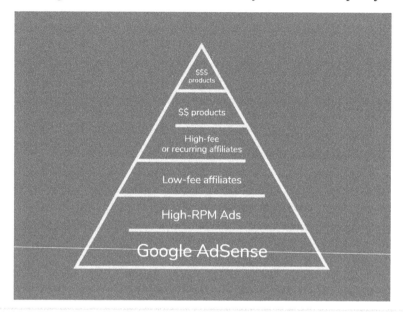

Figure 20—The common, flawed approach to blogging monetization

An overwhelming majority of bloggers who try to monetize their blogs will take the path of least resistance and opt to simply place AdSense ads on their blogs. Doing so doesn't take much effort and in turn, it typically leads to receiving very little return, perhaps a few dollars a month, unless they have monthly six-figure page views or they cover a very specific niche that happens to have extremely high advertising costs, like law or insurance, and therefore pays out at a much higher rate.

A smaller percentage will then seek higher RPM (revenue per thousand impressions) ad networks (either because of the nature of the ads or because it's a network specific to the topic covered in their blog). This will typically improve one's blogging income a little, but it will still be quite limited for sites that don't receive massive amounts of traffic.

An even smaller percentage of bloggers will try their hand at affiliate marketing, typically with a program like Amazon Associates or the eBay Partner Network. Assuming they're accepted and that they do a good job reviewing or discussing specific products in their blogs, these bloggers will generally start to see some extra revenue in the form of a percentage commission.

Some, but not many, will seek high-paying affiliate programs where the commission will be substantial (e.g., $50+) or recurring each month if the buyer remains a subscriber of whatever product/service the referral was made for. Having huge traffic becomes less necessary when a single person buying the product (e.g., a hosting package you recommend) can generate $50 or more for you.

Whether people visiting your blog have the right intention (e.g., they're looking for hosting recommendations) and whether you're a credible source of said recommendations become much more important factors. But, of course, "the more traffic the merrier" still applies.

A tiny percentage of bloggers will end up creating their own product targeted for their audience (think an ebook for $39, for example). Those who do a good job by creating a genuinely useful product and then marketing it correctly to their readers can start to see income that would take decades to accrue with AdSense at their current traffic level (think of five- [and more rarely six-] figure incomes per year, depending on how successful they are).

An even smaller percentage of bloggers will add a final high-ticket item to their marketing funnel. This is typically an expensive course (in the $297–$1,999 price range) or some exclusive, direct mentorship offer for an equally substantial fee. The sky's the limit here in terms of income. If successful in this approach, your blog will qualify as a bona fide digital business at that point.

The Inverse Pyramid of Blogging Income

There's a positive correlation between the effort required and the economic reward, as well as a negative correlation to how popular the approach is.

The least rewarding, AdSense, requires the least effort, produces the least amount of revenue for the blogger, and in turn is the most popular monetization method among bloggers.

The most economically rewarding option, creating your own high-price items, requires the most amount of effort both in terms of creating something of so much value and marketing it (e.g., $297 is definitely not an impulse buy for most people). But you can make scary amounts of money from it.

The real problem is that most bloggers looking to monetize their blogs tend to follow the pyramid presented in Figure 20, The common, flawed approach to blogging monetization, on page 224. Many will stop at the first three steps, at best, never venturing into high affiliate offers or making their own products.

The secret to increasing direct blogging income, if that's your goal, is to invert the pyramid and focus your efforts and priorities accordingly, as shown in the following figure.

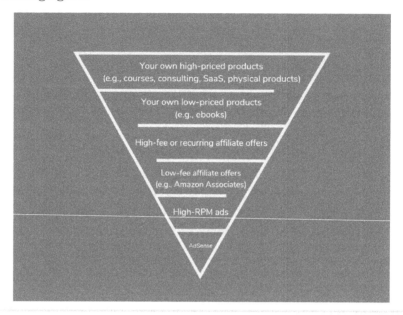

Figure 21—The most efficient approach to monetizing your blog

Now this doesn't mean that you can't have AdSense, but you should prioritize the high-reward items because they're the ones that are most likely to make you serious extra income—even if you only get a few thousand visitors a month to your site.

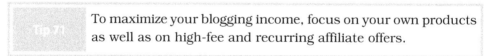

Tip 71 | To maximize your blogging income, focus on your own products as well as on high-fee and recurring affiliate offers.

How the Pros Do It

That's how serious bloggers make money! They create what's essentially a funnel that's laser-focused on getting readers to buy the useful product they've made.

They attract a lot of visitors with great free content that's relevant to their blog topic, content that both helps people and establishes the blogger's authority on the subject at hand. Then they'll typically offer some sort of valuable freebie, like an email course or a PDF guide to turn their site's visitors into email subscribers (the aforementioned lead magnet).

They'll continue to provide value to their subscribers with great content, for free, as well as making them aware of some kind of offer related to their products (remember, people love sales). Some will even first sell the inexpensive product (e.g., a cheap ebook or course) and then upsell true believers to their more expensive products and/or services. If you are familiar with Tony Robbins, that's what he does. But pretty much anyone raking in big bucks through digital sales adopts a similar strategy.

There's a reason for the common mantra, *The money is in the list.* Nothing beats having regular readers you can continue to communicate with directly. You'll be able to email them useful information on a regular basis and sell them valuable products that will help them, and in turn, help you achieve your financial blogging goals in the process.

It's worth noting that depending on your reasons for blogging, optimizing monetary gain might not be a concern. And that's okay. Your career itself might be the high ROI "product" in that case.

Take Action

Your main homework for this chapter is to define what benefits you're most interested in. Then maximize for those. If you're looking to advance your career, don't waste time trying to monetize your blog directly. Instead, focus on increasing your influence and the reach of your blog.

If you wish to transform your blog into a side business of its own, then by all means define a clear strategy to maximize profits instead.

Whatever you decide to do, be deliberate. Don't let chance decide for you or wander around aimlessly. Decide what you want from your blog, and then go get it.

What's Next

We covered a lot in this chapter. You should now have all the tools you need to start experimenting with proven methods that can benefit your career (or income, if that's one of your goals).

In the next chapter, we'll explore how to blog for your business or the company you work for. In the process, we'll also cover the most remunerative approach to monetizing your blog—namely, the creation of your own products.

Next to doing the right thing, the most important thing is to let people know you are doing the right thing.

    John D. Rockefeller

CHAPTER 12

Promoting Your Own Business

This chapter is dedicated to the topic of promoting your own business through blogging. This is beneficial to two types of readers: people who are interested in promoting and growing their company (or their employer's business) and bloggers who'd like to increase their income by selling their own products.

The distinction between the two isn't that important because the information I provide here serves both categories of business well.

A company blog is not very different from a regular technical blog. What this chapter does is build on top of the knowledge you've acquired so far to help you hone a blogging strategy that's specific to your company.

A Checklist for Company Blogs

Let's start by reviewing some of the startup/company-specific concepts that have been introduced so far. This list acts both as a checklist and a quick recap.

- Identify why you're blogging. Is it for customer acquisition and to increase sales? Providing support to existing customers? Finding moral support and sharing war stories with fellow entrepreneurs? Expanding your team by recruiting new hires? Get to the root of what you want to accomplish with your company blog.

- Identify who you're blogging for. Now that you know why you're blogging, try to understand who your target readers are. This will help you determine what to blog about, with what degree of detail, what kind of tone, and so forth.

- Keep your blog on the same domain as your company. Opt for yourcompany.com/blog over blog.yourcompany.com to maximize the SEO benefits.

- Prominently link between your blog and your site. Anyone landing on your site should be able to check out your company blog with ease. Much more importantly though, someone landing on a random post should immediately be able to find out more about your company and products. Whether the two sections of your site share the same navigation bar or not, the main marketing purpose of your blog is to get readers to discover your products. Make it easy and obvious.

• Use the same logo and general look and feel for your blog, even if the layout and style is slightly different from that of your main site.

• Don't place ads and offers from third parties on your company blog. As a business, income from sales should overshadow any extra income ads can provide. You don't want your blog readers to leave the site. Instead, have buttons, banners, and other ads for your own products in multiple spots around your blog template.

• Host your blog on a different infrastructure from your company site. If your site were to become unavailable, you'd still be able to communicate with your customers through your blog. This isn't by any means necessary, especially now that you can use Twitter for the same purpose, but it's a good trick that can facilitate more extensive communication during outages.

• Make it a team effort. Unless you're a one-person startup or a micro-ISV, you should try to enlist the help of others on your team when it comes to keeping the blog going strong. Depending on your company's age and structure, you can turn to cofounders or fellow team members. Even if you plan on doing most of the blogging yourself, don't forget to enlist the help of other experts on your team to enrich your collective company blog.

• Determine if you need more than one blog. Some companies choose to have two blogs: one for customer-facing announcements and news and another for their "From the Trenches" or "Behind the Scenes" posts for fellow techies and entrepreneurs. Try to determine if a second blog could help you better achieve your blogging goals.

This last point is the one we've discussed the least throughout the book, yet it's an important early decision for company blogs. Let's take a moment to talk about it.

Do You Need More Than One Blog?

Maintaining one blog is a sizable effort. Of course, it's one of the best marketing tools at your disposal. There's no denying, though, that it still requires work, consistency, patience, and commitment.

Marketing is hard work (contrary to what some believe). The moment you introduce a second blog, you have if not doubled, then at least significantly increased, the challenge and responsibility you face. You'll also need to clarify which blog is for what so you don't confuse your customers.

As a big believer in the power of simplicity, my default stance is that you should focus on one company blog only unless you have a good reason not to. An obvious advantage of going the one-blog route is that your announcements and news will be shown to subscribers who mainly follow your site for the subject matter expertise you share. Remember that such posts are another occasion to get your products in front of your prospective customers.

To help you decide on this issue, ask yourself the following questions:

- Do I have enough product announcements and news to justify creating a separate blog?

- Do I have the workforce and drive to manage two blogs?

- Is there a big disconnect between the content and audience of my main company blog and those of a blog about my products? Keep in mind that this gap between the two is only justifiable if the purpose of your non-product-related blog isn't to acquire new customers (e.g., hiring, finding business partners). If your main objective is to get new customers and increase sales, the content of your company blog should be crafted accordingly and it makes sense to focus on one blog.

- Do I post so often in my company blog that I want to provide a second, less frequently updated blog for those who are solely interested in news and announcements from our company?

If you answered yes to one or more of these questions, then, by all means, consider the second blog option. Perhaps host it on yourcompany.com/news or something equally telling, so that its purpose is readily apparent.

Likewise, ensure that your nonproduct blog (which is usually aimed at expertly discussing topics related to your niche or activity) has a clear title and/or tagline to identify its purpose.

Some companies go so far as to have a multitude of blogs, and it's not rare for large companies to have various blogs operating on a department or an industry basis. Don't get ahead of yourself, however. Start with one blog first.

Blog vs. Company Site

When I refer to having a blog on your company site, I'm working under the assumption that your company already exists and you have a site that sells products or services.

If you're a blogger who managed to attract a following and is now trying to earn more money by selling information products such as ebooks, you don't need a separate site. Simply prepare sale pages on your blog that include some form of checkout functionality. These will act as landing pages for your products. Then link to and advertise those pages and products from your posts, your sidebar, and throughout your blog.

To begin selling digital products, if you are such a blogger, look into e-commerce providers that handle everything for you, including payments and download delivery. A popular option for digital products is Gumroad.[1]

For subscription-based services, Stripe Billing, Rebilly, Chargify, or Recurly are all viable options.[2] I would argue, however, that these solutions are created for startups with SaaS needs. If your needs are more modest, the membership options mentioned in the previous chapter (including Patreon) may suffice here.

If you're integrating full-blown e-commerce into your blog, with several products for sale, look into WooCommerce (for WordPress) and Shopify.[3]

Identify and Understand Your Readers

Now that your company blog is in place, you'll likely be wondering what you should blog about. As you probably know by now, the answer is that it depends on your goals. But let's narrow things down.

Most companies are after new customers, increased sales, retaining customers, increased loyalty, and other traditional marketing purposes. So your main goal is likely to be getting your products in front of as many prospective customers as possible.

With such a customer acquisition goal in mind, you should blog about topics that deeply interest your prospective customers. Answer their pressing questions, clarify their doubts, stimulate their curiosity, inspire them to achieve their full potential and succeed (particularly with your products). Become that comforting, expert voice in their industry that readers can rely on and trust.

---

1.   gumroad.com
2.   stripe.com/billing, rebilly.com, chargify.com, and recurly.com, respectively.
3.   woocommerce.com and shopify.com, respectively.

Meet Laura

Before you tailor content to your customers and answer their needs with your expert voice, you must first understand who your prospective customers really are.

Most marketers will tell you to think in terms of demographics. Your customers are in such and such an age group, are of this gender, and earn within a given salary range. All that info may be useful to know, but it's not the way to penetrate the minds of your customers.

To really feel empathy and understand what your customers want, what confuses them, and what inspires them, you need to get personal. You can't put yourself into the shoes of a whole demographic, but it is possible to imagine one typical prospective customer and work towards getting to know that person better.

Let's say that your company sells educational iPad applications that are designed for young children. Who is your prospective customer? Well, let's see. She is a mom; let's call her Laura. How old is she? Let's say 33. OK, how many children does Laura have? Probably two. What ages? Hmm, a three-year-old daughter and a five-year-old son. What's her profession? She used to be an accountant, but now she does bookkeeping for small businesses from home so that she can spend more time raising her kids.

You get the idea. You can use this thought process to create a detailed profile of a possible customer and ask yourself questions in your head to get to know your target users better. Now assume that Laura doesn't know about your iPad applications and you want to reach her through your blog.

Will Laura find you when researching Swift vs. Flutter mobile apps? Well, based on Laura's profession, that's very unlikely. What does Laura, a concerned parent who wants the best for her children, care about? What worries Laura? What's Laura's main objective? What's her problem in relation to the solution you have to offer?

Laura probably doesn't care about your product. She doesn't care about features. She cares about her kids. If your product helps her and her kids' needs, then she might care about what you have to say.

It's easier now to understand your customer because you can imagine how this person would react to what you write. You can also better assess what kind of questions your customer has and answer them. If you are an iPad developer, you may take many of your customers' questions for granted.

What's obvious to you may not be to Laura. When you think about Laura, you can come up with all sort of questions that your posts should answer:

- Are iPads safe for young children to use? For how long?
- Which iPad should you buy for your young children?
- Is the iPad a good educational tool for children ages three to six?
- Can you use a pen to write on the iPad screen?
- What are some clever ways to use mobile devices to encourage children to learn?
- Are there fun iPad games aimed at young children?
- Is an iPad or an Android tablet better for educational purposes?
- Should parents buy their children an iPad?
- What can children learn through the iPad?
- What are the best iPad apps for young kids to use?
- Should children spend their time on the iPad?
- How do you teach mathematics to preschool kids?
- What software can teach young children how to read?
- Is software beneficial for the development of your child's brain?
- How can you assess and improve your child's IQ?
- How can you prepare your children for elementary school?
- How can parents and children use the iPad together to learn and bond?
- What's the difference between the iPad Wi-Fi and the iPad Wi-Fi + Cellular?

These are just a few random examples of questions your posts could answer. Notice that some of these questions aren't even iPad-specific. Laura is interested in her kids' education first, and the iPad is just a tool that can help her with that goal. Talk about the iPad by all means, but focus on what the customer really wants to know.

Though this exercise may appear silly, you really need to connect with your customers at this depth in order to help them find your blog and, in turn, your products. Put yourself into their shoes, and if you have access to early customers, listen to what they tell you so you can better gauge how to address their questions.

 Use the SEO tools we discussed to better identify customer questions.

Craft Your Content for Your Prospective Customers

You can, and should, talk about your products at length in your blog. Showcase how they work, what they're good for, what's possible to achieve with them, announcements you'd like to make (unless you have a separate blog dedicated to covering announcements), and so on. However, if you focus on your products alone, the audience you'll end up attracting will be rather limited.

You need to reach a wider audience of prospective customers with your content and then gently introduce them to what you have to offer. The key here is to persuade customers to purchase by first offering value so as to win their trust and respect. Once a relationship is in place, you won't have to rely on *hard selling* by being obnoxious and pushy in your efforts to have them purchase what you're selling.

Instead, you'll be able to perform a so-called *soft sell* on your landing pages. Your sales copy (the text in which you explain your offer) will be able to focus on the benefits of your product, and the reader will have more reason to believe your claims. Your friendly and conversational tone won't look out of place or unfamiliar, because it's the same clear and expert voice that's been providing valuable advice and knowledge, without any strings attached. In other words, your sales message will be more effective and welcomed.

You could, for example, append a banner ad at the bottom of each of your posts detailing what your company does and how it can benefit your readers. You are definitely selling, but you aren't coming across as imposing or annoying. All you're saying is, hey, by the way, here's an offer that may interest you if you found this post interesting or useful.

For example, if you are blogging about nutrition and you're hoping to sell your diet ebook or meal plans, you might want to write a large post that explains the core principles of the diet, something very useful and appealing to readers. By the end of it, they'll want to learn more, and that's where a soft pitch for your ebook won't be out of place.

Returning to the example of the educational applications for the iPad, you could conclude a post entitled "How to Use the iPad to Teach Your Children the Joy of Learning" with the following paragraph:

> Thank you for reading this post. I hope you and your child will have tons of fun playing with your iPad and learn a lot in the process. If you are looking for an application to help your child learn basic numeracy, check out XYZ in the App Store. We built it specifically for children between the ages of two and five.

In this fictitious example, our small ad in the text of the post (or highlighted just below it) does not come across as invasive or out of place. If that helpful and inspiring post were read by thousands of parents like Laura, you'd be guaranteed to receive a significant boost in sales.

> Tip 73   Be a person, not a corporation, when you blog.

Case Study: How I Promoted Db2

A few years back, one key responsibility I had at work was the technical advocacy of Db2 (a commercial database produced by IBM). To further back up the approach I just suggested, let me tell you what I did to promote downloads of Db2 on my personal programming blog.

You'd think that the best approach would be for me to talk about Db2 every chance I got (on my blog)—maybe even go so far as to call the site "Programming with Db2" and grab a domain name along the same lines.

That approach would have enriched the Db2 ecosystem but would have been suboptimal in terms of actually reaching new developers. Who searches for a Db2-related blog? For the most part, people who already use Db2.

Instead, I blogged about all sort of interesting topics for programmers who may have never heard of Db2. This way I built a large, receptive audience composed of the exact people IBM would have loved to see adopt Db2. Every time someone read an article on programming in general or on, say, Ruby, they'd see a Db2 download button toward the top of the sidebar. Out of thousands of readers, quite a few end up clicking and investigating what it's all about.

Then when I occasionally posted about Db2, I had a very sizable audience of subscribers reading about that very database. Those articles were hosted on my popular blog, which in turn helped them obtain better search engine positioning. Guess what happened? Over the years, hundreds of thousands of people heard about Db2 through my blog, and many thousands have tried it or switched over. It would have been virtually impossible to achieve this with a blog focused solely on Db2.

In your company blog (or side project blog), you should do the same thing. Mix some posts about your products with content that's not about your products per se but is highly interesting and valuable to the people you are targeting. Check out the Buffer blog to see a company that nails content marketing by understanding who its core audience is and speaking to them.[4]

> Tip 74   If you're promoting an open source project, consider having a guide on how to contribute to it.

---

4.   blog.bufferapp.com

From the Trenches Blogs

It's very tempting to use your company blog to share all the good things you're doing from a business or development standpoint. Your "From the Trenches" blog can motivate you, help you clarify your thoughts and vision, and psychologically help you cope with the challenges that entrepreneurship will inevitably throw your way.

Remember, however, that if you're blogging for customer acquisition, your focus has to be on blogging for prospective customers. Of course, if your customers are fellow entrepreneurs, then you have a match between your marketing goals and your desire to share your business experiences and lessons learned.

In fact, if your customers are entrepreneurs, typically because you have a B2B (business-to-business) product, you may even go so far as to share detailed statistics about your success. People are attracted to successful companies and their stories. By showcasing how well you're doing, you might inspire and attract a serious following from the very people you're trying to market to. In addition, your articles will be generously shared by these potential customers on social media.

I've mentioned Basecamp (formerly 37signals) before in the book, which is a great example of a company using this technique to earn respect (and new customers). Balsamiq is another company that shared its figures publicly from the very beginning, documenting its own journey from day one. This unconventional approach truly paid off; there was a time when you couldn't stop hearing about Balsamiq on Hacker News, Twitter, and the like. The figure-sharing approach worked.

It's not just the strong allure of wanting to emulate and listen to someone who's making money; it's that when you're sharing your figures, you're being specific. And readers trust and appreciate specifics far more than vague statements such as, "We did X and it's working for us."

If there isn't a fit between what you'd like to share and what your audience wants, consider starting an additional company blog or launching your own separate blog on the topic of entrepreneurship and startups. The former approach has SEO advantages, while the latter may put a greater emphasis on you, thereby boosting your personal visibility in the industry.

Convert Readers into Customers

By now, you should have a clearer picture of what to blog about in order to promote your business. What's left to explore in depth is how to convert the audience you're attracting into actual customers.

Your Company Blog Layout

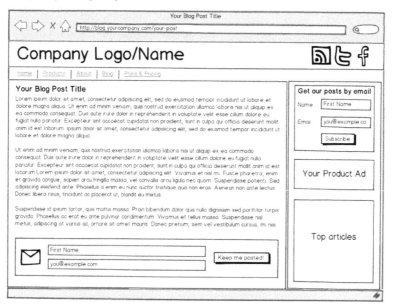

Figure 22—A sample company blog layout

Just like your content, your company blog should be laid out in agreement with what you're trying to accomplish.

Consider Figure 22. This layout has the following characteristics:

- The company logo or title will typically link to your company site. This helps increase the number of people who'll end up on your actual product site. Just ensure that there's an easy way to access your blog's home page (in the example in the figure, the Blog link in the navigation bar does that).

- The blog shares the same navigation bar with the company site.

- The sidebar gives priority to the newsletter and to your own product ads without ignoring the promotion of other blog articles. Note how the RSS feed and the company's social presence are easily accessible as well.

- At the end of each post, regardless of whether the content promoted your products or not, the layout embeds a sign-up form.

This is the type of template that will help your readers discover your commercial offerings.

When in doubt, use a heatmap service like Crazy Egg to see where on the page your readers are focusing. Ensure that the attention is on your brand, your call to action (e.g., newsletter subscription), or whatever else you're trying to highlight.

Get and Promote Your Newsletter

You should know by now that a newsletter is your most valuable asset as a marketer. To show this, let's compare the interactions of three visitors on our site.

- Visitor A checks out a blog post and leaves.

- Visitor B checks out a blog post and clicks on our product ad. Visitor B may buy or may not be ready to commit to purchasing our product or service, so B leaves.

- Visitor C checks out a blog post and signs up for the newsletter before leaving.

Visitor C is far more valuable than B. Only a tiny percentage (e.g., 2%) of B visitors will buy our product. The rest may never come back to the site, and thus we won't have a way of communicating with them again. C visitors, on the other hand, are *leads*. They'll be reminded about us and our products every single time a new post is published, a new offer is sent out directly to subscribers, and so on.

This repeated exposure greatly increases our chances of making a sale. In fact, have you ever visited a site and in doing so seen ads for that particular site that suddenly pop up seemingly everywhere? This is called *retargeting*, and it's very effective due to the repeated exposure (if albeit a bit spooky).[5]

So in your template, emphasize newsletter sign-ups. If possible, as mentioned before, create a lead magnet freebie only available to subscribers to get more people to sign up. Make it a short guide, white paper, ebook, video, or anything else that your visitors will perceive as being valuable and useful.

---

5. adroll.com/learn-more/retargeting

If you're monetizing your blog through digital products, make this resource a lightweight version of your full offering so that readers are primed to buy your main product.

In fact, if you're a blogger trying to come up with ideas for digital products to sell to your readers, you should investigate your most popular content and create a valuable digital resource (like an ebook) that expands, or at least organizes in one place, what you have to say on the topic.

> Tip 75   Cross-role ebooks tend to do well (e.g., design for developers).

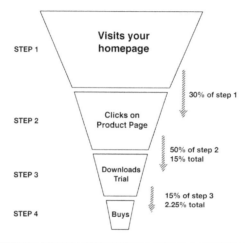

Figure 23—A sample sales funnel

Track the Impact of Your Blog

OK, you're writing great content and promoting it as described earlier in the book. You check your statistics and notice that your blog obtained 40,000 pageviews during the past month.

That number makes you feel good, but for someone promoting a business, it's just a vanity metric. On its own, it doesn't really tell you much. All you really can claim is that you attracted some traffic to your blog.

What did these people do when they landed on your blog? How many subscribed? How many ended up visiting your product pages? And how many went from being visitors to being customers? It's particularly important to distinguish between vanity metrics and actionable metrics if you operate a business.

The first thing you need to do is to ensure that you understand which spots on your blog (or which email campaigns) are sending traffic to your product pages.

For newsletters, providers like MailChimp will automatically tag your URLs for you. As mentioned before, tagged URLs have a series of parameters that uniquely identify campaigns so you can understand where traffic is coming from when using Google Analytics and other analytics suites.

For your blog you may want to manually craft a different URL for, say, your product ad in the sidebar and the pitch at the bottom of your posts. You can do so by using the Campaign URL builder in Google Analytics.[6]

You can now track traffic that comes from your blog and newsletter to your product pages with a finer degree of control. There's still one other step, however, before you can fully make sense of that data and try to take action in response to the information you've collected.

Keep Track of Your Sales Funnel

You need to understand your sales funnel so you can determine and improve your conversion rates. You have a large group of people reading your blog, but how many of those visitors will actually end up clicking your product page? And of this smaller group, what percentage will actually buy your product? (See Figure 23, A sample sales funnel, on page 240.)

You can obtain these types of conversion rate metrics by defining your goals in Google Analytics. Alternatively, you can use a dedicated conversion rate tracking tool like the aforementioned KISSmetrics.

When you do so, you'll quickly discover what is and what isn't working (and isn't providing a return on investment) for your company.

As a reminder, if you want to introduce changes and see how your conversion rate is affected, you should look into A/B testing tools or services, because these allow you to test two different versions of a given page in parallel. Doing so will determine how a change affects the conversion rate in the next step of the funnel.

Small changes on your site can have a significant positive impact on your conversion rates within the funnel. Others won't, though, and some may even make your conversion rate worse. For example, adding social proof, such as showcasing a large number of Facebook fans, should theoretically increase your conversion

---

6. ga-dev-tools.appspot.com/campaign-url-builder/

rate. But there's always the risk that users will get distracted and end up on Facebook instead of completing the steps you want them to take.

How will you know for sure? Run an A/B test long enough to obtain statistically significant results. Every A/B testing tool worth its salt will automatically calculate this for you, so you don't really need a knowledge of statistics. Just have the patience to wait for conclusive results.

Your ultimate goals as a marketer are to attract a large targeted audience and to increase the efficiency of the sales funnel by improving your conversion rate at each step of the process.

Other Approaches to Selling More

It's beyond the scope of this book to provide an extensive tutorial on marketing in general. That said, here are some promotional techniques that shouldn't be overlooked when it comes to marketing your product or company.

- Approach fellow bloggers and offer them the chance to receive your product for free in return for a review of that item, service, and so on. Many people will take you up on the offer and you'll end up leveraging the existing audiences that those bloggers have already established. Guest blogging, extensively discussed before, is also a great tool for this purpose.

- Consider establishing your own affiliate program. Good affiliates are formidable marketers who can help you connect with prospective customers that may otherwise be tricky (or even impossible) for you to reach.

- Consider a live chat widget or a chatbot for your site to support and engage your prospective customers.

- Don't ignore paid advertising, such as Google Ads, Facebook Ads, or Twitter Ads. Free traffic from SEO, blogging, and social media is probably the best tool you have in your marketing utility belt. It would be foolish, though, to put all your eggs in one basket if you have the budget for more. Always diversify your customer acquisition efforts, provided each channel continues to give you a positive ROI.

- Don't forget offline marketing efforts either. Companies are still out there doing extremely well through traditional advertising and publicity channels. Augment your online efforts by recruiting prospective customers in the offline world as well.

> Tip 76   Bookmark all press and blog mentions of your company.

Take Action

If you are blogging for a company or have your own digital product, you should focus on two things:

1. Focus your writing on what's genuinely useful to your prospective and existing customers, not the product itself.

2. Fine-tune your blog to promote your product(s) as a premium offering for those who found your free content valuable.

What's Next

This concludes our second chapter on direct strategies to help you benefit and earn money from your blog.

In the next and final section of the book, we'll look at how to take your blogging to the next level by scaling your activities (if you so desire), as well as at useful social media strategies that complement your online content marketing approach.

Part V

Scale It

Ambition is the germ from which all growth of nobleness proceeds.

   Oscar Wilde

CHAPTER 13

Scaling Your Blogging Activities

By following the advice provided within this book so far, you should be able to create a fairly successful blog. This may be enough for you, or you may have even bigger aspirations.

For those readers, we'll now look briefly at the topic of scaling your blogging activities, both scaling vertically by stretching your blog's potential to the limit and scaling horizontally by creating further blogs.

Scale Your Blog Vertically

The growth of most people's blogs is not limited by the size of the niche they're part of. In fact, even successful bloggers rarely manage to reach the majority of their target audience.

The real limit is often the amount of content that a single person can produce. Excluding a few bloggers who manage to obtain a celebrity-like status online despite publishing infrequently, there's a strong correlation between how much you publish and how popular your blog is.

By now, I'm operating under the assumption that your content is good, that you've presented it well, and that you've promoted your work through all the legitimate channels you can think of.

The easiest way to rapidly scale your blog at this point is to transform it into an online magazine or news site.

Online Magazine vs. News Site

Online magazines and news sites are collective blogs that enlist the help of other writers. They mostly differ in their frequency and content type.

An online magazine like *Smashing Magazine* typically publishes several articles per week.[1] These articles tend to be HOWTOs about accomplishing certain web design–related tasks.

A news site like *The Next Web* publishes dozens of posts per day on tech-related events and announcements.[2] Smaller news sites or those operating in narrower niches, however, could get by with just a few stories per day.

Magazines tend to require a few writers who can publish in-depth, informative articles on the topic at hand. News sites will require many writers who are on the ball with what's happening in their niche and can quickly write a 500-word piece before other news sites do as well (or at least create better content than their competitors while remaining timely).

> **Tip 77** It's far easier to evolve a technical blog into a magazine than into a news site.

Remember this important point when searching for writers to hire: Before transforming your blog into a magazine or news outlet, consider what's made it successful so far. If it was the excellent writing, ensure that the writers you hire are on par with your own writing. If you adopted a particular style or covered various topics in a certain manner, see if the same traits can be maintained as you expand your blog.

As usual, treat the process of expanding as an experiment. Make a gradual switch and see how your audience responds. Perhaps announce that a new writer is coming on board and then invite the community surrounding your site to welcome that person. If your audience is happy about it, slowly add more writers. Keep your readers in the loop and explain what benefits your decision to scale will bring their way.

Hire a Team of Bloggers

So you're getting serious about your blog and are now looking for new writers to help you produce a substantial amount of content every week. Here's how to go about it.

From Guest Bloggers and Your Community

The cheapest approach is to recruit guest bloggers, as discussed in Chapter 6, Producing Content Regularly, on page 111.

---

1. smashingmagazine.com
2. thenextweb.com

The main advantage is that you don't pay them. They're happy enough to do it for a backlink to their own site. The main disadvantage is that you don't pay them. How much can you really rely on someone you don't pay? I don't doubt you can get good articles from your most prolific guest bloggers, and you should certainly continue to promote your availability for guest posts.

Unfortunately, you can't expect these people to either post on a regular basis or (necessarily) respect your editorial schedule, nor can you request a specific number of articles per week from them. Unless you pay your guest bloggers, you should consider their efforts to be an occasional extra to your regular content. Every week you may have zero to n new posts coming from guest bloggers. These are certainly nice, but again, you can't rely on their presence or frequency.

If you introduce economic rewards, you can start to fish for writers from your existing pool of guest bloggers. You already know who did a great job and who didn't, so you can approach the right people with your proposition. Since you're paying them, if they accept, you can now rightfully request that they publish at least one article per week, or whatever schedule you agree upon.

Insightful commenters are another pool of prospective writers. Contact people that fit this description and explain what you're trying to create and what's in it for them. Keep in mind that people are not solely interested in money (particularly if you can't offer much). People yearn to belong to something important. Give your project a compelling mission statement that makes it that important something that will appeal to people.

If you can't find the right amount (or type) of writers from among your guest bloggers and top commenters, consider asking your community directly in your posts. Post announcements should attract a variety of candidates. The trick will be selecting those who can write well and can keep up with a regular schedule.

> Tip 78   Create a We're Hiring page and post about it from time to time.

Specify how much you'll be paying up front to prevent wasting yours and other people's time should economic expectations be too far apart.

The amount you pay your bloggers is a business decision you need to make. It's common to pay per article, per word, or per hour. I do not recommend paying per hour because you and your writer's incentives are not aligned.

Try to figure out how much additional income you receive on average per additional post. If you can't calculate that, guesstimate how much value you get out of it; then pay your writers less than that number, thereby leaving room for your profit.

Your topic, requirements, the research level required to write an article, and the blogger's level of experience all affect the going rate. The range varies from five to several hundred dollars per article, though some mainstream publications offer well above $1000 per piece. More commonly though, you'll see midsize reputable blogs offering in the neighborhood of $20–$100 for an article of 500–1000 words.

From Job Boards, Freelance Sites, and Outsourcing Services

In addition to paying guest bloggers and recruiting from your community, you should consider placing local ads, listing projects on freelance sites, using outsourcing services, and posting on niche job boards.

Local Ads

The advantage of using ads on places such as Craigslist or Kijiji is that you may be able to find local talent that you can interview and meet in person and who can regularly contribute as a contractor to your blog. Your local college or university's bulletin board may also work.

You could use this approach to assemble your own newsroom locally rather than virtually. In turn, this grants your team a better environment for communication and collaboration.

Of course, this also implies a more serious commitment to blogging as a business than your average virtual team of bloggers. Depending on where you live, it might also be hard to find qualified candidates locally. This isn't a problem in a major city, but it's certainly an issue if you live in the middle of nowhere.

Freelance Sites

Freelance sites like UpWork and Freelancer are also decent venues to find people who are willing to write for truly reasonable rates (e.g., $20–$30 for a usable article).[3] The main problem is that, in my experience, you'll have to be very selective and go through a series of low-quality writers before you find a person you can trust and rely on to deliver the kind of posts you're seeking.

Paying a little more and aiming to hire (actually) native English speakers is the way to go (assuming your blog is in English), if you want to keep the number of unsuccessful paid writer experiences to a minimum.

---

3.   upwork.com and freelancer.com, respectively.

Being clear and detailed about what you want is also a must. Some people even go as far as to include special requests in their job description in order to filter out those who apply without having carefully read the description. You could, for example, ask candidates to include an out-of-context word (e.g., tapioca) in their application to demonstrate that the candidate actually read your job description carefully before applying.

This is reminiscent of Van Halen's "no brown M&Ms" contract clause for their concerts. (If you are not familiar with the story, Google it, as it's quite fascinating.)

It's also a good idea to check out the feedback and comments left by other employers, but view such comments with a grain of salt. In my early days of hiring paid writers, I had a few bad experiences with contractors who had fantastic feedback. Always remember that people who are desperate for work will go to great lengths to game the system.

Often contractors on freelance sites don't mind if you want them to act as ghost-writers whose name won't be attributed to the posts they write for you. This has its advantages in some contexts, but I personally prefer not to publish other people's writing under my own name. Either way, specify in your requirements regarding whether the article will be published in your name or in theirs.

Start with a small assignment for a specific article you have in mind, but explain that you can provide much more work should the arrangement work out.

Outsourcing Sites

Alternatively, you can consider outsourcing to services that provide articles on demand. The advantage of such sites over freelancing ones is that you don't have to go through the process of selecting writers, which will save you a considerable amount of time.

These types of services take care of assigning a prescreened writer to your article. If you order a set of posts in bulk, you may have several authors assigned to you who work in parallel, therefore reducing turnaround time and introducing a greater variety of writing styles.

On the lower end of the spectrum, you can get articles written for as little as $0.01 per word, which equates to a mere $5 for a 500-word news article (in the same range of writers available on Fiverr).[4] And such a piece will, generally speaking, be unusable. This approach works for MFA (made for AdSense) sites and content farms that don't really care about the quality of the content, but it's absolutely useless for reputable technical or business blogs.

---

4. fiverr.com

If you want to rely on these services for the convenience they offer, you need to aim for the higher end of the scale. For example, if you use Textbroker,[5] a reputable outsourcing service, aim for their four- or five-star writers. At Textbroker's current rates, you can expect to spend in the range of $10–$40 for a 500-word article.

> **Tip 79**   Opt to fund fewer articles but of a higher caliber.

The quality is still highly variable, but your odds of obtaining a well-written article increase. Start with four-star writers, and if you're not happy and your funds allow it, consider trying five-star ones. In my experience, five-star writers on TextBroker are definitely better than four-star ones, but they cost roughly three times as much.

Once you find a writer you like, you can request that same person again the next time you place an order (if the person is available), hence introducing some consistency to the writing you've outsourced. This is equivalent to hiring them directly, with the added convenience of having the site handle payments and disputes.

Niche Job Boards

If you're looking for a longer-term relationship with a blogger who will produce content on a regular basis, you might also want to try job boards that are specifically targeted toward bloggers or at people in your niche. The Jobs board on ProBlogger is an example of the former.[6]

For regular writers, you would typically establish requirements up front regarding the frequency, length, and types of posts you expect to see and offer a monthly payment. If you look around, you'll quickly notice that the going rate is not particularly high.

Of course, the more technical and specialized the content, the harder the time you'll have finding someone who's willing to work on the lower end of the scale. In other words, while some people may have lower income expectations when blogging for hire, you still get what you pay for.

More elaborate arrangements exist, such as offering 50 percent of the ad revenue, but such terms would generally not attract or convince many qualified writers to come work for you.

---

5. textbroker.com
6. problogger.com/jobs/

Hiring bloggers can be a great business decision, but it's one that requires an investment of time and money. This is the sort of option that's best left for when you have a clearer indication of the economic potential of the blog you're trying to scale.

Build Your Blogging Empire

What do you do when you feel you have exhausted the economic opportunities your blog can provide? You can scale horizontally rather than vertically. Instead of diminishing your returns by putting much more effort into a blog that's already providing as much as is reasonable to expect, you can start a second blog.

The idea is that, at times, it may be easier to grab a second orange rather than try to squeeze every last bit of juice out of the current one.

Blog Networks

It's not rare to see wildly successful blogs launch sister blogs. If a multitude of blogs are born over time, they'll progress into a network.

Some blog networks allow third-party blogs to join under certain mutually beneficial conditions (sometimes economical). But in this section, I'm referring to a small network of blogs you own.

Each site promotes the network, typically at the top and the bottom of each site, in turn sending each other visitors, as shown in Figure 24, A network bar, on page 254.

One such example is the Cheezburger network.[7] It all started with the popular LOLCat blog *I Can Has Cheezburger?* and has expanded to now include dozens of blogs, including *FAIL Blog* and *Know Your Meme*.

Despite the humorous nature of these sites, networks like this can be very serious business. For instance, the aforementioned network received a $30 million investment even though it struggled to evolve over time and was eventually acquired for an undisclosed sum by a larger company in 2016.[8]

Keep in mind that you don't always have to come up with new domain names. At times you may want to simply create new sections in your existing blog and dedicate the same kind of effort to them as if they were their own sites.

---

7. cheezburger.com
8. blog.cheezburger.com/miscellaneous/omg-30-million1-thats-a-lot-of-cheezburgers

Figure 24—A network bar

For example, *VentureBeat* has a series of channels that act as categories within the same domain name.[9] This approach certainly has SEO advantages.

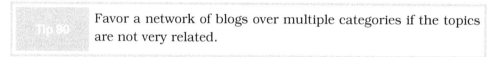

Tip 80   Favor a network of blogs over multiple categories if the topics are not very related.

Launch a Second Blog

As you can probably imagine by now, it's possible to create a media empire online by running a series of successful sites that promote each other. Is it easy? Certainly not, but once you've established one blog and managed to make it very popular, launching a second one and making it successful, too, is usually not terribly hard.

Picture this: you're running a successful blog about cars, and you now want to launch a blog about motorbikes. Your second blog won't start from scratch. In fact, you've got the invaluable asset of firsthand experience under your belt now. Not only that, but you'll announce and talk about your new blog on your existing site so your current readers can learn about it. And if you have a powerful presence on social networks like Twitter, your followers there will also learn about your new venture.

From an SEO standpoint it's beneficial to link to your new blog from such a popular preexisting site, even if both are on the same server. Search engine optimization specialists will give you all sorts of tricks, such as hosting the

---

9. venturebeat.com

sites on different Class C IP addresses to convince Google that the two sites aren't related and therefore the links from the popular one to the new one should be valued more. Ignore all that. It's not worth your time or money in most cases.

Remember to have links in your navigation bar and perhaps an ad in the sidebar, and remember to mention the new blog several times in your posts as your new site begins to get off the ground. Chances are that a percentage of your car-enthusiast audience will also be into bikes and will, therefore, check out your new blog. Ta-da! Instant traffic for your second site.

> **Tip 81** Giveaways are a great way to draw the attention of your existing readers to your new blog.

Rinse and repeat the process of promoting new online properties from existing ones. Just be warned that if you're trying to create a network on your own, it can quickly become overwhelming. If you were posting ten times per week, now you need to post twenty, thirty, or more times, depending on how many sites you launch.

Networks are definitely not for everyone. They require multiple writers, ideally a few editors, and good management to ensure things run smoothly. You'll also need a good hosting solution to handle all the traffic that an entire series of successful blogs will attract.

On the plus side, networks have huge economic and influence potential. If you manage to attract a few million visitors a month with your network, you'll also have much more bargaining power when dealing with advertisers and sponsors, be able to command higher CPM rates, and also get larger deals. And as you already know, advertising is just the tip of the iceberg.

Take Action

Revisit this chapter after having achieved success with your existing blog. At that point decide whether you want to make it into an online magazine or news site for your niche with the help of outsourced writers, or whether you want to launch a network of related blogs.

Consider the pros and cons of each solution and the time and money investment required to scale your blogging activities to that degree.

What's Next

This chapter should have provided you with a picture of what it takes to scale your blogging activities. It was included for the most ambitious readers, but remember that it's perfectly fine to run a single successful blog that doesn't morph into a news site or branch out into becoming a series of different blogs.

In the next chapter, we'll go beyond blogging and enter the fascinating world of social media. We'll dispel some of the myths that surround it and establish evergreen guidelines to help you succeed in creating a remarkable social media presence that further amplifies your influence.

CHAPTER 14

Beyond Blogging: Strategizing for Social Media

Social media adoption has exploded over the past decade. It's become an integral component of many people's lives and created a wide range of opportunities for businesses in the process. In this chapter, I'll provide you with a balanced approach to incorporate it within your existing content marketing strategy.

I believe social media has become so prominent due to the innate desire we have to get together, belong to something, and share with other people what we know, what we think, and what we do.

We are increasingly lonelier in real life, and social media offers a refuge to connect with other human beings, participating in virtual tribes of sorts, without the commitment requirements and challenging logistics of real encounters.

Unlike full-blown blogging, social media also requires significantly less effort to set up and contribute to on a regular basis, so far more people partake in social media.

It's an incredibly fast-moving target, so I won't provide detailed sign-up instructions that will become obsolete before the ink on this page has even dried. Case in point, Google+ didn't exist when I started writing the first edition of this book and the announcement of its demise (for consumers) arrived as I was penning this second edition.

Instead, we will focus on the essential notions you need to learn in order to establish yourself or your business on common social networks. You'll then be able to apply the same principles to whatever social networks you choose now or in the future.

Why Bother with Social Media?

By now, you should know that I care about you and won't sell you pipe dreams. This chapter is about social media because I think you should engage in it to further amplify your influence online. But social media is not a bed of roses. There's a dark side that's worth contemplating for a moment.

Social networks, Facebook in particular, have been all over the news lately. They possess an enormity of data about us, and that data hasn't always been guarded with due care. Data breaches are a privacy nightmare when the one holding the data knows everything about you and your family.

Privacy concerns aside, many believe that Facebook has acquired too much power. Enough power, in fact, to interfere with and sway national elections, affect the collective perception of right and wrong through political biases, and even run psychological experiments without consent.[1] While writing this chapter, the news broke that Facebook even used a research app to collect mobile data from teens.[2]

The argument has been made that (along with Google) Facebook contributed to dismantling the business model that made journalism viable, on top of making us, somewhat ironically, more depressed and lonely.[3]

In the past, trusting Facebook backfired for many companies. They promoted their Facebook page instead of their own sites (including in prominent ad campaigns featured during the Super Bowl) under the assumption that they could always freely communicate with the audience who liked (a.k.a. subscribed to) their Facebook pages. Not long afterward, Facebook changed its approach to requiring people to pay to fully reach their own page subscribers. It was within its right to do so, but it clearly had a bait-and-switch feel to it that left a bad taste in many marketers' mouths.[4]

Mind you, I'm not picking on Facebook (which, while problematic, I also find useful as someone with friends and family around the world). Twitter has its own challenges too. Many believe it's far too lenient with radicals who should be booted off the platform, while others feel that it tends to stifle free speech far too often. Regardless of your stance on the issue, even ignoring politics, it's undeniable that conversations on Twitter often devolve into the online

---

1.   www.theguardian.com/technology/2014/jul/02/facebook-apologises-psychological-experiments-on-users
2.   www.recode.net/2019/1/30/18203231/apple-banning-facebook-research-app
3.   www.vox.com/policy-and-politics/2018/3/21/17144748/case-against-facebook
4.   theoatmeal.com/comics/reaching_people

equivalent of high school behavior: cliques, name-calling, and bullying very much included.

Many find it both useful and stressful at the same time. Paul Graham even asked the question, "When you meet people who don't use Twitter, do you tell them they should try it out, or do you say, 'You're so lucky. Don't start!'"[5] and generated some good takes on the issue in the replies.

So why do we want to bother with social media at all? For all its negative aspects, there's still a lot of value that can be captured if we approach it with the right business mindset. In fact, within this chapter, I'm not advocating for or against using social media at a personal level. That's your choice. Instead, I'm recommending how to leverage this important channel to further extend your professional reach.

It's a massive oversimplification, but I like to think of this in terms of push and pull. For the most part, when you publish content on your blog, people will find out about it through a pull process. They have a particular question, they'll search for it in Google, and your blog post might just happen to be one of the first results for that specific query.

Social media allows us to engage in a push process. Our account or page will have some followers and we'll seed the content to this initial group. If the group members engage with it to some degree by liking it or sharing it, the followers of our followers will be exposed to it. It's a network effect that can make us known to people we wouldn't normally reach otherwise. Some of these people might like our content enough to start following us, subscribing to our newsletter, and so on.

When other people discover us through the pull process (say Google) and decide to share it with their followers, we'll still benefit from the potential network effect. If we have a social media presence on the given social network, however, the person might also tag us, directly or indirectly suggesting to people to follow us. It all adds up to a bigger following over time.

Another underrated advantage is connecting and building genuine relationships with influencers within your particular niche. On Twitter, in particular, they become quite reachable, and interacting with them isn't uncommon.

Realistically, I think your biggest risk is spending too much time on social media. After all, it's intended to solicit as much use as possible by design.

---

5.   twitter.com/paulg/status/1088375110258569217

Provided you can stick to the plan below, however, I think it's a worthwhile endeavor that will complement your blogging activities.

> **Tip 82**   Disable social media notifications on your phone.

Define a Social Media Strategy

Social media doesn't have to be complicated. Here's a simple step-by-step plan to get you going.

1. Identify the social networks you intend to target.
2. Create your social media profiles.
3. Cross-promote your site and social properties.
4. Post frequently and engage with people in your niche.

The devil, of course, is in the details. So let's address how to approach each of these steps, including what to post.

Identify the Social Networks You Intend to Target

There are countless social media sites. What's not countless is your two most valuable resources—your time and your energy. You need to be ruthlessly selective in deciding which social networks you're going to invest in. Okay, Antonio, spill it! Which ones?

Our goal for social media is to spread our message further, reach new audiences where they happen to be, connect with our followers and other influencers, and in the process amplify our own influence. Your choice needs to be strategic and calculated, as each social network you add will generally require further promotion and attention on your part.

So I wouldn't waste my time on minor social networks, unless they happen to be specific to, and well known in, your particular niche. In that case, even an audience of a few thousand users could make it worthwhile, much like your presence in niche-specific forums and Slack groups can be a valuable investment of your time.

> **Tip 83**   Research niche-specific social networks.

For example, Hashnode is a community for developers.[6] It's barely a dot compared to Twitter, but it might be a worthwhile investment of your time if you're targeting developers.

---

6. hashnode.com

In Chapter 8, Promoting Your Blog, on page 141, where we already covered social media to some extent, I recommended some major options: Twitter, LinkedIn, Facebook, and (if you felt up to them) Instagram and Pinterest as two visually rich social media options. I'll add YouTube to the list of general social media sites as one more option.

> Tip 84   If targeting a younger crowd, also consider Snapchat.

Twitter

Twitter allows you to reach new people every time one of your followers engages with your short messages (i.e., tweets). As mentioned above, when they like or share a tweet of yours (i.e., retweet you), a portion of their followers will be notified and exposed to your tweet even if they don't follow you.

If the tweet resonates enough with these folks, they might, in turn, engage with your tweet by liking it or retweeting it, which in turn is then shown to some of their respective followers. Rinse and repeat enough, and your best content could potentially become viral through a cascade effect. These people, impressed by your content, might also decide to check out your profile and timeline, and if they like what they see, follow you. When that happens, your following grows and so does your influence.

In short, Twitter is an ideal way to reach new people with your message and get them to know you and your blog in the process. It's also a favorite among technical folks, so it might give you an opportunity to engage with some of the most prominent figures within your niche or industry, potentially forming friendships and alliances with them in the process. If I were to pick just one social media site, without knowing anything else about you, it would likely be Twitter.

LinkedIn

LinkedIn is the most popular professional network. To some degree, the same advantages as Twitter apply. People can like and share your content, allowing you to reach audiences who aren't yet familiar with you. It's a less-open system than Twitter, but it directly links your social media updates and the content you share with your professional profile.

If you're blogging in an attempt to establish yourself professionally, LinkedIn is definitely a good place to promote your blog posts and industry-related content. You may be noticed and receive professional opportunities there, so I wouldn't ignore it.

Facebook

Facebook is somewhat controversial these days due to all the reasons mentioned before, so it's okay if you feel like skipping it on ethical grounds. If you don't, however, there's still lots of value to be captured there. I'm not suggesting the promotion of your content with your friends and family, as much as your uncle might support you and give you a like regardless of the content you post.

Instead, once you have an account there you can create a page for your blog or the topic of your niche and leverage people who are interested in the topic on Facebook to further extend your reach. You can also use Facebook groups as a way to create a community dedicated to your niche (a remarkably effective technique if done well).

Just keep in mind that Facebook is fairly aggressive in limiting the number of people you can reach organically without paying, even among the people who expressly subscribed to your page. There's also much less interaction with influencers or peers compared to Twitter. In short, have a presence on Facebook, but don't set your expectations too high.

Instagram and Pinterest

Instagram and Pinterest are both visual and extremely popular. The former, in particular, is incredibly popular among the newer generations. Today, I wouldn't say that either is overly popular among programmers. Most have Instagram accounts, but they tend to be more personal in nature, since most programming discussions don't happen on either Instagram or Pinterest.

You can still use them to promote your programming blog, and it might actually be easier to stand out as a result, but it's not a requirement by any means. If, on the other hand, your niche happens to be popular on such platforms, your presence becomes somewhat expected by your followers. I wouldn't want to be a fitness blogger without an Instagram account, or a food blogger without an Instagram account plus some pretty compelling Pinterest recipe boards.

YouTube and Twitch

I'm including YouTube because it has the biggest potential to increase your influence online among these social networks (even more than Twitter). If you create an interesting channel, push content regularly, and market it right, you can really distinguish yourself in your niche. Unfortunately, it's a bit of a lottery ticket and it requires a massive commitment. Whether you vlog regularly or simply post there occasionally,[7] it's not a platform where you quickly rebroadcast your new posts like you can on Twitter, LinkedIn, or Facebook. It's a new endeavor altogether that requires some serious time commitment.

If video calls to you, however, YouTube could elevate your status within your community. Yes, it's a lot more work, but because of that, way fewer people in your niche are likely doing it. For technical topics, particularly programming, YouTube is also a natural fit, since you can post screencasts and other technical tutorials that can benefit from you showing others what you're doing.

While on the subject of video, I want to mention Twitch,[8] a platform that's particularly popular among gamers streaming themselves live. I'm seeing more and more developers and makers there,[9] live-coding or building projects for a live audience who can interact with you, ask you questions in real time, and even tip you.

YouTube also supports live streaming, so if you decide to launch a YouTube channel, streaming there is an option. If you're simply streaming, however, Twitch appears to be more popular at the time of writing. At any rate, video (whether live-streamed or not) is yet another way for you to raise your status within your niche and amplify your online influence in the process.

Create Your Social Media Profiles

Now that you've decided which social networks you intend to target, you should immediately try to secure your *social properties* (e.g., accounts on these sites with your desired usernames).

For example, the fictitious Acme Fireworks Inc. will want to register the Twitter account @acmefireworks, if available. If already taken, a variation using an underscore, prefix, postfix, or abbreviation may be necessary.

When it comes to Facebook and LinkedIn, things are a little different. These sites require you to sign up as an individual first and then allow you to add a company identity that you manage and represent.

For Facebook, once you have a personal account, you'll be able to create a page for your blog. On LinkedIn, you'll likely want to create a company. This will, in turn, be added to your LinkedIn profile (e.g., Blogger at [Your Blog]).

---

7. en.wikipedia.org/wiki/Vlog
8. twitch.tv
9. github.com/bnb/awesome-developer-streams

Personal Presence vs. Business Presence on Twitter

My Twitter handle is @acangiano (by the way, feel free to follow me there).[10] If I were to launch a consulting practice tomorrow, I would probably keep using my personal handle for that business because the company would be focused around me and its success would greatly depend on my personal online presence.

But what about a business that sells products as an online retailer or a SaaS? In that case, I would absolutely need to create a dedicated account for the company. My prospective and existing customers would search for and refer to the company name on social networks, since very few people would even know who the founder of the company was. I could, and would, promote my company with my personal presence as well (e.g., @acangiano); however, the business's identity would be key.

OK, those two cases are straightforward enough. What about edge cases, such as a blog that's not a business per se? Ask yourself if the blog is mainly a single-person operation or whether it's a collective. Collective blogs get their own account because they transcend your personal identity.

If I had a technical blog whose domain was not my own name, I would probably go through the effort of securing a Twitter account for it if I were serious about the project. When I started on Twitter over a decade ago, I didn't bother doing that for my sites *Programming Zen* and *Math-Blog*, but I would if I were starting out today, and certainly I did when I launched *Any New Books* (i.e., @anynewbooks).

Brand Your Social Properties

Much like you customized your blog to make it unique to you, you should consider branding your social properties to make them specific to you, to be instantly recognizable, and to draw attention to your call to action.

For Twitter, you'll need to use a custom image (i.e., an avatar) representing your blog or business. Your avatar will be shown along with each of your 280-characters-or-less tweets. You want to be identifiable among the stream of tweets shown to your followers, so make sure to pick a good avatar. For your blog, your logo (or an adaptation of it) is a logical choice. For your personal account, you want a nice photo of yourself.

Accounts with the default Twitter egg icon rarely attract followers. Likewise, you should make or commission a nice header image for your Twitter profile.

---

10. twitter.com/acangiano

Canva, mentioned before, is a nice tool to create one with the right specifications (i.e., 1500px x 500px) for free (just search for "Twitter header" once you're logged in). In fact, I used Canva to quickly update my Twitter header image once this book became available for purchase.

This updated header announces to anyone who checks out my profile that I have a new book out, and it provides them with a shortened (using bit.ly) link where they can buy the book. That's my key call to action at this time, as far as my personal Twitter account goes, and my Twitter header photo reflects that.

Headers on Twitter can be used in other clever ways. Some people opt to create a collage of tweets from customers and influential early adopters who have praised them, their blog, or their company. Showing testimonials in this manner is a powerful kind of social proof that increases your conversion rate from profile visitors to followers.

Some people have opted for this strategy but turned it on its head. Instead of including praise, they included negative tweets, comments, or reviews from people who are generally disliked. The basic idea is the same—social proof for the tribe of people who agree with the despicability of the featured critic.

The name you display should be your own, or that of your blog if you're creating a Twitter account for it. Some people get really creative (or funny) here. You know your audience and whether doing so is appropriate. You can even include emojis in your name to express yourself or quickly signal to others what you're about.

For example, a lot of developer evangelists have begun adding an avocado emoji to their name to indicate that they are developer advocates. Be aware that some seemingly innocent emojis have been adopted by particular groups of people and you could inadvertently identify yourself as a member by using their emoji.

Be sure to include an enticing description in your profile (as well as your URL in the appropriate field), as this will be shown at the top of your profile page and will help convince visitors to follow you. A few hashtags in your description are okay, but don't go too crazy.

A display of wit in your description is always beneficial to get people to follow you. "Tweets are my own" might also be needed as a disclaimer if required by your employer.

That's pretty much it when it comes to customizing your appearance on Twitter (it's really quite easy).

For Facebook, after you have created a page for your blog, you should provide a cover image (again Canva comes in handy), profile image, a URL, and a description. You'll also be offered the chance to choose a URL for your Facebook page (e.g., facebook.com/cognitiveclass).

Unlike Twitter, Facebook enables you to create custom tabs that you can use for newsletter sign-up forms, sweepstakes, and other activities that can reinforce your brand and help you interact with your followers. It even allows you to add a button (e.g., Shop Now) for your main call to action. You should take advantage of this feature.

To kick things off, you should post a welcome message announcing your new page, describing its purpose, and asking people to participate. Being informal and relaxed is far better than portraying a corporate image. This is the microblogging equivalent of your welcome post on a blog.

Customize other social networks you are targeting (e.g., LinkedIn) in a similar fashion. Some are more liberal than others when it comes to customizations. You should strive for a professional yet approachable look, one that invites people to interact with you as you guide them to the action you wish them to take.

Social properties are an opportunity to reach new customers and readers as well as to strengthen your relationship with them. But if you use these sites incorrectly, they can do more damage than good. Start out on the right foot with a good branding effort.

You're trying to inject yourself into the active discussion going on within a community of prospective and existing customers (or readers, in the case of a blog). The objective here is to obtain social currency, which is about affiliation, conversation, utility, advocacy, information, and identity.[11]

How to Get Your Initial Followers

All right, let's assume that by now you have your branded pages on a bunch of social networks that you intend to target. Everything is in order.

The problem is that you have zero followers to start with. How do you go from zero to hundreds or thousands of followers? We'll discuss techniques to attract followers in an ethical way in a moment. But first, it's worth restating that the viral nature of the beast requires an initial group of followers who can amplify your messages by rebroadcasting your updates to their followers.

---

11. en.wikipedia.org/wiki/Social_currency

On Facebook, as a page admin, you'll be able to invite your existing Facebook friends to like your page. When I launched *Cognitive Class*'s page, I selected a couple hundred Facebook friends that I already knew were into data science and programming. Many of these friends, colleagues, and acquaintances liked the page. Some did it because they were already existing users of Cognitive Class, others because they were genuinely interested, and some, I'm sure, just to humor me.

Either way, it got my page some initial likes. This means that new updates I posted on the page were shown to a subset of these fans, who could then interact with the updates by liking them, commenting on them, or even sharing them with their friends. Today I certainly don't know most of the 60,000 people who subscribe to the page. But the initial seeding from my contacts helped.

> **Tip 85** Announce your social media properties on your blog, inviting people to follow you on them.

As mentioned before, if your updates are engaging and your fans loyal enough, more of them will see your updates, and you can leverage a network effect to reach thousands of people's news feeds very quickly.

For Twitter, I did something similar. I announced the new account from my personal Twitter account, leveraging my existing contacts in this case as well.

If you don't have the luxury of an existing account and network, fear not. We'll delve right in to how to acquire fans/followers in the next few sections.

Cross-Promote Your Site and Social Properties

You have a successful blog and you've created various accounts on social networks. Cross-promoting those accounts means promoting your social properties on your site and, in turn, your blog on your social properties.

A successful blog has a constant stream of new visitors. Many of these readers will have accounts on major social networks. Your goal is to let them know about your presence there as well.

This will not only allow you to better connect with visitors in an environment that they're already familiar with, it will also help you grow your presence there. Furthermore, search engines are now considering social media signals when determining the ranking of your pages. Articles that are popular on social media have an advantage over those that don't receive any attention from social media users.

Your network of followers and fans can quickly expand if your site or blog visitors engage with the social call to actions on your pages.

For all these reasons, you should announce your social media properties on your blog when you create them. You should also include social media icons or widgets that invite people to like your Facebook page, follow you on Twitter, follow you on Instagram (if you opted to have an account there) and so on. You can find all sorts of widgets and snippets of codes to achieve these actions if you just search online, and your blog theme might already have such features built in. On blogs, such widgets are typically placed in the header area or at the top of the sidebar.

When visitors follow you on Twitter, your follower count increases, which in turn shows social proof as well. Finally, when visitors like your Facebook page through your site, they'll increase the Facebook counter shown to your visitors, automatically subscribe to your updates on Facebook, and broadcast that they just liked your page to a subset of their friends.

For Facebook, opt to use the official Like button or the Page plugin to show a sample of your existing followers to prospective followers.[12] Faces add a human element that may increase engagement from your visitors as well as trust for your blog or business (after all, other humans trusted you enough to like you already).

For Twitter, opt for its Follow button or one of the many other options available on the official site (e.g., showing your tweet timeline in the sidebar).[13]

> **Tip 86** Use the Tweet button to invite your readers to tweet prepopulated salient quotes within your posts.

Your follower count should be shown (both for Facebook and Twitter). As we discussed before when talking about other counters, showing that you have a large following acts as social proof that what you're doing is worthwhile, interesting, and worth paying attention to. If your numbers are very small initially, you might consider switching to a counter only after gathering a sizable following.

Most major social networks have equivalent buttons, widgets, and counters available, so you just need to pick which ones and add them to your blog.

---

12. developers.facebook.com/docs/plugins/page-plugin/
13. developer.twitter.com/en/docs/twitter-for-websites/follow-button/overview

If you're trying to attract a large following, you can make your social properties part of your call to action. At the bottom of your blog posts, for example, you could invite readers to like your page, follow you on Twitter, and so on. However, too many calls to action become a distraction for the user and will kill your conversion rate to your true desired outcome (e.g., joining your newsletter).

> **Tip 87** Add your social media calls to your welcome email or confirmation page of your newsletter sign-up.

Don't expect miracles, but between the announcements you'll make, your invitation to your existing network of contacts, and the follow buttons/widgets on your blog, you should create an initial following so that you don't post updates on social media like a performer in an empty concert hall.

With the rise of social media, we've seen mentions of social properties become increasingly popular in offline advertisement campaigns (e.g., fliers, billboards, and TV commercials and programs). Even software programs integrate social features in an attempt to have users share with their friends the fact that they're using that particular software, achieved a particular milestone (e.g., introducing an element of gamification), and so on.

It's all fair play as long as you understand that your social media presence is an important but distant secondary goal to the growth of your newsletter. Your Facebook page, Twitter handle, or other social media pages can be included in your other marketing activities to draw attention to them, but they shouldn't be included in lieu of your blog. This is especially true if you're doing any paid advertisement.

For example, Facebook will tempt you to pay to reach a larger number of people, inviting them to like your page. If you're going to pay, you may as well run the campaign to get people to sign up to your newsletter in exchange for an alluring lead magnet or buying a particular product you created.

After you're done setting up a way for your visitors to discover your social properties, you should ensure that the same is true the other way around, too. People may come to know you via social networks by way of their friends or by randomly searching for a word used by your status updates (e.g., people searching JavaScript on Twitter). You want them to immediately be aware of your site when they discover you this way.

This is why I recommended earlier that you include the URL of your blog (or site if you're representing a business) on sites like Twitter and Facebook.

Include it in your header image as well (in the case of Twitter and Facebook) and whenever possible in your status updates. Whatever you opt to do, don't be shy with your main URL on social properties (within the limits of each site's policy and the netiquette for that particular community).

Post Frequently and Engage with People in Your Niche

By far the easiest way to grow a following, everyone will tell you, is to be interesting and approachable. It's not that different from real life. The problem with this type of advice is that it's quite generic. It's like me telling you, "If you want to lose weight, eat less and exercise more." It's technically true, but it's not overly helpful in actually getting you started. So let's dig deeper into some specifics.

Post Frequently

Take a look at most great artists and you'll find a prolific body of work that ranges from mediocre to extraordinary. You'll increase your odds of success if you are prolific. You'll want to post on social media multiple times a day. On Twitter, Facebook, LinkedIn, and similar social networks, I recommend posting 10–20 times a day. If you created an account on Instagram, you can get away with posting less frequently, but you should still aim for 1–4 posts per day, if possible.

> Tip 86   Consider Planoly or Later to schedule your Instagram posts.

I know what you're thinking. This sounds both insane and a full-time job, but hear me out, as there is a method to this madness. If after reading this chapter you still feel that it's too much for you, it's okay to post less frequently. You'll continue to benefit from social media, just to a lesser extent.

This approach does have a few advantages. More post updates means a greater likelihood of being noticed, followed, and going viral. It also means more opportunities to reach most of your followers, given that modern algorithms on social networks tend to show your posts only to a selected subset of your followers and then expand that circle on the basis of their engagement.

Not everyone is online at the same time or lives in the same time zone, so posting throughout the day ensures that you'll catch people regardless of when they tend to be online or where they live.

The downside is finding the time to add so many updates and the possibility that if your updates are low quality, your engagement level will be very low.

We'll cover the quality of your social media updates and what to post in the next section, but let's first address the issue of posting numerous updates.

I'm not advocating that you spend your day looking for something to post and then posting when something worthwhile comes up. What I'm suggesting instead is to schedule your daily posts. Schedule some time in your calendar to sit down and come up with a series of posts for your social networks each day, and then use a tool like Buffer to add them to a queue. You can even customize Buffer to decide when posts in your queue should be published.

> **Tip 89** Schedule and cross-post your social media updates to multiple social networks with tools such as Buffer.

This way, investing some time each day can lead to a consistent posting schedule. You also get to post the same updates on multiple social networks at once (e.g., Twitter, Facebook, and LinkedIn), saving you time. And if during the day you do come up with a nice idea for a new social media post or find an interesting link that you intend to share with your followers, you can either simply add it to the queue or immediately post it (if you want to prioritize it).

Speaking of useful social media tools, I'm partial to Buffer for its simplicity, but you should definitely check out Hootsuite and SocialOomph as well,[14] since they offer more advanced features that you might find useful (particularly when it comes to tracking mentions of your brand and following conversations happening in your niche).

What to Post on Social Media

Why should people follow you? Because you post great links and insight about your industry or niche. In short, you should post things that are valuable to your followers. Valuable can mean various things to various people. A joke or meme image that amuses your followers can have high entertainment value.

You want to establish yourself as a useful go-to person for the niche that you're targeting. The updates you post don't need to be solely original content. In fact, in most cases, they won't be. Your job is to filter and aggregate the most valuable information for others within your niche or industry.

If your blog is about JavaScript programming, your social properties should be used as microblogs that focus on JavaScript and related technologies. By all means, rebroadcast your own blog posts by linking to them through these

---

14. hootsuite.com and socialoomph.com

channels. In fact, you should repost your most useful blog posts (those that are still relevant) on social media often, not just when they are first published. Over time, as your followers grow, you end up exposing your blog content to new audiences.

> **Tip 90**   Reschedule your best blog content frequently.

Don't limit yourself to self-promoting your blog, however. To attract more followers, you need to come across as a thought leader or trend spotter in your industry. People should see you as a subject matter expert who offers relevant quotes, insight, comments, and trends and who share links to interesting stories (from other sites) related to your niche. These stories— whether opinion pieces, tutorials, or videos—will be, for the most part, published elsewhere by other people, not by you on your own blog.

Put yourself in the shoes of your followers. What would you want to see? What's useful to them? Remember when we talked about Laura in Chapter 12, Promoting Your Own Business, on page 229? Do the same type of thought experiment here for social media.

Here are a few extra suggestions as you go about populating your queue of scheduled social media posts:

- Humans are visual creatures. When given the chance, we generally opt for visually rich content over simple text. Images and videos do much better than simple text in terms of social media engagement. Sometimes you can easily transform simple text into something more compelling by slapping a background image to your text in a fancy font. Again, Canva and Pablo are great tools for this.

- Your tweets can easily be lost in the sea of other tweets your followers will be shown. Consider making them stand out more in their streams by formatting them with ample space. Take a look at Figure 25, Two different ways of spacing the same tweet, on page 273 (from the popular placeholder text Lorem Ipsum).

  Which one do you think will attract more attention while quickly scrolling the page? Don't go overboard, but if the spacing makes sense, use it freely.

- Include a few relevant #hashtags in your social media posts. Use just a handful of the most relevant ones. If the particular topic you're covering is trending right now, include the hashtag that everyone else is using to attract even more eyeballs to your status updates. In fact, if a hashtag is trending, many people who are interested in the topic will monitor it to read updates

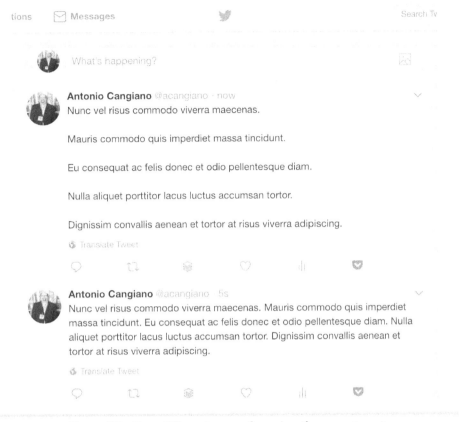

Figure 25—Two different ways of spacing the same tweet

on that particular topic. The same is true when attending a conference or event or participating in one of the many online Twitter chats.[15]

> **Tip 91** Participate in and even host Twitter chats relevant to your niche.

Some social networks don't support hashtags or downplay their importance since they're not an integral part of the platform. See what other users are doing. If you see them using hashtags, use them as well. For Facebook Pages and LinkedIn, I'd recommend using hashtags for the extra discoverability, even though users on these two platforms tend to use them less than Twitter users.

---

15. blog.hootsuite.com/a-step-by-step-guide-to-twitter-chats

- Your posting style on social media should be consistent with that of your blog, but it's okay to relax a little. People expect to interact with a real person and not an emotionless corporate robot. Being witty and giving your audience a laugh here and there will do wonders for your brand, even if you're representing a Fortune 500.

- Memes applied to your particular niche or industry (as well as jokes) are an easy way to get people to like and share your content. For an example in action, see my tweet on how every programmer over 30 feels, which has received, at the time of writing, 828 retweets and 747 likes so far.[16]

- Be polarizing. Thought leaders tend to take a stand and express their opinions with conviction, whether they're controversial ideas or not.

- What's obvious to you might not be obvious to other people from a different background or at a different stage of their career. So feel free to post what you might consider as platitudes if they might end up helping or at least motivating others. You might be surprised by how popular some of these can get.

- Don't beg for retweets or shares. Occasionally you'll post something really important and it's okay to ask your followers to share the message as much as possible, but don't make a habit of it or it gets old fast.

- Speaking of retweets, do share the best posts from other people you follow. On Twitter, these would be retweets. On Facebook and LinkedIn, you'd use the share function. Just don't copy and paste them as your own without crediting them, of course. When retweeting or sharing someone else's post, try to inject your own commentary for your followers, whether to add context, your opinion on it, or a simple endorsement.

- Sassy accounts can do extremely well on social media, but it's a risky game. It's very easy to come across as rude or a bully, so I would keep the level of sass to a minimum unless you really know what you are doing. To see a true master of this, check out Wendy's (the fast food chain) on Twitter. This account routinely roasts other fast food chains and have witty comebacks for anyone who tries to play the same game back.

- To further promote your account on Twitter, you should also create lists of users who tweet about topics related to your main niche (a list of AI researchers, for example, if you're into AI). When people search for such a topic, they'll discover you and possibly end up following you. It's also a

---

16. twitter.com/acangiano/status/545963947179114496

great way for you to keep tabs on discussions within your niche on that particular social network.

- Politics will get you into a lot of arguments on social media. If your niche is related to politics, then you don't have much of a choice. Otherwise, I'd suggest keeping it to a minimum.

  Discussing politics can potentially make you a target for people who disagree with you. In rare instances, it can escalate to threats or attacks on your livelihood. I'm not necessarily saying ignore politics. I'm saying expect arguments and possibly some degree of trouble if you engage in it on social media. It's up to you to decide whether it's worth it.

  Interestingly, some publications leverage hateful clicks. For example, VICE Magazine will often post shocking articles on Facebook. Most of their followers find its takes outrageous, and this in turn drives clicks and engagement. In fact, VICE gets a huge number of comments, most of which are negative toward the publication.

  For a myriad of reasons, including some mentioned above, I don't suggest you adopt this technique, however.

- Find interesting stories that are relevant to your niche by following the most influential people in your field on Twitter and LinkedIn; subscribing to relevant blogs, news, and market research sites (if applicable to your niche); subscribing to your niche's podcasts and YouTube channels; setting up Google Alerts; and exploring Google Trends to spot trends within your niche. Essentially, be on the ball when it comes to what's going on within your own specific niche. Find the cool, interesting, useful stories and share them with your followers.

  > **Tip 92** Post interesting stories to social media directly from your feed reader (e.g., Feedly).

- Narrow your focus. Just as niche blogs are easier to popularize than general blogs, so too are highly specific social media accounts. It's far easier to become popular within a niche if, say, your Twitter profile is a stream of useful content related to that niche than it is if you mix it up with a multitude of interests. If your profile is all about Elixir programming for example, and I'm an Elixir programmer, I'd be very tempted to follow you. If I'm a Java programmer, I'm not likely to follow you. You want to appeal a lot to a small group of people, rather than appeal a little to a lot of people. Hell yeah or no, so to speak.

It's fairly easy to respect this last recommendation if your Twitter account is one specifically made for your blog, and that's part of the reason why I really recommend that you create an account specifically for it. It becomes a lot trickier if you opt to go with a personal account instead. Naturally, your stream of tweets there is likely to be more heterogeneous.

I highly recommend that you avoid the approach I took many years ago. Have your personal accounts for fun, if you wish, but be laser-focused with your blog accounts. Alternatively, if you opt to simply have one personal account on Twitter, try to narrow the focus to one or two main topics (one of which should be your niche or industry).

I don't do so myself and it's my biggest shortcoming as far as Twitter goes. I have many interests I tend to discuss on this platform, including self-improvement, productivity, programming, IBM-related stuff, chatbots, technical marketing, my photography,[17] weight loss and fitness, math, science, business, a bit of politics, random jokes and memes, and so on.

There is no, "You must follow Antonio if you want to know about X." For the five of you who also happen to be into all those topics, I'm your guy. Follow me. Everyone else may enjoy some tweets and ignore the rest as irrelevant, killing my engagement and seriously limiting the growth of my social media account (which currently sits at a little over 4,200 followers on Twitter).

> Tip 93   When in doubt, narrow your focus.

This section should give you plenty of ideas about what to post on social media. Review the list from time to time and pay attention to what other popular folks in your niche are doing on social media.

Interact with Your Followers

What's the point of having a hundred thousand followers if they're not personally interested in your brand? If they're not involved? Along with being interesting, you need to be approachable and ready to converse with your audience.

When people ask you questions, try to reply to them whenever you can. When they praise you, thank them, and if the compliment is worth bragging about, rebroadcast it to your followers (on Twitter a simple retweet will do). Doing so will give your followers further confirmation for their existing positive bias toward you and your brand. You'll also make the original commenter happy that you noticed and acknowledged them, increasing their loyalty to you.

---

17. instagram.com/acangiano

As a matter of fact, don't just retweet praise. Retweet interesting replies to you. You don't need to write panegyrics, but don't forget to do your own praising of people you admire. Make sure you're genuine and specific in your praise and that you tag them (on Twitter, you'd write @acangiano to tag me). If you're lucky they'll even share your tweet or post with their large following, giving you some extra exposure.

If you take the time to interact with your followers, you'll naturally grow your brand and, as a result, people will be more likely to notice your important announcements, posts, and sale offers.

> Tip 94   Pin your current sale or call to action at the top of your social media profiles.

Remember that it's not just about being responsive on social media; you should be proactive in the way you interact with followers. Social media is an ideal place to ask questions and run quick polls of your audience. These tend to do well there because they naturally engage people who want to express their opinion on the subject.

If you're a company selling books, ask your followers what books they're currently reading, what the latest book they bought was, whether they give books as gifts for the holidays, what their favorite book ever is, and so on.

So long as you don't constantly bombard your readers with questions, you'll see a great deal of participation from people who are eager to connect with you and share their knowledge or enthusiasm for the subject you're covering.

On Twitter, you can also actively search for people who ask questions that you may be able to answer. In fact, you can even use the search function to find people who are interested in your specific topic. Follow and reply to the most interesting people you find this way. They'll take notice and some will start following and interacting with you as well.

How to Interact on Twitter

Resist the urge to game the system. The Twitter API has limits in place to prevent you from automatically following thousands of users at once, so if you had a bot that follows people in your niche in place, it would have to be a bit clever to bypass Twitter's detection. If you're caught doing such things, your account may be suspended, so it's not worth the risk.

A lot of self-defined social media marketing experts will have thirty thousand or more followers on Twitter. When you take a closer look, you'll find that they often follow a roughly equivalent number of people as well. More often than not they used software or third-party services that allow them to follow thousands of people over time and then automatically removed those who didn't follow them back. Or alternatively, they may have bought their social media followers in bulk (something that also violates the terms of use of most social networks).

I suggest you ignore both techniques and instead opt to manually follow anyone who actually interests you within your niche. On that note, you might wonder if you should follow people who follow you. Scroll through the list of people who follow you on Twitter and, again, simply follow the people that you genuinely find interesting or who are clearly part of your niche, industry, or community.

Find out who the influencers and thought leaders are in your niche and follow them on social media. Engage and interact with them, being mindful of the fact that they receive a significantly larger volume of interactions and will therefore likely not engage back with you in most instances.

You can even tag influencers and other relevant parties, but don't abuse this ability. You shouldn't tag influencers every time you post a link. That's an easy way to get blocked or called out as a spammer. Instead, only tag them when the story is very relevant to them personally or if you're asking, occasionally, for their thoughts on something.

Resist the temptation to spam even regular users by tagging them with their @handle. For a real life example of how this can backfire, check out the "Ragu Hates Dads" disaster at cc-chapman.com/2011/ragu-hates-dads.

For example, the following message would be considered spam:

> @arrington check out my new book notification service at
> https://anynewbooks.com.

Alternatively, let's look at a different scenario, one where I'm monitoring the keywords *new book* on Twitter, where someone has posted the following tweet:

> I loved Infinite Jest. Can someone recommend a new book like it to me?

I could respond from my @anynewbooks account, even if the person is a perfect stranger, with book suggestions, and doing so would not be considered spam.

However, if I were to reply automatically through software or manually with the following tweet, it would be seen by many as spam.

> You can find out about new books on https://anynewbooks.com.

It's spam because it pushes my link but doesn't actually directly help the user. If I recommended a few books and then mentioned that my service can help them discover new books they'll love, then it would be a little aggressive but probably okay.

When you monitor keywords, be sure your reply adds value and doesn't just push your product or site. Your site or blog can also be mentioned if in itself it's a good answer to a specific question from the user. For example, picture the following conversation on Twitter:

> Where can I find out about new book releases?

> @example You could try our free service at https://anynewbooks.com. Please let us know if this works for you.

This would not be classified as spam. But should you do it on a daily basis? It's time-consuming and likely not the best use of your time. It also portrays you in a negative light if those are the only interactions you have with other users on the platform. You don't want your brand to come across that way.

Final Tips for Social Media

Here are a series of final tips to help you succeed on your path to mastering social media.

- Check your Google Analytics statistics and any dashboard your social media tools provide you with. If possible, try to figure out how well your social media traffic converts to desired calls to action compared with your other types of traffic. Much like the epigraph at the beginning of the chapter, however, don't focus too much on immediate ROI. You're playing the long game here.

- Monitor how your following and engagement grow over time. Are you gaining followers? At the same time though, don't obsess over numbers. Focus on adding value and building relationships with your customers or readers. Twenty early adopters who are raving fans of your blog or business are better than a thousand apathetic followers who tiptoed into following you.

- Social networks are made up of people. Never forget to treat everyone with respect by making them feel welcome and part of your conversation. Also, cultivate your relationship with early adopters as much as you can; they'll provide invaluable feedback and help you increase your reach on social networks.

- Hecklers will criticize and attack you on social networks as much as commenters do on blogs. Follow the usual guidelines. Ignore trolls, but politely address valid criticism or misguided folks without belittling them.

- Don't waste money on pay-for-tweet services. Paying up to thousands of dollars to have influencers plug your message or account isn't the way to go about building a loyal following.

- Imposing a Like or a tweet before granting the download of a given product is not liked by many, but it can be very effective.[18] Likewise, sweepstakes, giveaways, and contests where participants must take some social action are a great way to spread the word about your blog or specific product.

- If you're running a business, don't forget to try out paid advertisements on social networks that permit this. If the ROI is there, it's a fast way to earn new customers. Just remember to start with a small budget to run experiments across multiple social networks to see what works best. You can then double down on that particular platform.

- What your friends buy often affects what you buy too. Social media is a huge opportunity from this standpoint. If you have a business, you can greatly increase your revenue by crafting your site to encourage customers to share the fact that they're interested in an item, or that they just bought one, with their followers. Don't forget social media on your e-cart thank-you page, either.

Take Action

This chapter is packed with tips and suggestions that will come in handy as you gain more experience and continue to grow your social media presence.

For the time being, your take-home assignment for this chapter is simply this:

1. Decide which social media sites you're going to target.

2. Create your accounts for these sites.

3. Brand each social media property to make it yours (and ideally match it with the name of your blog).

4. Cross-promote your blog and social properties.

5. Follow influencers and other users within your community.

---

18. seomoz.org/blog/how-to-win-tweets-and-influence-search-engines-with-paywithatweet

6. Engage with them by replying, mentioning (sparingly), liking, and sharing their content (freely).

7. Focus on your niche and your niche only on social media.

8. Stay on top of the news within your niche or industry by subscribing to valuable resources and feeds and then share that information with your followers.

9. Schedule many posts per day to really maximize the growth of your accounts. Don't be afraid to reshare your blog posts several times long after they've first been promoted.

What's Next

This chapter provides a solid framework to get you started with your social media efforts. It's a very fast-evolving world, but the principles and the human element aren't going to change anytime soon.

Get started as soon as possible, because building a solid presence on social media can take several months. Freely experiment and don't be afraid to deviate from the guidance provided within this chapter.

You'll make mistakes, but the best way to learn is by practice and firsthand experience. Just remember to be genuine and honest. Readily take ownership of your mistakes and apologize; that way you shouldn't face any long-term consequences from errors you might make.

This chapter also concludes the instructional part of this book. Congratulations on reading this far. The remaining couple of pages are the conclusion, with a few final words of advice. Don't skip these pages, as this is where we'll say goodbye and share important details on how to stay in touch.

The credit belongs to the man who is actually in the arena, whose face is marred by dust and sweat and blood, who strives valiantly, who errs, who comes short again and again, because there is no effort without error and shortcoming.

Theodore Roosevelt

CHAPTER 15

Final Words of Advice

I started this book by telling you how blogging has the potential to change your life. I hope I've persuaded you about the actual possibility of that bold claim by this point. I also hope that the road map, or at least the principles I've outlined, will work for you, whatever your blogging goals may be.

Try It Out

It's my sincere wish that the preceding pages have managed to inspire and motivate you to take action and give blogging a try. If you don't take action, as discussed in the beginning, all of this information will have been only marginally useful.

Implementing every single suggestion within this book would be overwhelming for anyone. So pick and choose the ones that resonate with you, one small step at the time.

Above all, be patient. Building a remarkable online presence takes months or even years, not days. You'll likely start to see benefits much sooner than that, but you're in this game for the long haul, not for short-term gain.

If you fail, change some aspects of what you're doing and see if your outcome improves. As mentioned before, you need to treat all of this as a series of experiments. You think that making a certain change will lead to a positive effect, but you won't know until you test it. Use iteration, trial and error, feedback, and analytics to figure out what works for you as a blogger.

Also, remember that blogging is mostly about spreading ideas. You want to do so with passion and professionalism. Put your heart into it, and chances are that blogging will give you what you're after, whether it's influence, recognition, a new job, some extra income, or something else altogether.

You know the classic adage that says, "With great power comes great responsibility"? Keep that in mind. Be genuine, respectful, and honest with the people you interact with online. Use your newly acquired influence to spread your ideas, to connect further, and to love, not to hate.

Blogs to Follow

If you want to read more about blogging and Internet marketing in general, I wholeheartedly recommend the following blogs. Consider subscribing by email or adding these to your feed reader:

- *Technical Blogging*: technicalblogging.com
- *The Ahref Blog*: ahrefs.com/blog/
- *The Moz Blog*: moz.com/blog
- *Buffer's blog*: blog.bufferapp.com
- *Neil Patel's blog*: neilpatel.com/blog/
- *Seth Godin's blog*: seths.blog

The first one on the list is my blog. I think it's a good complement to the book you've just finished. Consider subscribing to the newsletter there to be informed of new posts relevant to your blogging interests.

You might also want to consider my personal blog for insight into productivity and self-development.[1]

Keep in Touch

You can further keep up with what I'm up to via Twitter (twitter.com/acangiano) and LinkedIn (linkedin.com/in/antoniocangiano). Feel free to connect with me, and don't be afraid to say hello.

Finally, let me just say that it's been an absolute pleasure writing this book and sharing my insight with you. Should you have any questions related to my book, feel free to email me at info@technicalblogging.com.

I wholeheartedly wish you the best in your career as a blogger, and I thank you deeply for reading my book.

---

1. antoniocangiano.com

List of Tips Within the Book

You'll find a list of highlighted tips throughout the book. For your convenience, we've collected them all in this appendix.

Chapter 1: What Kind of Blog Are You Going to Run?

1. Collective blogs can benefit greatly from an editor-in-chief.

2. Don't betray your readers' expectations.

3. Do one thing, but do it well.

4. Niche blogs are more likely to become successful.

Chapter 2: Rock-Solid Planning for Your Blog

5. Focus your elevator pitch on the why, not the how.

6. Always set verifiable goals.

7. For company blogs, prefer a subfolder over a subdomain.

8. If your target audience is local to a specific country, favor ccTLDs.

9. Enable WHOIS privacy when registering your domain name.

Chapter 3: Setting Up Your Blog

10. Don't use a free subdomain for your blog URL.

11. Specify a canonical URL when republishing your content.

12. Opt for WordPress-specific hosting plans.

13. Only install plugins that you strictly need.

14. Promptly update WordPress and its plugins.

Chapter 4: Customizing and Fine-Tuning Your Blog

15. If you run a company blog, prominently link to your main site from it.

16. Android users can glance at stats on their home screen via the handy WordPress widget.

17. Feature your newsletter sign-up form near the top of your sidebar.

18. Use a mini-course for your lead magnet. It'll get people used to receiving and opening emails from you.

19. Ensure your theme is responsive.

20. Use a CDN to speed up your blog.

Chapter 5: Creating Remarkable Content

21. Write epic content you'd love to read yourself.

22. Write your headline before your post. This will give focus to your writing.

23. Use an odd number for your listicles. They perform better.

24. When possible, establish credibility in the first paragraph.

25. Ensure your font size is large enough to be read comfortably.

26. Have your computer read your post to you. If something is off, you'll immediately catch it when you hear it.

27. Don't ever belittle or mock others in your posts.

28. Have at least three backups in different places.

Chapter 6: Producing Content Regularly

29. Have 3–5 posts in your blog "savings account."

30. Contact people who guest-blog on blogs that you follow.

31. Discuss your post prior to writing it down.

Chapter 7: Finding Time to Blog

32. For each goal you set, write down WHY it matters to you.

33. Keep track of appointments in your calendar, not in your to-do list.

34. Do not assign artificial due dates to tasks.

35. To-do programs have many advanced options. To keep your overhead to a minimum, err on the side of simplicity.

36. Avoid installing known time waster apps on your phone.

37. Take at least one day off each week to recharge.

38. If you find 25-minute dashes to be too short, set your pomodoro length to 50 minutes with 10-minute breaks.

Chapter 8: Promoting Your Blog

39. Check your blog with website.grader.com.

40. Install an SEO extension for your browser (e.g., SEOquake).

41. Read the Google webmaster guidelines in full.

42. Establish a relationship with a blogger before proposing a guest post.

43. Submit your best content when guest blogging.

44. Remember the golden rule: treat others as you'd like to be treated.

45. Install Buffer's browser extension.

46. Make sure your links are posted on social sites with a preview.

47. Submit your stories between 9 a.m. and 1 p.m. eastern time (ET) to maximize votes and exposure.

48. Participate in social news sites; don't just submit your own blog entries.

Chapter 9: Understanding Traffic Statistics

49. Trust the process: continue to publish even in the face of disappointing statistics.

50. Pay close attention to engagement metrics such as pages per session.

51. Spend some time investigating all the reports available within Google Analytics.

52. Watch out for referral spam.

Chapter 10: Building a Community Around Your Blog

53. Prioritize and aim for tasks that have a great reward-to-effort ratio.

54. Slack and Facebook groups are valid alternatives to traditional forums.

55. Don't spread yourself too thin when it comes to community-building initiatives.

56. Smaller subreddits tend to be friendlier.

57. If you actually wish to be notified of mentions around the web, use Google Alerts.

Chapter 11: Advancing Your Career with Blogging

58. Blog for the position you want, not the one you have.

59. Include a link to your blog on your traditional résumé.

60. If you're available for hire, mention it in your author box at the bottom of your posts.

61. As a freelancer, include content that appeals to prospective clients, not just fellow developers.

62. Consider Rafflecopter for your giveaways.

63. Put your blog URL and Twitter account on your first and last slides when giving a presentation.

64. Keep an eye on fellow bloggers in your niche to spot niche-specific ad networks.

65. Don't place ads on your blog at least until you have 10,000 pageviews per month.

66. Diversify your sources of blog income.

67. Aim for high-quality, niche-relevant sponsors only.

68. Review technical and business books you read.

69. Promote only products you'd buy yourself.

70. For one-off donations, consider ko-fi.com.

71. To maximize your blogging income, focus on your own products, as well as high-fee and recurring affiliate offers.

Chapter 12: Promoting Your Own Business

72. Use the SEO tools we discussed to better identify customer questions.

73. Be a person, not a corporation, when you blog.

74. If you're promoting an open source project, consider having a guide on how to contribute to it.

75. Cross-role ebooks tend to do well (e.g., design for developers).

76. Bookmark all press and blog mentions of your company.

Chapter 13: Scaling Your Blogging Activities

77. It's far easier to evolve a technical blog into a magazine than into a news site.

78. Create a "We're Hiring" page and post about it from time to time.

79. Opt to fund fewer articles but of a higher caliber.

80. Favor a network of blogs over multiple categories if the topics aren't very related.

81. Giveaways are a great way to draw the attention of your existing readers to your new blog.

Chapter 14: Beyond Blogging: Strategizing for Social Media

82. Disable social media notifications on your phone.

83. Research niche-specific social networks.

84. If targeting a younger crowd, also consider Snapchat.

85. Announce your social media properties on your blog, inviting people to follow you on them.

86. Use the Tweet button to invite your readers to tweet prepopulated salient quotes within your posts.

87. Add your social media calls to your welcome email or confirmation page of your newsletter sign-up.

88. Consider Planoly or Later to schedule your Instagram posts.

89. Schedule and cross-post your social media updates to multiple social networks with tools such as Buffer.

90. Reschedule your best blog content frequently.

91. Participate in and even host Twitter chats relevant to your niche.

92. Post interesting stories to social media directly from your feed reader (e.g., Feedly).

93. When in doubt, narrow your focus.

94. Pin your current sale or call to action at the top of your social media profiles.

Bibliography

[Nöt09]   Staffan Nöteberg. *Pomodoro Technique Illustrated*. The Pragmatic Bookshelf, Raleigh, NC, 2009.

Index

Thank you!

How did you enjoy this book? Please let us know. Take a moment and email us at support@pragprog.com with your feedback. Tell us your story and you could win free ebooks. Please use the subject line "Book Feedback."

Ready for your next great Pragmatic Bookshelf book? Come on over to https://pragprog.com and use the coupon code BUYANOTHER2019 to save 30% on your next ebook.

Void where prohibited, restricted, or otherwise unwelcome. Do not use ebooks near water. If rash persists, see a doctor. Doesn't apply to *The Pragmatic Programmer* ebook because it's older than the Pragmatic Bookshelf itself. Side effects may include increased knowledge and skill, increased marketability, and deep satisfaction. Increase dosage regularly.

And thank you for your continued support,

Andy Hunt, Publisher

Land the Tech Job You Love

You've got the technical chops — the skills to get a great job doing what you love. Now it's time to get down to the business of planning your job search, focusing your time and attention on the job leads that matter, and interviewing to wow your boss-to-be. Land the tech job you love.

Andy Lester
(280 pages) ISBN: 9781934356265. $23.95
https://pragprog.com/book/algh

The Passionate Programmer (2nd edition)

This book is about creating a remarkable career in software development. In most cases, remarkable careers don't come by chance. They require thought, intention, action, and a willingness to change course when you've made mistakes. Most of us have been stumbling around letting our careers take us where they may. It's time to take control. This revised and updated second edition lays out a strategy for planning and creating a radically successful life in software development.

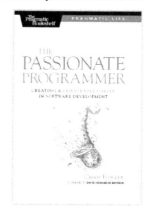

Chad Fowler
(232 pages) ISBN: 9781934356340. $23.95
https://pragprog.com/book/cfcar2

Create Your Successful Agile Project

You think agile techniques might be for you, but your projects and organization are unique. An "out-of-the-box" agile approach won't work. Instead, unite agile and lean principles for your project. See how to design a custom approach, reap the benefits of collaboration, and deliver value. For project managers who want to use agile techniques, managers who want to start, and technical leaders who want to know more and succeed, this book is your first step toward agile project success.

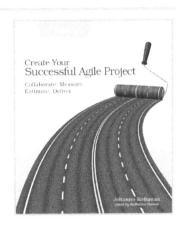

Johanna Rothman
(290 pages) ISBN: 9781680502602. $45.95
https://pragprog.com/book/jragm

Creating Great Teams

People are happiest and most productive if they can choose what they work on and who they work with. Self-selecting teams give people that choice. Build well-designed and efficient teams to get the most out of your organization, with step-by-step instructions on how to set up teams quickly and efficiently. You'll create a process that works for you, whether you need to form teams from scratch, improve the design of existing teams, or are on the verge of a big team re-shuffle.

Sandy Mamoli and David Mole
(102 pages) ISBN: 9781680501285. $17
https://pragprog.com/book/mmteams

Genetic Algorithms and Machine Learning for Programmers

Self-driving cars, natural language recognition, and online recommendation engines are all possible thanks to Machine Learning. Now you can create your own genetic algorithms, nature-inspired swarms, Monte Carlo simulations, cellular automata, and clusters. Learn how to test your ML code and dive into even more advanced topics. If you are a beginner-to-intermediate programmer keen to understand machine learning, this book is for you.

Frances Buontempo
(234 pages) ISBN: 9781680506204. $45.95
https://pragprog.com/book/fbmach

A Common-Sense Guide to Data Structures and Algorithms

If you last saw algorithms in a university course or at a job interview, you're missing out on what they can do for your code. Learn different sorting and searching techniques, and when to use each. Find out how to use recursion effectively. Discover structures for specialized applications, such as trees and graphs. Use Big O notation to decide which algorithms are best for your production environment. Beginners will learn how to use these techniques from the start, and experienced developers will rediscover approaches they may have forgotten.

Jay Wengrow
(220 pages) ISBN: 9781680502442. $45.95
https://pragprog.com/book/jwdsal

The Ray Tracer Challenge

Brace yourself for a fun challenge: build a photorealistic 3D renderer from scratch! It's easier than you think. In just a couple of weeks, build a ray tracer that renders beautiful scenes with shadows, reflections, brilliant refraction effects, and subjects composed of various graphics primitives: spheres, cubes, cylinders, triangles, and more. With each chapter, implement another piece of the puzzle and move the renderer that much further forward. Do all of this in whichever language and environment you prefer, and do it entirely test-first, so you know it's correct. Recharge yourself with this project's immense potential for personal exploration, experimentation, and discovery.

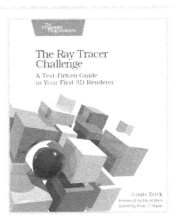

Jamis Buck
(290 pages) ISBN: 9781680502718. $45.95
https://pragprog.com/book/jbtracer

Mazes for Programmers

A book on mazes? Seriously?

Yes!

Not because you spend your day creating mazes, or because you particularly like solving mazes.

But because it's fun. Remember when programming used to be fun? This book takes you back to those days when you were starting to program, and you wanted to make your code do things, draw things, and solve puzzles. It's fun because it lets you explore and grow your code, and reminds you how it feels to just think.

Sometimes it feels like you live your life in a maze of twisty little passages, all alike. Now you can code your way out.

Jamis Buck
(286 pages) ISBN: 9781680500554. $38
https://pragprog.com/book/jbmaze

The Pragmatic Bookshelf

The Pragmatic Bookshelf features books written by developers for developers. The titles continue the well-known Pragmatic Programmer style and continue to garner awards and rave reviews. As development gets more and more difficult, the Pragmatic Programmers will be there with more titles and products to help you stay on top of your game.

Visit Us Online

This Book's Home Page
https://pragprog.com/book/actb2
Source code from this book, errata, and other resources. Come give us feedback, too!

Keep Up to Date
https://pragprog.com
Join our announcement mailing list (low volume) or follow us on twitter @pragprog for new titles, sales, coupons, hot tips, and more.

New and Noteworthy
https://pragprog.com/news
Check out the latest pragmatic developments, new titles and other offerings.

Save on the eBook

Save on the eBook versions of this title. Owning the paper version of this book entitles you to purchase the electronic versions at a terrific discount.

PDFs are great for carrying around on your laptop—they are hyperlinked, have color, and are fully searchable. Most titles are also available for the iPhone and iPod touch, Amazon Kindle, and other popular e-book readers.

Buy now at *https://pragprog.com/coupon*

Contact Us

Online Orders:	*https://pragprog.com/catalog*
Customer Service:	*support@pragprog.com*
International Rights:	*translations@pragprog.com*
Academic Use:	*academic@pragprog.com*
Write for Us:	*http://write-for-us.pragprog.com*
Or Call:	+1 800-699-7764

Milton Keynes UK
Ingram Content Group UK Ltd.
UKHW012339190824
447149UK00007B/135